Israel
&
the Arabs:

The June 1967 War

Israel
&
the Arabs:
The June 1967 War

Edited by Hal Kosut

FACTS ON FILE, INC. NEW YORK, N.Y.

Israel
&
the Arabs:

The June 1967 War

Library of Congress Catalog Card No. 68-23430
ISBN 0-87196-172-5
9 8 7 6 5 4 3
PRINTED IN
THE UNITED STATES OF AMERICA

CONTENTS

i

BACKGROUND

The 6-day Arab-Israeli war of June 1967 was the 3d major struggle waged by Israel to maintain its existence since it became a state in 1948. In the brief but bitter fighting of June 1967, as in the 1948 war of independence and in the 1956 Sinai campaign, Israel emerged victorious over its Arab neighbors. But Israel's confidence in its ability to defend itself was tempered by the reality of the Arabs' continued implacable hostility and by the imponderables of the world power rivalry in the Middle East.

The Arab-Israeli antagonism is deeply rooted in ancient rival claims to the area known as Palestine, cradle of 3 great religions—Judaism, Christianity and Islam. Although Palestine's political boundaries had shifted frequently, its geographic area had always been regarded as including the territory between the Mediterranean Sea and the Jordan River and between Egypt and Syria. The name Palestine comes from the Arabic, Falastin. It derives from Pleshet, the Land of the Plishtim (Philistines), a people who came from Crete or the shore of Asia Minor and settled in the southern coastal plain in the 12th Century B.C.

According to the biblical account, the Jews—originally known as Hebrews (Ibrim)—were first identified with Palestine with the appearance of Abraham, the first Jewish patriarch, in what was known in biblical times as the Land of Canaan. Driven to Egypt by famine in their own land, the Hebrews endured a period of Egyptian enslavement until they were led back to the Land of Canaan in the 2d millenium B.C. by Moses in a pilgrimage referred to in the Old Testament as the Exodus. The Jews emerged as a political force in about 1025 B.C. with the establishment of a Hebrew kingdom under Saul. Saul was followed by Kings David and Solomon. In about 930 B.C. Solomon's realm was split into the northern kingdom of Israel and the southern kingdom of Judah. Israel was conquered by the Assyrians in 726 B.C., and Judah fell to the expanding Babylonian empire in 586 B.C., at which

1

time many Jews were exiled to Babylonia. The Land of Israel later came under the sway of the Persians and Greeks, but the Jews enjoyed self-rule for 4 centuries during this period. Syrian attempts to interrupt Jewish autonomy in 168 B.C. led to the Maccabean revolt and the establishment of the Hasmonean and later Herodian dynasties, which lasted for more than 2 centuries until the arrival of the Romans. A majority of the Jews fled the country and dispersed throughout the world following their unsuccessful revolts against Roman rule in 66-70 A.D. and 132-135 A.D.

Although most of their compatriots had scattered, some Jews had always maintained a foothold in Palestine in small settlements, where they lived under the invaders and conquerors who succeeded the Romans: the Byzantines, Arabs (637-1072), Seljuks (1072-1099), Crusaders (1099-1291), Mamelukes (1291-1517) and Ottoman Turks (1517-1917). During World War I, a force of about 5,000 Jewish volunteers, armed by the British and fighting as a separate unit, helped the British armies wrest control of Palestine from the Turks. The force was made up of Jewish refugees from Palestine and Jews from Russia, Britain, Canada, the U.S. and Argentina.

Jews, largely from Europe, had begun to trickle back to Palestine in the 1880s, and by the time of British occupation in 1918, their numbers totaled about 70,000, compared with 630,000 Arabs. The immigration was spurred by anti-Semitism and deteriorating economic conditions for Jews in Eastern Europe. The Jews' centuries of yearning for a return to their ancestral homeland was further intensified by the publication in 1896 of *The Jewish State,* by a Viennese journalist, Dr. Theodor Herzl, and the subsequent formation in 1897 of the World Zionist Organization (WZO) in Basle, Switzerland. Herzl's document and the WZO sounded a call for political action to re-establish a Jewish state in Palestine.

Throughout World War I Zionist leaders negotiated with British officials in London for a Jewish homeland in Palestine. Britain declared in Feb. 1917 that it was prepared to fulfill the Zionists' objectives and incorporated this policy in the Balfour Declaration, issued Nov. 2, 1917. The declaration was first made known in a letter British Foreign Secy. Lord Arthur James Balfour had sent to a British Zionist leader, Lord Rothschild. It said: "His majesty's government view with favor the establishment in Palestine of a national home for the Jewish people, and will use their best endeavors to facilitate the achievement of this object, it being clearly understood that nothing shall be done which may prejudice the civil and religious rights of existing non-Jewish communities in Palestine, or the rights and political status enjoyed by Jews in any other country." The text of the Balfour Declaration had been submitted to U.S. President Woodrow Wilson and was approved by him before being published. The Allies formally turned over Palestine to Britain as a mandated territory April 19, 1920.

The Arabs' historic claims to Palestine were based on their presence in the country since it came under the rule of the first Moslem caliph in the 600s A.D. The Arabs regarded their claims as having been further bolstered by a "secret agreement" of 1915, made in an exchange of correspondence between Sir Henry McMahon, British high commissioner in Egypt, and Sherif Hussein of Mecca, one of the holy Moslem cities of Hejaz, in the northwestern part of the Arabian peninsula. In compensation for Arab assistance in fighting the Ottoman Turks, the agreement promised that Britain would "recognize and support independence of the Arab regions [formerly belonging to the Ottoman Empire in the Levant] within the limits demanded by the sherif of Mecca." But subsequent British statements, including one made in 1922 by Winston Churchill, then secretary of state for the colonies, insisted that it had never been Britain's intention to include Palestine in the 1915 pledge to the Arabs. Churchill also reaffirmed Britain's adherence to the Balfour Declaration.

The Balfour Declaration signalled the start of Palestine's modern development. Jewish immigration grew, communal agricultural settlements (*kibbutzim*), which had already begun to appear in the early 1900s, expanded, and industries were established. Arabs also started to immigrate to Palestine, from Syria and other nearby countries.

In a move to quiet Arab fears of an expanding Jewish population, the British in 1920 issued the first of a series of ordinances limiting the immigration of Jews to Palestine. The population of the country at that time was 757,182—78% Moslem, 11% Jewish and 9% Christian.

Britain's ambiguous policy toward Arabs and Jews on the development of Palestine fanned the hostility of the Arabs. On Easter Sunday in 1920 Arabs rioted against Jews in Jerusalem and killed 5. This was the first of a series of violent anti-Jewish incidents that continued through the 1920s and into the early 1930s. Arabs also suffered casualties, inflicted by British troops suppressing the disorders. The Jews formed a self-defense organization in the late 1930s, and the Haganah, which was to spearhead the battle for independence in 1948, became the principal guard force.

The Arabs sought to win by political as well as violent means, and in 1935 a group of United Arab Parties was formed in Palestine. It demanded that Britain establish an independent Arab government, prohibit the sale of land to Jews and halt Jewish immigration.

In 1937 a British Royal Commission proposed a plan to terminate the British mandate and to partition the country into a Jewish and Arab state. The British intention of ending the mandate was reiterated in a White Paper of Feb. 1939. The document also imposed a quota of 75,000 Jewish immigrants during the next 5 years, after which any further Jewish immigration would be subject to Arab approval.

Palestinian Jews and world Jewish leaders were outraged at Britain's restrictive immigration policy. It came at a time, they held, when the emergence of the anti-Semitic Nazi regime in Germany and the subsequent persecution of Jews there and elsewhere in Europe made it vital that Palestine remain open as a haven of refuge. An illegal movement of Jews into Palestine was therefore started. Accompanying this movement was the first organized armed Jewish resistance to British policies.

With the outbreak of World War II, the Jews and Arabs in Palestine observed a temporary truce as the Middle East faced a threat of invasion by advancing German armies in North Africa. The Arabs halted their attack against the Jews, and Jewish armed groups suspended their campaign against the British. But even before the Germans were expelled from North Africa by resurgent Allied troops in 1942-43, the Zionists intensified their political drive. This was evidenced in the Biltmore Program of May 1942, which demanded replacement of the British mandate by a Jewish state, withdrawal of the 1939 White Paper and unrestricted Jewish immigration. The program was drawn up at a meeting of world Zionist leaders in New York.

At the conclusion of World War II, an Anglo-American inquiry into the Palestine question was undertaken. In a report published in April 1946, the inquiry group recommended the admission of 100,000 European Jews into Palestine. It also called on the Jewish Agency, which represented the interests of the Jewish community in Palestine, to "resume active cooperation with the mandatory power in the suppression of terrorism and illegal immigration." (The agency, a body of world Jewish leaders, had been set up under the terms of the mandate in 1920.) The Arabs continued to protest against the entry of Jewish refugees.

British insistence on limiting Jewish immigration precipitated a new wave of anti-British violence carried out by the Haganah as well as by dissident Jewish terrorist groups. British reprisals followed and led to counter-military action by the Jewish groups. Exasperated by the continuing Arab and Jewish disagreement, Britain April 2, 1947 called on the UN to convene a special session of the General Assembly to find a solution.

A UN Special Committee on Palestine (UNSCOP) was formed. After hearings in New York, Palestine, Lebanon, Transjordan and in Jewish refugee camps in Austria and Germany, UNSCOP issued its report August 31, 1947. UNSCOP recommended in its majority report: (a) the partitioning of Palestine into separate independent Arab and Jewish states with economic union; (b) the creation of a separate enclave for Jerusalem, which would be placed under the supervision of the UN Trusteeship Council; (c) the admission of 150,000 Jewish immigrants; (d) the abolition of restrictions on the sale of land to Jews in areas alloted to them. UNSCOP's minority report recommended the creation of a bi-national Arab-Jewish state, with autonomy for each national sector.

UNSCOP's majority report was approved by the U.S. and the Soviet Union and accepted by the Jewish Agency but was assailed by the Arab states and the Arab Higher Committee. The

UN General Assembly Nov. 29, 1947, by a 33-13 vote (10 abstentions), approved the partition plan.

The Arab response to the UN partition plan was adamant opposition and a call for a war of extermination against the Jews. The appeal was issued by Haj Amin el Husseini, the ex-mufti of Jerusalem, and his followers in Palestine. It was supported by the Arab League states of Egypt, Iraq, Syria, Lebanon, Jordan, Saudi Arabia and Yemen. (The league, formed in 1945, was a loose confederation of 7 states; its purpose was to hold periodic consultations to formulate common policy.)

The start of the withdrawal from Palestine of Britain's 100,000 troops, police and civilian personnel paved the way for the opening round of attacks against Jewish settlements in Palestine by Arab guerrillas in Palestine and by irregular forces from the Arab League states. Jewish forces succeeded in containing the Arab attacks by mid-April 1948. The Egyptian secretary general of the Arab League then requested that the league states' armies intervene in the fighting.

Britain's mandatory rule in Palestine ended May 14, 1948. On the same day the Jewish National Council proclaimed the establishment of the state of Israel and the formation of a provisional government. On the following day, May 15, Arab armies invaded Palestine in a determined effort to crush the new Jewish state. The Israeli armed forces repelled the Arabs, and the fighting halted temporarily June 11 with the acceptance by both sides of a UN Security Council truce. Fighting resumed July 9 and was halted again by UN intervention 10 days later. Arab-Israeli clashes erupted several times thereafter and came to a full stop Jan. 7, 1949.

By the end of the war—Israel's "war of independence"—Israel was in control of more territory than had been alloted to it under the UN partition plan. The captured territories included the western Galilee, the city of Jaffa, the modern section (New City) of Jerusalem and the corridor from Jerusalem that extended to the coastal plain. The proposed Arab state never came into existence; instead Jordan seized the territory west of the Jordan River and captured the Old City of Jerusalem, and Egypt seized the Gaza Strip.

Israel signed UN-mediated armistice agreements with the 4 Arab belligerents in 1949—with Egypt Feb. 24, with Lebanon March 23, with Jordan April 13 and with Syria July 20. But a UN Conciliation Commission (established Dec. 12, 1948) failed in efforts to translate the armistice into a stable, permanent peace.

Unreconciled to their defeat and to the existence of Israel, the Arab states embarked on a campaign of harassment against the new Jewish state. They proclaimed an economic boycott of Israel; Egypt barred Israeli ships from the Suez Canal; Arab infiltrators attacked Israeli border settlements; the Arabs expressed vehement opposition to Israeli efforts to divert water to the arid southern parts of Israel. (The potential sources of water bordered Syria and Jordan.) Israeli fishing in the Sea of Galilee encountered Syrian interference. Israel's relations with the Arab states was further exacerbated by the Arab refugee problem created by the 1948 war. Thousands of Arabs had fled Palestine in the wake of the fighting, and most of them encamped in crowded refugee centers in the Gaza Strip and in Jordan. The Arab states insisted on the return of the refugees to their former homes in Israel.

(The Arab defeat in Palestine precipitated a series of revolts against upper-class leaders in neighboring Arab countries. In Syria 3 *coups d'état* in 1949 brought about the dictatorship of Col. Abid Shishakli. In Egypt, King Farouk was overthrown in 1952 by a military coup led by Col. Gamal Abdel Nasser. Nasser, who eventually became president of Egypt, emerged in the 1950s as the leader of the Arab world's struggle against Israel. Egypt and Syria merged as the United Arab Republic in 1958, but Syria withdrew in 1961, and Egypt remained as the United Arab Republic's sole member.)

Alarmed by the continued Arab-Israeli clashes, the undiminished animosity, the absence of a permanent peace treaty and the stocking of arms by both sides, the U.S., Britain and France May 25, 1950 issued a joint statement designed to promote peace and stability in the area. Known as the Tripartite Declaration, it expressed opposition "to the use of force or the threat of force between any states of the area." In the event of a breach of the frontiers or armistice lines, the U.S., Britain and France pledged in the declaration to "take action, both within and outside the UN, to prevent such violation."

The Tripartite Declaration failed to ease the tense situation. Arab infiltration attacks against Israeli border areas continued and intensified in 1953. Events were rapidly building up to another showdown. In 1955 Egypt concluded a deal for the Soviet Union to supply Cairo with war planes and modern arms. The Egyptian army had clamored for modern weapons following an Israeli retaliatory raid on Gaza in Feb. 1955 in which 40 Egyptian soldiers were killed. The arms transaction enabled the Soviet Union to resume an active role in Middle Eastern affairs and raised Israeli fears that the military balance in the region had been upset in favor of the Arabs.

Adding to Israel's feeling of insecurity were an upsurge of attacks on its borders with Egypt by Arab *fedayeen* (suicide commandos) from bases in the Sinai and an agreement reached by Egypt, Jordan and Syria Oct. 23, 1956 on the establishment of a unified military command. Six days after the creation of the 3-nation Arab command, Oct. 29, Israeli troops crossed the Egyptian border in a massive assault, penetrating deep into Sinai. By Nov. 3 the Israeli forces reached the Suez Canal and were in control of most of the peninsula. They also captured 6,000 Egyptian prisoners and huge quantities of arms and ammunition.

The Israeli Foreign Ministry, on the opening day of hostilities, had described the attack as "security measures to eliminate the Egyptian *fedayeen* bases in the Sinai Peninsula." The Ministry also cited Nasser's persistent declarations that "his country remains in a state of war with Israel." Egyptian threats of "annihilating" Israel, the statement said, had been "crowned a few days ago" by the establishment of the 3-nation command under Egyptian leadership.

A few days after Israel had launched the drive into Sinai, Britain and France called on both sides to stop fighting and to withdraw 10 miles from the Suez Canal and to let British and French troops occupy the intervening zone. Israel agreed but Egypt refused. Cairo's rejection of the ultimatum led Oct. 31 to an Anglo-French invasion of the specified zone, accompanied by the bombing of Port Said and adjacent areas. British, French and Israeli troops were forced to withdraw from Egyptian territory under pressure of a UN Security Council resolution, approved Nov. 7, 1956 and supported by the U.S. and the Soviet Union.

A UN Emergency Force (UNEF) was established under a General Assembly resolution in 1957. UNEF troops were stationed in Sinai to guarantee Israeli ships passage through the Gulf of Aqaba and to serve as a buffer between Israeli and Egyptian troops. But future events proved that the UN's pacifying efforts were of a temporary nature; violence and military retaliation persisted as the pattern of Arab-Israeli relations. According to Israeli records, 7,506 Israelis were killed in the 3 wars and the many between war Arab commando operations in the 20 years since Israel became a state. 4,487 were slain in the 1948 war of independence, 191 in the 1956 Sinai campaign, 759 in the June 1967 war and 2,069 in the guerrilla raids.

Geographical Profile of Israel

The geography of Israel (not including Arab territories conquered in June 1967):

Israel lies on the eastern seaboard of the Mediterranean, near the meeting-point of Europe, Asia and Africa, between latitudes 29°30′ and 33°15′ North, and longitudes 34°17′ and 35°41′ East. Its area is 7,992.6 square miles, of which 171.8 square miles are water. The frontiers are disproportionately long: 590 miles on land and 159 on water.

The country is an irregular, narrow strip some 265 miles long, stretching from the hills of Galilee in the north to the Red Sea port of Elath (Eilat) in the south, bounded in the north by Lebanon and Syria, in the east by Syria and Jordan, and in the southwest by Egypt and the Gaza Strip.

North of Tel Aviv, the country is only 12 miles wide. At its widest, south of Beersheba, it is 70 miles across; from there the triangular blade of the Negev tapers off southwards to its tip at Elath, where it is only 6 miles in width.

The highest point is Mt. Meron (3,692 feet); Sodom, on the Dead Sea (1,286 feet below sea level) is the lowest point on the earth's surface.

The coastal plain borders the Mediterranean for 117 miles. It broadens out north of Haifa (Zebulun Valley), south of Haifa (Sharon Plain), and again south of Tel Aviv (Plain of Judea). Except for Haifa Bay, the coast is unindented and lined with sand dunes.

The coastal plain is the most thickly populated part of Israel; within it, from north to south, are: the ancient town of Acre; Haifa, the main port; Tel Aviv, the largest city; Lod (Lydda), international airport; Ashkelon; and Ashdod, where a new deep-water harbor has been built.

The mountains, the central column of the country, average 2,000 feet in height and stretch 200 miles from Lebanon to Sinai. Near the coast, the slopes are gentle; further inland are the rounded, stone-ribbed, rain-eroded hills of Samaria, Ephraim and Judea, sloping steeply eastwards to the Jordan. In the arid Negev there are high mountain ranges. The mountain backbone is cut across by several valleys. The largest, the Valley of Jezreel (Esdraelon), stretches from Haifa to the Jordan Valley; it is 30 miles long and, at its widest, 12 miles across.

In Galilee, the northern part of the mountain complex, are the old towns of Tiberias and Safad.

Jerusalem, the capital, occupies a commanding position in the Judean hills and is connected with the coast by the "Corridor," a flourishing belt of mountain villages.

In Jordan Valley, from the Hula Valley in the north, the Jordan River plunges 3 miles southwards to the Sea of Galilee (also called Lake Kinneret, Sea of Tiberias and Lake Gennesaret), 665 feet below sea level, and flows down into the Dead Sea.

The Negev comprises about half the country's area. In the north it is an extension of the coastal plain, which, eastward, tilts up towards the cliffs and crags overlooking the Dead Sea and the Arava Valley.

PRELUDE TO WAR
1962-67

The military victory over Egypt in the Sinai campaign of 1956 removed the immediate threat to Israel's security. Israel regained freedom of passage through the previously Egyptian-blockaded Gulf of Aqaba, and its frontiers with Egypt remained relatively calm. But the Israeli border again came under sporadic attacks in 1957, this time largely from Syria. Between 1957 and 1962, Israel filed no fewer than 422 complaints with the UN, accusing Damascus of infiltration attacks and breaches of the 1948 truce. The pattern of violence continued on a relatively smaller scale through 1964. There were incursions against Israeli border settlements, attacks on Israeli patrols, Israeli retaliatory strikes into Arab territory and, in many instances, skirmishes between Israeli soldiers and regulars of Egypt (the United Arab Republic, or the UAR) Jordan and Syria.

As the violence continued, a series of political events in the Arab world foreshadowed preparations for a major Arab showdown with Israel. At summit meetings held in 1964, 1965 and 1966 Arab leaders mapped joint strategy against Israel. Arab refugees who had lived in the territory currently part of Israel formed a "Palestine Liberation Organization" in May 1964 to "recover their usurped homes." An extreme wing of the Socialist Ba'ath party seized power in Syria in Feb. 1966 and pledged greater support for Arab terrorists in their campaign of sabotage along the Syrian-Israeli frontier. Arab unity was further strengthened when Egypt and Syria, whose 1958 merger had been rescinded by Damascus' secession in 1961, resumed diplomatic relations in Nov. 1966 and agreed to establish a joint defense command.

The Israeli-Arab frontiers were punctuated by almost constant and fierce clashes between 1965 and April 1967. The infiltration of Arab terrorists in this period emanated from Jordan as well as Syria and were mounted with greater frequency and violence. An

11

important aspect of the Arab terrorist strikes was the emergence of Al Asifa (also called El Asifa [Hurricane], the military arm of the Palestinian Arab nationalist Al Fatah or El Fatah). Israel claimed that the organization consisted of former Palestinian refugees who operated from Syria, where they were organized and financed by the Damascus government. Syria repeatedly denied the charge.

Israeli troops responded to the infiltration raids with more powerful counter-strikes, which, in turn, led to more frequent clashes with Syrian and Jordanian forces. The most serious Israeli act of retaliation was directed against Es Samu, Jordan Nov. 13, 1966. The Israeli attack caused widespread destruction in the town in reprisal for Jordanian-originated raids on Israel. The UN Security Council censured Israel for the attack. A side-effect of the raid was the precipitation of violent political upheavals in Jordan itself.

The demilitarized zone between Israel and Syria in the Galilee region remained a source of friction between the 2 countries and was the scene of constant fighting. The most serious outbreak, prior to the June 1967 war, occurred April 7, 1967, when Israeli pilots shot down 6 Syrian MiGs in an aerial clash that followed sharp ground fighting.

Arab Summit Conferences

The first of the Arab summit sessions took place Jan. 15-17, 1964, when the chiefs of state of the 13 Arab League nations met in Cairo to map common strategy against Israel. The conferees agreed at the Jan. 15 session to establish a unified military command. Lt. Gen. Abdel Hakim Amer, the UAR's chief of staff, was named chief of the proposed command, which was to have a permanent headquarters and "financial capabilities."

In another accord announced Jan. 15, Jordan and the UAR agreed to resume diplomatic relations. The UAR had severed relations with Jordan in Sept. 1961 after the Amman government recognized a Syrian revolutionary régime that seceded from the UAR union with Egypt.

A final communiqué issued at the conclusion of the summit meeting Jan. 17 announced agreement on the "necessary practical resolutions" to frustrate an Israeli plan to divert the waters of the

Jordan. Although the communiqué did not say what specific measures were envisaged, it was reported that the Arab counter-plan called for the building of dams in Syria and Lebanon to drain off the headwaters of the Jordan River before they reached the portion of the river flowing through Israel.

Israel's official reaction to the Arab League meeting was voiced by Premier Levi Eshkol Jan. 20. In a statement to the Knesset (parliament), Eshkol warned that Israel would "oppose unilateral and illegal measures by the Arab states" and would "protect her vital rights." The premier charged that the Cairo conference had "proclaimed a plan of sabotage." In defending Israel's Jordan River project, Eshkol said that his country would not use more water than was allotted to it under the plan proposed in 1953 by Eric Johnston, Pres. Dwight D. Eisenhower's special envoy for a U.S.-backed scheme for joint Arab-Israeli development of the Jordan River Valley. The plan, accepted by Israel but rejected by the Arabs, would have permitted Syria, Jordan and Lebanon to use all the Jordan River waters they needed for irrigation, with the remainder (about 40%) going to Israel.

The 2d summit conference, attended by 11 Arab heads of state, was held in Alexandria, Egypt Sept. 5-11, 1964. A conference spokesman announced Sept. 8 that the conferees had reached unanimous agreement on military measures to block Israel from diverting the waters of the Jordan River. Egypt's Middle East News Agency said the agreement provided the UAR commander, Gen. Amer, with "the right to move military forces from one Arab country to another in case of war." The agency said that the conference had agreed "that the 3 key countries on Israel's border—Jordan, Syria and Lebanon—must have more arms and presumably bigger armies; 7 countries should pay $14 million a year for the next 5 years toward this, in addition to a sum of perhaps $42 million already promised by all countries together."

A spokesman at the conference reported Sept. 10 that the UAR, Saudi Arabia, Kuwait and Iraq had pledged to finance an army of former Palestinian Arabs. The UAR said it would permit the new army to train on Egyptian territory in the Gaza Strip and Sinai Peninsula.

A final conference communiqué Sept. 11 said it was agreed that work would start immediately on projects to prevent Israeli diversion of Jordan River waters.

The Israeli government reacted to the Arab summit meeting Sept. 13 by denouncing its decisions as a virtual declaration to destroy Israel. The government statement insisted that Israel would "draw water from the Sea of Galilee within the quantities alloted to her in the unified plan" proposed by Eric Johnston, representing Pres. Eisenhower. "Israel will oppose unilateral and illegal measures by Arab countries and will act to preserve her rights," the statement said.

Arab League heads of state met in Cairo May 26-30, 1965 to devise a unified political and military policy against Israel. In a statement issued May 30, at the conclusion of the discussions, League Secy. Gen. Abdel Khalek Hassouna said the conferees had agreed to consolidated action to liberate Palestine, to press for military unity and to continue projects to divert Jordan River waters to the detriment of Israel. The meeting, however, failed to agree on the deployment of Arab troops under a unified command in countries bordering Israel. The resolutions adopted at the meeting were kept secret, and this was taken as an indication of deep disagreement on unified action against Israel. The talks were preparatory to another Arab heads-of-state meeting that was held in Casablanca, Morocco Sept. 13-17. The May 26-30 sessions were boycotted by Tunisia, which had felt it would be used to discredit Pres. Habib Bourguiba for his relatively conciliatory attitude toward Israel.

In a speech at the opening session of the Palestine National Congress in Cairo, UAR Pres. Gamal Abdel Nasser May 31 emphasized that the UAR would not participate in a war against Israel if Israel confined its military activities to attacks against water diversion projects in Syria.

Syrian Pres. Amin el-Hafez declared at a rally in Damascus June 3 that the Arab League meeting in Cairo was a "conspiracy against Syria" because the Arab states had no intention of helping Syria if it were attacked by Israel.

The Casablanca conference, officially the 3d chiefs-of-state conference of the Arab League, was again boycotted by Tunisia.

In a final communiqué issued Sept. 17 at the close of the Casablanca conference, the league announced that it had decided to "reinforce the Arab unified command and to pursue work to exploit the waters of the Jordan and its tributaries in accordance with the agreed plans." The plans referred to the anti-Israel diversionary water measures proposed at the 2 previous league meetings. Arab differences over diverting the Jordan River waters had been evidenced at the Sept. 15 meeting. Gen. Amer reiterated Cairo's proposal that Jordan permit the entry of Iraqi and Saudi Arabian troops on its soil to help protect dam-building and other water diversionary sites near the Israeli frontier. Jordanian King Hussein was said to have replied that it was "not the right time" to bring foreign troops into Jordan because Israel would regard the move as provocative and launch counter-military measures. The UAR, Iraq and Syria were said to be the only league nations that favored Amer's proposal.

Palestine Liberation Organization

A Palestine Liberation Organization (PLO) was formed at a meeting of the Palestine National Congress May 28-29, 1964 in the Jordanian sector of Jerusalem. It was the congress' first meeting since the 1948 Arab-Israeli war. The conference was attended by the congress' refugee representatives from Jordan, Syria, Lebanon, Iraq, the Gaza Strip, Qatar (Katar) and Kuwait.

Ahmed Shukairy, Palestinian delegate to the Arab League, declared that the new organization "will act to mobilize the Palestinian people to recover their usurped homes," (Shukairy, who headed the PLO, had actually formed the organization in the 1950s, but the PLO was little more than a paper force until it received international Arab support after its rebirth in 1964. The PLO's striking arm was its Palestine Liberation Army, commanded by Shukairy and consisting ultimately of an estimated 10,000-15,000 Palestinian Arab refugees trained largely for guerrilla fighting.)

King Hussein of Jordan had opened the congress with a speech urging the Palestinians to unite to recover their former homeland.

Israeli-Arab Border Clashes

The first of a series of clashes between Israeli and Arab border forces in 1965 erupted on the Syrian frontier Mar. 2 and continued sporadically through Mar. 21. Most of the fighting took place in the demilitarized zone north of the Sea of Galilee. The clashes largely involved Syrian attacks on Israeli tractors attempting to plow inside the zone near the Israeli farming settlement of Almagor. UN observer teams halted the shooting in incidents that took place Mar. 2 and 3.

Two of the most serious clashes occurred Mar. 16 and 17. One Israeli was killed and 4 were wounded Mar. 16 near Almagor in a tank-mortar exchange. Damascus radio charged Mar. 17 that Israeli troops that day had crossed into the demilitarized zone and fired on a Syrian project for diverting the Jordan River headwaters "in the Dan and Doka areas." Damascus said a Syrian bulldozer driver had been killed and 2 bulldozers destroyed. An Israeli spokesman said at UN headquarters in New York Mar. 17 that the Israelis had not started the fighting but had fired back after being attacked.

The Arab "General Command of Arab Storm Troops" (Al Asifa) claimed Mar. 4 that its raiders had attacked and destroyed an Israeli army barracks near Kfar Hess Feb. 27 and had killed 20 soldiers. The command's report, appearing in the Beirut pro-Nasser newspaper *Al Moharrer,* said the Arab infiltrators also had blown up the Kfar Hess commander's office, killing its occupants. An Israeli army spokesman Feb. 28 had acknowledged that 2 buildings in Kfar Hess had been damaged by explosives, but he said there were no casualties.

Israeli forces fought May 25-June 5, 1965 with Arab soldiers and armed irregular infiltrators from Jordan and Lebanon. Acting in retaliation for infiltration attacks, Israeli soldiers May 27 crossed the Jordanian frontier and attacked the towns of Shuneh (about 2 miles east of the Jordan River), Jenin and Qalqilya.

An Israeli communiqué said the attacks were in reprisal for raids on Israeli territory earlier in the week by armed members of El Fatah. The communiqué said that the infiltrators, in 2 separate raids from Jordan, had wounded 7 Israeli civilians in attacks on homes and installations at Ramat Hakovesh May 25 and at Affuleh May 26. (Israel lodged a complaint May 27 with the Jordan-Israel Mixed Armistice Commission.) The communiqué said Israel had informed Jordan that it held the Amman government responsible for the raids and that Jordan had ignored Israeli demands that it take "measures to curb this activity." A Jordanian army spokesman denied that the attackers had come from or had returned to Jordan.

Israel announced that in the reprisal raids the El Fatah base at Shuneh was destroyed, a flour mill and ice factory were destroyed at Jenin and a large gasoline tank was set afire at Qalqilya. The Israelis claimed that Shuneh had served the El Fatah group "as a center for training, storage of arms and explosives and as a base for sabotage squads." The announcement said the Israeli soldiers sought to avoid civilian casualties. But Jordan claimed that the Israeli raiders had killed 4 Jordanian civilians and wounded 4 others.

Maj. Gen. Itzhak Rabin, Israeli chief of staff, said May 28 that the raids were "warnings and not reprisals" for 9 acts of sabotage committed in Israel by Arab infiltrators during a 6-month period.

At a meeting in Amman with the U.S., British and French ambassadors, Jordanian King Hussein complained May 28 that Israeli raids "endangered regional security and world peace." The U.S. State Department May 28 deplored the use of force along the Arab-Israeli frontier. The statement appealed for the use of "established UN machinery for dealing with" "violations of the armistice."

Israeli Foreign Min. Golda Meir May 30 took issue with the State Department complaint. She asserted that the U.S. had not reacted to "acts of sabotage" committed on Israeli territory by Arab infiltrators from Jordan. Mrs. Meir recalled that Israel had filed a complaint with the UN Security Council Mar. 1 about a series of raids in Israel by saboteurs allegedly from Jordan. She said that while UN observers were investigating one of the complaints, "the Jordanians were occupied in another dastardly assault."

Israeli and Jordanian forces were reported to have engaged May 31 in a 20-minute exchange of gunfire between their respective sectors of Jerusalem. Two Israeli civilians were killed and 4 were wounded by the shooting.

Arab infiltrators attacked the Israeli settlements of Beit Jibrin (southwest of Jerusalem) June 1 and Yifta (north of the Sea of Galilee) June 2. No injuries were reported in either incident.

The U.S.' May 28 appeal for restraint was again criticized by Israel in discussion of the border incidents in the Knesset (parliament) June 2. Premier Eshkol said his government had sought to inform Israel's friends of the situation "so they should know where the trouble is coming from and who is responsible and so our friends should not give us pointless moral advice."

An Israeli military spokesman disclosed June 6 that an Israeli military court June 3 had sentenced to death one of 6 El Fatah guerrillas who had entered Israeli territory Jan. 7 in an unsuccessful attempt to blow up a well at Nehosha, southwest of Jerusalem near the Jordanian frontier. The 5 others escaped.

Israel Prevents Water Diversion

Maj. Gen. Itzhak Rabin asserted July 15, 1965 that Israeli attacks had deterred Syria in its efforts to divert the sources of the Jordan River. "The Arab diversion plan," he said, "did not stand the first test of attack. Already the Syrians have ceased their diversion work after 2 Israel army blows against their equipment." But Lebanon was "continuing the diversion work and will have to face the consequences," he warned. According to the London *Times* of July 16, Israeli shells in March and May 1965 had destroyed Syrian equipment being used to clear a channel from the Baniyas River eastward to the Litani River in Jordan.

Fighting between Israeli and Syrian border troops erupted again July 18. An Israeli communiqué charged that the Syrians had first fired on Israeli farmers. Damascus sources said the Syrians had opened fire when Israeli tractors entered a restricted area on the frontier, and Israeli guns had fired back. The UN Mixed Armistice Commission obtained a cease-fire ending the clash.

A 2-hour exchange of tank and artillery fire occurred Aug. 12 on the Israeli-Syrian border at the Jordan River north of the Sea of Galilee. Four Arab civilians were reported killed on Israeli territory by Syrian shells, and 3 children were reported wounded. Israeli sources said 2 Israeli soldiers were wounded and a number of Syrian troops killed in the engagement.

An irrigation pipeline in Ramin, Israel was blown up Aug. 27 reportedly by 2 Lebanese saboteurs. Footprints were discovered leading from the pipeline to the Lebanese border, 400 yards away.

Israeli soldiers blew up 11 water pumps in the Qalqilya area of Jordan Sept. 5. They left leaflets stating that the raid had been in reprisal for Jordanian-based raids from Qalqilya over the preceding 10 weeks. A few hours after the Israeli action, Jordanian and Israeli patrols near Gesher, in the Jordan River Valley, exchanged small-arms fire for 3 hours. A report issued by the UN Mixed Armistice Commission Nov. 10 called the Israeli attacks on the Qalqilya water pumps a "warlike act."

Israeli army units Oct. 28 raided 2 Lebanese villages, Houle and Meis Ejj Jebel, in retaliation for the blowing up of an empty house in the Israeli village of Margaliot Oct. 26. Israel had charged that the infiltrators had come from Lebanon. In Houle, the village *mukhtar*'s house was blown up after its occupants had been led out; in Meis Ejj Jebel, 3 reservoirs were destroyed. (Earlier the same evening Israeli Premier Eshkol had said in a speech near Margaliot that "while Israel would not be provoked into hasty action, she could not afford to remain silent forever.") The Lebanese delegation to the UN Mixed Armistice Commission filed a protest Oct. 29.

Border fighting between Israeli and Jordanian units took place Oct. 30-31 in the valley of Ayalon, 10 miles west of Jerusalem. The fighting started Oct. 30 as tractors belonging to both sides began cultivating the land, an area under dispute since the 1948 armistice. Each side accused the other of opening fire. An Israeli army spokesman said 2 Israelis were wounded slightly before UN truce observers halted the fighting; the Jordanian radio claimed 15 Israelis killed. Fighting erupted again Oct. 31. A Jordanian army spokesman claimed 5 Israelis killed, 6 wounded and several pieces of equipment destroyed or damaged with no Jordanian losses; Israel denied suffering any casualties or losses of equipment. The battle was stopped after 2 hours by UN intervention. Jordan, in a letter to the UN Security Council, accused Israel of a border violation; Israeli UN delegate Michael S. Comay denied the Jordanian charge.

King Hussein, speaking in Amman at the opening of parliament Oct. 28, announced a general military mobilization in anticipation of Israeli "aggression" during work on a dam that would divert Jordan River waters.

Army Seizes Power in Syria

The moderate Ba'ath government of Premier Salah al-Bitar of Syria was overthrown Feb. 23, 1966 by a bloody *coup d'état* carried out by extreme leftwing military dissidents of the Ba'ath party. A military-appointed cabinet headed by Dr. Yussef Zayen as premier took office March 2. Zayen had been replaced as premier by Bitar Jan. 1.

Heavy fighting raged in Damascus Feb. 23 before the rebels defeated the pro-Bitar army forces. According to official casualty figures, 41 persons were killed and 95 wounded. But Baghdad radio reported Feb. 24 about 400 killed. Other sources placed the death toll as high as 1,000.

The leader of the coup was identified as Maj. Gen. Salah Jedid, ex-army chief of staff, who had been ousted from the Ba'ath party in Dec. 1965. Jedid and 4 other officers were said to have staged the uprising after Bitar Feb. 21 had ordered them transferred to military command posts outside Damascus.

The rebels dissolved the ruling executive Presidency Council, headed by Lt. Gen. Amin el-Hafez as chairman, and replaced it with a 14-man military junta that they dubbed the Provisional Command of the Syrian Ba'ath party.

Hafez was arrested after being wounded during fighting at his home in Damascus. At least 100 military guardsmen around Hafez' home were reported slain. Bitar was said to have escaped along with Maj. Gen. Mohammed Omran, defense minister, Michel Aflak, a founder of the Ba'ath party, and Mounif Razzaz, a Jordanian, who was secretary general of Ba'ath's international wing. A curfew was imposed throughout the country. The borders were closed Feb. 23 but reopened March 2.

On seizing power, the junta leaders denounced Hafez as a dictator and Bitar as a rightwinger. Ba'ath newspapers charged that Bitar had planned to denationalize Syrian industries and that his statements on Vietnam had shown "secret sympathy" for "American imperialist aggression." The Ba'ath faction that seized power reportedly stressed doctrinaire Socialist goals and revolutionary pan-Arabism, while the moderate elements they replaced favored reviving the economy and promoting internal stability.

The junta announced Feb. 25 the appointment of Zayen as premier and Dr. Nureddin al-Attassi, 38, a physician, as chief of state. (In a purge of the Ba'ath party Dec. 21, 1965, Hafez had forced the resignation of Attassi as deputy chairman of the Presidency Council and of Zayen as premier.)

Arabs Warn U.S. vs. Arming Israel

Foreign arms shipments to Israel was a major topic of consideration at an Arab League summit conference in Cairo March 14-17, 1966. The conferees adopted a resolution that declared: "The supply of arms to Israel by the United States or any other country constitutes support of aggression and flagrant denial of rights of the Palestine people to their homeland." The U.S.' policy of sending arms to Israel and denying arms to the Arab states "will push American policy to consequences harmful to Arab-U.S. ties."

At a simultaneous meeting of the league's Defense Council, a "secret report" was filed on the diversion of Jordan River waters. According to the Jordanian newspaper *Al-Diffa*, Lt. Gen. Abdel Hakim Amer (of the UAR), commander of the United Arab Command, had reported to the council March 14 that the league states had raised no more than £40 million of the money needed to finance Jordan River "diversion work." According to *Al-Diffa*, another "secret report" filed with the council by League Secy. Gen. Abdel Khalek Hassouna said that the diversion plans had been modified and that, therefore, there would be a delay in the implementation of the "immediate stage" of the plan.

The Israeli government announced May 20, 1966 that the U.S. had agreed to sell Israel "tactical" military aircraft. The State Department confirmed the sale later May 20: State Department press officer Robert J. McCloskey said the decision to sell an undisclosed number of the aircraft to Israel "reflects our due regard for security in the Near East, our wish to avoid serious arms imbalances that would jeopardize area stability and our general restraint as to military equipment supplied to that area." "Imbalances," he said, had been caused by "Soviet sales of arms to certain countries in the Near East." The U.S. sale to Israel reportedly had been concluded in mid-February during a visit to Washington by Israeli Foreign Min. Abba Eban.

(In April 1966 the U.S. had confirmed the sale of fighter-bombers to Jordan and in February the sale of 200 M-48 tanks to Israel.)

Retaliatory Raids on Jordanian Villages

Israeli army units crossed into Jordan April 29, 1966 and raided 2 villages in retaliation for alleged Arab terrorist attacks on Israeli territory. The raiders struck the villages of Qalat (2 miles inside Jordan), south of the Sea of Galilee, and Rujum Madfa, 5 miles west of the Dead Sea. The Israeli soldiers blew up 4 houses in Qalat and 10 in Rujum Madfa. The buildings were believed to have been used as bases by El Fatah terrorist raiders. A Jordanian military spokesman said Apr. 30 that 37 Israeli solders had been killed or wounded and 11 Jordanians slain, including 4 village guards and 7 civilians. An Israeli spokesman said Jordanian civilians had been removed from the buildings before they were blown up. According to another Israeli official, 4 Israeli soldiers were wounded in the operation.

Jordan May 2 filed a complaint with the UN Security Council. It called the Israeli assault an "unprovoked vicious attack" in "flagrant violation" of the 1949 armistice agreement. An Israeli reply to the Council said the Israeli government "deeply regrets the necessity for taking the action." The note said the military strikes were in response to acts of sabutage against Israel from Jordan.

These were among the alleged Jordanian-based incidents that prompted Israeli forces to act: (a) An Israeli army jeep was damaged Apr. 28 when it ran over a mine near Masada, 5 miles from the Jordanian border; the explosive was believed to have been planted by Arab terrorists. (b) 2 Israelis were injured Apr. 24 by explosive charges at Bet Yosef, near the Jordanian border south of the Sea of Galilee.

Syrian-Israeli Clashes

A Syrian army spokesman in Damascus reported Apr. 30, 1966 that 2 Israelis had been killed and 2 wounded Apr. 29 in a one-hour exchange of gunfire across the Syrian-Israeli border.

Syrian Foreign Min. Ibrahim Makhous warned the U.S., French, British, Soviet and Communist Chinese ambassadors in separate meetings May 5 that Syria would blow up the oil pipelines on its territory if Israeli troops invaded Syria or if the Damascus regime was threatened by "imperialist reaction." Makhous said Israeli units were massed near the Syrian frontier. The Syrian Ba'ath newspaper *Al-Ba'ath* warned May 5 of "imperialist and Israeli activities"; it alluded to Israeli Premier Eshkol's charge the previous week that Syria was responsible for raids on Israeli territory by the El Fatah and Al Asifa terrorist groups.

Beirut newspapers reported May 15 that Syria had ordered the evacuation of villages near the southwestern border with Israel. The newspapers said Syria had acted after accusing Israel of planning to move troops into the demilitarized zone between the 2 countries.

Israeli air force jets carried out a 25-minute daylight raid 8 miles inside Syria north of the Sea of Galilee July 14. Israeli officials said the attack was in retaliation for the killing July 13 of a soldier and a civilian by a Syrian-planted land mine in the Israeli village of Almagor. The Israeli planes struck a Syrian water-diversion project 10 miles southeast of Almagor. Israeli officials reported the destruction of 5-8 tractors and excavators, which they said had been engaged in diverting the Baniyas River, a tributary of the Jordan River. (The project was part of the joint Arab plan to prevent Jordan River waters from reaching Israel.) During the raid, Israeli pilots flying escorting Mirage fighters encountered 4 Syrian MiG-21 jets and claimed to have destroyed one. Maj. Gen. Itzhak Rabin denied a Syrian claim that 2 Israeli planes had been shot down during the operation. Syria said one civilian had been killed and 9 wounded in the Israeli raid.

The UN Security Council Aug. 3 rejected a resolution introduced by Mali and Jordan to censure Israel for the July 14 air attack. The vote was 6-0 (9 abstentions) in favor of the resolution, but 9 votes were required for adoption. In addition to Jordan and Mali, the resolution was supported by the USSR, Bulgaria, Nigeria and Uganda. Most of the delegates who abstained contended that the resolution was one-sided because it did not take into account Syrian provocation of Israel. The Council had started discussing the border clashes July 25 after receiving requests for a meeting from Syria July 21 and from Israel July 22. The Council had received 2 separate reports on the incidents July 27 from Lt. Gen. Odd Bull, chief of the UN Truce Supervision Organization (UNTSO). One report confirmed Israel's account of the air attack and the other cited evidence that saboteurs from Syria had planted mines on Israeli territory.

UN Meets on Israeli Complaints vs. Syria

The UN Security Council convened Oct. 14, 1966 on an Israeli charge of Syrian "acts of aggression." An Israeli delegation note of Oct. 12 had complained to the Council of a series of attacks on Israeli border positions the previous weekend by marauders operating from Syrian territory. Israel had claimed that the infiltrators were members of El Fatah and/or Al Asifa guerrilla-terrorist forces and that the Syrian government had initiated and supported the terrorist attacks. The Damascus régime had argued that it had no control over Arab infiltrators using Syrian soil to attack Israel. The Israeli note also cited "threats by Syria against the territorial integrity and political independence of Israel."

Following the killing of 4 Israeli soldiers on the Syrian border Oct. 8, Israeli Foreign Min. Abba Eban and Michael S. Comay, head of the Israeli delegation to the UN, had met Oct. 10 with UN Secy. Gen. U Thant and Lord Caradon of Britain, Security Council president. The Israeli officials had asked Thant and Caradon to get Syria to agree to halt the raids on Israel. In a note to the Council Oct. 13, George J. Tomeh, head of the Syrian delegation, denied the Israeli charges and disclaimed responsibility for the acts of the Arab infiltrators. Tomeh said the Israeli accusations were being used as a pretext for a possible Israeli attack on Syria.

As Council debate opened Oct. 14, Eban called on the Council to condemn "hostile acts and illicit infiltrations" against Israel "supported by the Syrian government." He said 61 acts of "murder, sabotage and mine-laying" had been committed since Jan. 1965 by armed infiltrators "who cross into Israel and, having carried out their attack, seek the shelter of Arab territory." In supporting his charge that Syria was responsible for these raids,

Eban said that Damascus radio Oct. 9 had broadcast in detail a report on the bombing of 2 buildings in the Israeli sector of Jerusalem Oct. 8. Eban also quoted an Oct. 11 speech in which Syrian Premier Yussef Zayen had warned that if Israel attacked Syria, "we would set the entire area on fire and turn it into a cemetery for Israel and all imperialist interests."

The Council Oct. 20 called for a report on conditions in the Israeli-Syrian demilitarized zone in the upper Galilee border region. The report, filed with the Council Oct. 22 by Lt. Gen. Odd Bull, commander of the UN Truce Supervision Organization (UNTSO), stated that Israel and Syria had both violated the armistice agreement by stationing armed military personnel in the zone. But, according to Bull, Syrian and Israeli inspection teams of 17 men each, each team accompanied by 3 UN observers, had found no evidence of a military build-up by either side during a surveillance of the border areas Oct. 19.

Following several hearings on the Israeli complaint, the Council Nov. 4 supported by 10-4 vote a resolution urging Syria and Israel to reduce frontier tensions, but the resolution was defeated by the USSR's 104th Security Council veto. Voting with the Soviet Union against the resolution were Mali, Bulgaria and Jordan. Nationalist China abstained.

Infiltrators Intensify Attacks

As the UN Security Council met on Israel's complaint against Syria, Arab infiltrators continued attacks against Israeli border areas. Israel charged that most of the assaults were by members of the El Fatah guerrilla group based in Syria, although some of the Syrian-based attackers had launched their forays from Jordanian territory.

Among incidents during the period Oct. 13 - Nov. 4:

■ An Israeli army vehicle was fired on Oct. 13 by terrorists 2 miles inside Israel, about 25 miles southwest of Jerusalem near the border village of Nehosha. Three Israeli soldiers were wounded. An Israeli army report indicated that the attack had been carried out by 4 intruders from Jordan.

■ One of 2 vehicles of an Israeli army patrol detonated a mine Oct. 18 near Tel Aziziyat in the upper Galilee area between

Lebanon and Syria. An Israeli soldier was wounded. The Israelis said they had discovered footprints of 2 men leading from the Syrian frontier.

■ An Israeli army patrol clashed Oct. 19 with 4 Arab infiltrators in the upper Galilee area west of the Israeli village of Ramot Naftali. Three Arabs and one Israeli were killed. One Arab was wounded and captured.

■ A Jerusalem-to-Tel Aviv freight train was derailed Oct. 27 when it struck and set off an explosive charge on a track several miles southwest of Jerusalem, near the Jordanian village of Battir. The blast coincided with shots fired at the train, an Israeli army spokesman said. One Israeli was injured. The derailment forced the Israelis Oct. 28 to cancel rail service from Tel Aviv, Haifa and Jerusalem. Repair work on the severed track was completed Oct. 30.

■ Terrorists Oct. 30 blew up an Israeli water pipeline between Arad and Massada in the northern Negev. According to Israeli officials, footprints of 3 men were traced back to the nearby Jordanian border.

El Fatah publicly claimed credit for carrying out 5 raids against Israeli installations during the period Sept. 26 - Oct. 8. The claim was published in Damascus newspapers Oct. 10. El Fatah said it had mounted 150 raids against Israel since the founding of the guerrilla group in Jan. 1965.

The Syrian government's support of the Arab infiltration attacks on Israel was affirmed in a broadcast by Premier Yussef Zayen Oct. 11. Zayen said: "We are not protectors of Israel. We shall never restrain the revolution of the Palestinian people who are seeking to liberate their homeland. Under no circumstances shall we do so. In the event of Israeli aggression against Syria we shall set this whole region on fire and turn it into a cemetery for Israel, imperialism and imperialist agents."

Israeli Premier Eshkol charged Oct. 17 that in addition to supporting El Fatah, the Syrian government also had trained, armed and financed marauders who had entered Israel from Arab states other than Syria. Eshkol denied that Israel was planning to attack Syria and offered Damascus "a mutual non-aggression pact" to allay such fears. Eshkol warned that if Syria persisted in continuing "the outrages" against Israel, "we have the strength to defend the right and lives of our citizens." Eshkol accused the Soviet Union of spreading a "foolish charge" that Israel was planning to attack Syria as part of an international plot to topple the Damascus government.

Reports from the Middle East included speculation that the Syrian régime, at odds with Jordan, was mounting attacks from Jordanian territory to trick Israel into retaliating against Jordan.

Israelis Attack Es Samu in Jordan

In one of the heaviest retaliatory raids of the undeclared Arab-Israeli conflict, Israeli forces Nov. 13, 1966 attacked the Jordanian village of Es Samu in the Hebron area, 3 miles inside Jordan. The UN Security Council Nov. 25, meeting at Jordan's request, approved a resolution censuring Israel for the raid and warning of possible sanctions in the event of future Israeli attacks. The Israeli raid precipitated widespread anti-Jordanian government riots in Jordan Nov. 14-25.

The immediate incident that had provoked the Es Samu raid had occurred only the previous day, Nov. 12, about 6 miles south of Arad, Israel. Three Israeli soldiers were killed and 6 wounded when their command car, on a routine patrol, detonated a mine. Footprints of 2 alleged infiltrators reportedly were traced back to the Jordanian border, one mile away. Israel filed a complaint with the UN Security Council.

Israeli soldiers, accompanied by tanks and armored cars, crossed into Jordan Nov. 13 and attacked Es Samu, a village of 4,000. The attackers soon fought a fierce battle with Jordanian soldiers who came to the defense of the village. UNTSO observers intervened and arranged a cease-fire 4 hours later, and the Israelis withdrew to their own territory. Israel charged that Es Samu had been used as a base by Arab marauders for attacks on Israel. The Es Samu raid, Israel asserted, was in retaliation for 13 recent acts of sabotage launched against Israel from Jordanian territory, 9 from the Hebron area.

Israel, Jordan and UNTSO observers gave conflicting accounts of casualties and property damage in the Es Samu battle. Major details of the various reports:

Israeli account—40 homes in Es Samu were blow up after their occupants were removed by Israeli soldiers. Israeli Mirage jets shot down one of 4 Jordanian Hunter jets 40 miles northeast of the battle area; all 4 Israeli jets returned safely. In the ensuing clash with Jordanian troops, one Israeli was killed and 10 wounded, 3 seriously. Fifteen trucks carrying Jordanian troops were destroyed. Three prisoners were taken, including a major who died of his wounds in an Israeli hospital. The invasion force consisted of 2 columns; one, including tanks and armored units, headed for Es Samu while the other moved toward 2 Bedouin encampments just east of Es Samu. The Israeli force came under Jordanian army attack at 2 approach roads to Es Samu; the Jordanians used tanks, recoilless rifles and smaller weapons.

Jordanian version—An Israeli brigade of about 1,000 men plus about "80 M-48 Patton tanks and a number of armored personnel carriers" were involved. Fifty Israeli soldiers were killed or wounded. Ten Israeli tanks were destroyed. The Israelis demolished 100 buildings in Es Samu, and several civilians in the village were killed by Israeli shelling. Six Jordanian soldiers were killed and 10 wounded. In the air clash, 2 Israeli Mirage jets were shot down and another damaged and possibly downed. One Jordanian plane was missing.

UNTSO report (based on a 4-day investigation, prepared by Lt. Gen. Odd Bull), filed with the UN Security Council Nov. 19— 15 Jordanian soldiers and 3 civilians were killed. 134 persons, 17 of them civilians, were wounded.

Preliminary UNTSO report read to the Council Nov. 16 by UN Secy. Gen. U Thant—At least 17 Israeli tanks and 80 armored half-track personnel carriers had taken part in the raid. At least 125 houses in Es Samu had been totally destroyed; 3 military jeeps, 17 military trucks and a civilian bus had been demolished. Fifteen stone huts in Jimba (about 5 miles southeast of Es Samu), which had come under Israeli attack, were destroyed.

In a speech to the Israeli Knesset Nov. 15, Premier Eshkol asserted that Syria was responsible for Israel's retaliatory attack on Jordan. Israel had "reliable information," Eshkol said, that Syria "encourages, maintains, organizes and trains saboteurs for operations in Israeli territory whether they come from Syria or via other countries." Citing the UN Security Council's failure Nov. 4 to act on Israel's charges against Syria, Eshkol told the Knesset that such inaction "encourages the aggressors to feel that they can get away with anything." Alluding to the Soviet veto that had defeated the Council's Nov. 4 resolution for easing border tensions, Eshkol warned the Syrian government not to "imagine that it is safe in the shelter of a big power." Eshkol called the Nov. 12 killing of 3 Israeli soldiers by a land mine near Arad "the gravest act of sabotage . . . so far perpetrated on the Jordanian border." He admonished "friendly" nations "who offer us advice and express indignation, without making any contribution to the stopping, or even exposure, of Arab aggression." He added: "To all of them, let it be said: After our people have suffered 2,000 years in exile, including the appalling Hitler period, we shall no longer allow Jews to be murdered again and again."

(Eshkol informed his cabinet Nov. 20 that Israel would begin a major effort to seal its borders against Arab marauders. He said measures would include strengthening the "deployment of forces" on the frontiers. In a previous action aimed at improving the Israeli army's "readiness and capacity," Eshkol had announced Nov. 8 the extension of military service for conscripts from 26 to 30 months.)

The UN Security Council, by 14-0 vote (one abstention: New Zealand) Nov. 25, approved a resolution that censured Israel for its "large-scale military action" against Es Samu "in violation of the United Nations Charter and of the general armistice agreement between Israel and Jordan." Asserting that "actions of military reprisal cannot be tolerated," the resolution warned Israel that "if they are repeated, the Security Council will have to consider further and more effective steps as envisaged in the Charter to insure against the repetition of such acts." (New Zealand delegate Frank Corner said he had abstained because he considered the resolution inadequate since it did not propose a long-term solution to the Israeli-Arab border tensions.)

After the vote, Michael S. Comay, Israeli representative to the UN, summed up the views his delegation had expressed during Council debate: "The fundamental cause of Arab-Israeli tension in the Middle East lies in Arab belligerence and military threat against Israel, in standing violation of the [UN] Charter and the armistice agreements."

A request for the Council session had been filed Nov. 15 by Muhammad H. el-Farra, Jordanian delegate, who called for "urgent steps to prevent any further deterioration" of the border situation. In opening Council debate Nov. 16, the U.S., Britain, France and the Soviet Union strongly assailed the Israeli raid on Jordan and called for measures to prevent future incidents.

Among major statements made during the Council session:

U.S. Amb. Arthur J. Goldberg—The Israeli raid "far surpass[ed] the cumulative total of the various acts of terrorism conducted against the frontiers of Israel."

Lord Caradon of Britain—Reprisal raids were wrong even when directed against those responsible for the precipitating incidents, but in this case the object of the reprisal (Jordan) was not responsible.

Nikolai T. Fedorenko of the Soviet Union—"Extremist forces in Tel Aviv," with the support of imperialist powers, were responsible for the Israeli raid. The raid was not a spontaneous move by individuals but "a premeditated planned operation by the armed forces."

Roger Seydoux of France—France "condemns unequivocally the military action planned and executed by the Israeli authorities." It was hard to understand why Israel attacked "a country that respects its obligations [Jordan]" in view of the fact that Israel's major complaint was directed elsewhere (at Syria).

Premier Eshkol Nov. 27 criticized the Security Council censure of Israel as "one sided." In a statement made at a cabinet meeting and broadcast over the state radio, Eshkol said: "So long as the Security Council has not adopted effective measures to stop the aggressor, it is the duty and right of an attacked state to defend itself. Our experience teaches us that self-defense is imperative for our survival."

The Israeli attack on Es Samu had precipitated violent demonstrations in the former Palestinian section of Jordan Nov. 14-25. At least 6 persons were reported killed in clashes with Jordanian police and soldiers in Ramallah, Nablus and Jordanian Jerusalem.

Outbreaks were reported also in Hebron and other cities in Jordan. The rioters first demanded arms to fight Israel but then directed their anger at King Hussein. They criticized his alleged policy of restraint toward Israel and expressed support for the Cairo-based Palestine Liberation Organization (PLO).

The first outbreak of anti-Hussein sentiment erupted Nov. 24 in a riot in Ramallah (8 miles north of Jerusalem). Palestinian refugees from 2 UN camps outside the town marched to the center of the city. They shouted slogans denouncing Hussein, demanding arms and calling for the leadership of Ahmed Shukairy, head of the PLO. Jordanian troops broke up the march. Several hundred persons were reported arrested. The Ramallah demonstrators were stirred up by a PLO broadcast from Cairo earlier that day. The PLO called on the Jordanian army "to join the people's rebellion and deal a crushing blow to Hussein and [Jordanian Premier Wasfi el-]Tell." It urged Jordanian cabinet members to resign by Nov. 26 "to avoid complicity with Hussein and Tell" and thus "save their honor and their lives."

The city councils of Jordanian Jerusalem and Nablus had petitioned Hussein to lift the ban on the training of saboteurs and commandos in Jordan to attack Israel. The councils had also urged the king to permit Shukairy and the PLO "free access to our people." Jordan had severed relations with the PLO in April, but the organization's office had remained open in Amman until the government ordered its closing Nov. 26.

The anti-Hussein riots spread to Jerusalem Nov. 25. Palestinian demonstrators shouted "Down with the monarchy" and demanded arms to "revenge our brothers in Es Samu." Jordanian troops had fired at the marchers and reportedly wounded about 40. Troops also fired over the heads of demonstrators in Ramallah, which had been placed under curfew. Nablus and Hebron were sealed off by troops.

Hussein Nov. 26 issued a decree authorizing the immediate military conscription of all Jordanians between the ages of 18 and 40. In an apparent move to mollify the Palestinian rioters, the Jordanian cabinet approved the establishment of military training camps in all Jordanian governorates and the issuance of arms to Jordanian villagers on the Israeli border.

In an interview in Cairo Nov. 25, Shukairy acknowledged that the PLO had instigated the riots in Jordan. But he assailed the Jordanian government for having carried out "an escalation of terror" in quelling the disturbances. Shukairy asserted that Premier Tell had known in advance that the Israelis planned to attack Es Samu but had done nothing to prevent the raid. Shukairy also said: During the past 6 months U.S. intelligence agents in Amman had helped Jordan in its "collusion" with Israel; Arab terrorists would soon increase their attacks on Israel and emulate the tactics of the Viet Cong (Shukairy had said previously that PLO representatives had been sent to Vietnam and Communist China to observe Communist guerrilla techniques); armed PLO troops (who, according to UN estimates, numbered more than 10,000 in the UAR-administered Gaza Strip) were receiving arms from Communist China.

Shukairy Nov. 27 announced plans to widen training of Palestinian Arabs to fight Israel. He said at a rally on the University of Cairo campus that additional training camps would be set up in the Cairo area. Shukairy said other Palestinians were being trained in Communist China, Syria and Iraq.

An Amman broadcast Nov. 25 made public a letter, sent to UAR Pres. Gamal Abdel Nasser Oct. 18, in which Hussein had protested the use of Egyptian territory for PLO attacks on Jordan. An Amman broadcast Nov. 26 blamed "seditious elements" for the Jerusalem riots of Nov. 25 and said the perpetrators had been arrested. Premier Tell charged Nov. 28 that "2 outside Arab sources" had expended "considerable amounts" of funds to finance the demonstrations in Jordan. Tell reportedly alluded to the UAR and Syria. Tell said Jordan was sympathetic to the PLO's aim of retaking Arab lands in Israel, but "we abhor and detest the opportunists who are exploiting the organization and want to use it for subversion." Tell accused Israel of harassing Jordan "to make us stop work and economic development and waste our time." Tell said the fatalities in the riots numbered 5: 2 in Nablus, 2 in Jerusalem and one outside a refugee camp at Ramallah (2 Ramallah deaths had been reported).

Hussein said Nov. 29 that "there was no justification whatsoever" for Israel's attack on Es Samu. Hussein discounted Israeli charges that Jordan had violated the armistice agreement by not preventing Arab marauders from infiltrating into Israel. He said: "If terrorists do infiltrate the border despite every preventive measure we take, Israel has equal responsibility to seal its side of the line. If it fails to do this it is equally to blame for whatever may follow." Hussein charged that there was "sufficient evidence of a new Soviet plan for this area, the result of setbacks the Communists have suffered at several points around the world, in Asia and Africa." Blaming the Communists for the riots that had swept Jordan, Hussein warned the Western powers that if Communist or pro-Communist governments assumed power in the Middle East, "the threat to them will be very, very severe."

(The Soviet Communist Party newspaper *Pravda* Dec. 4 said Moscow was "interested in lessening tensions and securing the peace in the Middle East." Citing the Soviet Union's technical aid to Syria, *Pravda* said: "It is not on the battlefield but on construction sites that people build their future. If this philosophy is not attractive to King Hussein, let him go his own way." *Pravda* denied Hussein's charges that the Soviet Union was responsible for the turmoil in the Middle East. It blamed "imperialists.")

UAR & Syria Resume Ties, Plan Joint Command

The United Arab Republic and Syria agreed Nov. 3, 1966 to resume diplomatic relations and to establish a joint defense command. The agreement was reached by UAR Pres. Gamal Abdel Nasser and Syrian Premier Yussef Zayen during talks held in Cairo Nov. 1-7. (When Soviet Premier Aleksei N. Kosygin had visited Cairo in May, he had urged Nasser to reopen political negotiations with Syria.)

The agreement to resume diplomatic relations, signed Nov. 3, called for an early exchange of ambassadors. Syria had not had diplomatic relations with Cairo since it broke away from the UAR union in 1961. The defense agreement, signed Nov. 4 by Zayen and UAR Premier Mohamed Sidky Soliman, stated that Syria and the UAR would come to each other's assistance if either came under attack by a 3d nation. Gen. Mohammed Fawzi, UAR chief of staff, was to be in command of UAR and Syrian forces in the event of joint military operations.

A communiqué issued at the conclusion of the talks declared that the UAR and Syria would undertake preliminary measures "in the spheres of economy, culture, information and other fields" leading to a possible reunification of the 2 countries in order to "defeat the offensive being launched by reaction to cooperation with imperialism and Zionism." Citing the bilateral agreement "on the coordination of political action," the joint statement said the UAR and Syrian defense and foreign affairs ministers would meet every 6 months or whenever conditions required.

Arabs to Aid Jordan Against Israel

In response to the Israeli attack on Es Samu, the Arab League's Defense Council convened in emergency session in Cairo Dec. 7, 1966. The Council Dec. 10 approved the conditional dispatch of Saudi Arabian and Iraqi troops to Jordan within 2 months to protect Jordan against possible attack by Israel. But Jordan rejected demands at the meeting that Syrian or PLO troops be permitted to enter Jordan "to take up positions on the front line against Israel."

The Defense Council meeting had been marked by sharp differences, according to an account of the 4-day conference provided by Jordanian Information Min. Sharif Abdelhamid Sharaf Dec. 11. Sharaf, a cousin of Jordanian King Hussein, said that Jordan had not requested Saudi and Iraqi military aid. He said that when this suggestion had been made the Amman government had insisted on the replacement of UN forces by UAR troops in the Sinai Peninsula and in the Gaza Strip (both areas bordering on Israel) as "a basic condition" for the entry of Saudi and Iraqi troops into Jordan. Describing the Jordanian proposal as a "real Arab mobilization against Israel," Sharaf said the UAR would first have to withdraw its troops participating in the Yemeni civil war before it could send its troops into the Gaza Strip and the Sinai Peninsula.

(An Israeli military spokesman had reported Nov. 29 that a Mirage jet of the Israeli air force had shot down 2 UAR MiG-19 jets that day 2-4 miles inside Israel. The engagement occurred between the Israeli border points of Beerrotayim and Har Lots. The 2 UAR planes were said to have crashed on Egyptian territory in the Sinai Pensinsula. A UAR announcement said the wreckage of a MiG-19 had been found in the area mentioned by the Israeli report. But the Egyptian statement made no mention of an air clash with Israeli planes.)

Galilee Border Battles

Israeli-Arab border clashes and Arab infiltration raids into Israel continued into 1967. There was little variation in the pattern of violence of previous years, except that the fighting this time was confined largely to Israeli and Syrian troops and involved the employment of a greater number of forces and of weapons heavier than those used before in the frontier battles.

The Israelis and Syrians clashed repeatedly in the Galilee border region Jan. 1-11, 1967. The most serious engagement occurred Jan. 11 near Notera, Israel, 15 miles south of the Sea of Galilee. Israel claimed that the 2-hour battle had started when a routine Israeli army patrol came under machinegun fire from Syrian positions at Darbashiya. In an ensuing exchange of mortar and tank fire, a Syrian Soviet-built T-34 tank was destroyed and an Israeli tractor damaged, according to the Israelis. Syria claimed that the fighting had started when "an Israeli tractor entered the demilitarized zone" and "simultaneously enemy positions at the [Israeli] settlement . . . opened fire with machineguns and mortars." The Damascus report said that in returning fire, the Syrian forces had destroyed 2 Israeli artillery pieces, a tractor and 4 blockhouses and had set a fuel depot afire.

Israeli Premier Eshkol had warned Syria Jan. 7 that it was "not immune to treatment in kind." He said that Israel would "not tolerate these incursions and murders." Israel would seek to limit its military action to self-defense, he pledged, "but I cannot exclude the possibility that we may have no other recourse but deterrent measures." After the Jan. 8 border clash, Eshkol said: Israel would "not tolerate developments likely to impair our sovereignty or the security of our citizens."

Israeli army tanks went into action for the first time Jan. 9 near Beit Katsir, south of the Sea of Galilee. Israeli armor was thrown into the battle after Syrian tanks opened fire from a position at Tawafik, overlooking Beit Katsir, the Israelis claimed. According to the Israeli account, 2 Syrian tanks were hit and abandoned. Asserting that until the Jan. 9 clash Israeli forces had employed only automatic weapons in defending the northern border areas, an Israeli Foreign Office spokesman expressed confidence that Israel's "limited escalation" of firepower would deter future Syrian attacks.

Israel and Syria filed protests with the UN Security Council Jan. 8-11 over the border clashes. An Israeli letter of Jan. 8 charged that Syria had attacked Israel "in flagrant violation" of the general armistice agreement and "in defiance of the commitment for an unconditional cease-fire pledged by the Syrian government" June 9, 1965. The letter cited 19 Syrian acts of "aggression" between Dec. 30, 1966 and Jan. 8, 1967. A 2d Israeli letter submitted to the Council Jan. 9 complained that the stationing of Syrian tanks along the Israeli border was forbidden by the armistice agreement. A Syrian letter to the Council Jan. 10 expressed fear that Israel was provoking incidents on the Syrian frontier "to make subsequent large-scale aggression look like the outcome of these actions." An Israeli charge that Syria had again violated the 1949 armistice agreement by using heavy weapons was brought to the Council's attention Jan. 11. The Israeli note said that in a clash that day Syrian forces had used 120-mm. mortars.

Syria & Israel Discuss Dispute

In early 1967 Israeli and Syrian representatives discussed their border dispute for the first time in 8 years. The talks took place at meetings of the Israel-Syria Mixed Armistice Commission held Jan. 25, 29 and Feb. 2. A scheduled 4th meeting was canceled indefinitely Feb. 15 by Lt. Gen. Odd Bull, head of UNTSO, who had acted as mediator at the 3 meetings. Bull said future talks would be pointless. Syria had first agreed to a single agenda dealing with cultivation in the 45-mile-long demilitarized zones between Syria and Israel. But at the meetings the Damascus delegation refused to discuss the matter.

Syria and Israel had agreed to the talks Jan. 16 after an urgent appeal by UN Secy. Gen. U Thant Jan. 15. Thant had made the appeal in the wake of the sharp border clashes of Jan. 1-11 and after the receipt of a report on the frontier situation from Bull. Thant told the Security Council Jan. 15 that Bull's report was "of such a disturbing nature as to impel me to communicate with Israel and Syria urgently." Thant said that according to Bull, the Israelis and Syrians had moved heavy arms, armored vehicles and troops into the demilitarized zones on both sides of the Syrian-Israeli lines. As a result of this build-up, Thant warned, "the situation threatens to erupt at any moment into a large-scale clash . . . in overt violation of Security Council resolutions and of the [1949] Israel-Syria General Armistice agreement." Thant said the purpose of the meetings was to seek agreement "on the problems of cultivation in the area, which have given rise to the situation of recent weeks." Thant, at a news conference Jan. 10, had attributed the latest border clashes to the opening of the cultivation season, when Israeli and Syrian farmers began plowing in adjacent sectors in the buffer area.

(Israel claimed both sides of the demilitarized zones, which were situated on the Israeli side of the former international frontier between Syria and Palestine. Syria had occupied the zones at the end of the 1948 Arab-Israeli war but later had withdrawn. Israel denied subsequent Syrian claims that Damascus had equal rights in the zones.)

At the first meeting of the Mixed Armistice Commission, held Jan. 25 on the Syrian side of the B'not Ya'akov bridge over the Jordan River, Syria and Israel pledged to observe the armistice agreement and to refrain from hostile military moves. Moshe Sasson, head of the Israeli delegation, said Israel was prepared to "negotiate a practical arrangement on problems of cultivation" in the demilitarized zones "without prejudice to our stated views on the broader political and juridicial issues" of border sovereignty.

Syrian claims to the border zones were stated at the 2d session, held Jan. 29 near Mahanayim, Israel, 2 miles west of the B'not Ya'akov bridge. The Syrian chief delegate, naval Capt. Adnan Abdullah, raised the question despite the fact that it was not on the agenda. Gen. Bull and the Israeli delegation objected. A Damascus broadcast later Jan. 29 said Abdullah had demanded: (a) that Israel withdraw its military forces from the demilitarized zones and remove fortifications from the buffer areas as the price of a truce in the area; (b) that former Arab inhabitants of the demilitarized zones be permitted to return.

The Israelis and Syrians met Feb. 2 on the Syrian side of the bridge. The conference was adjourned after an hour following Syrian refusal to discuss the topic on the agenda.

Israeli Premier Eshkol had pledged Jan. 17 that his government would "exhaust every available remedy before allowing Syria to drag this country into war." Speaking to the Knesset, Eshkol criticized the language of U Thant's Jan. 15 appeal to Syria and Israel. Thant had made "no distinction between this country, which had been attacked, and Syria, which is the aggressor," Eshkol complained. Eshkol also took issue with Thant's view that the Syrian-Israeli tension stemmed from a dispute over cultivation rights in the demilitarized zones. Eshkol said border incidents had occurred in areas that had no connection with cultivation and were not in the vicinity of the demilitarized zones.

A series of border incidents, attributed to Arab terrorist infiltrators, erupted prior to, during and after the Syrian-Israeli talks.

Among major incidents:

■ An Israeli youth was killed and 2 others injured Jan. 14 when a mine exploded in a soccer field at Dishon, a cooperative settlement at the western edge of the Sea of Galilee, near the Lebanese border.

■ Israeli and Syrian forces exchanged gunfire across the Sea of Galilee Jan. 14 and 15. In both incidents, Israeli patrol boats fired back at Syrian gun emplacements that had first opened up against Israeli fishing boats with machineguns and mortars.

■ Arab infiltration from Syria into Israel's Dan region north of the Sea of Galilee precipitated an exchange of gunfire between Israeli and Syrian soldiers Feb. 13 and 14. In the 2d incident, Israeli and Syrian soldiers fired at each other for 45 minutes after an Israeli patrol had chased 5 Syrian infiltrators who had crossed into Israeli territory. One Israeli soldier was wounded in the exchange.

■ Israeli forces Feb. 18 shot and killed a Syrian soldier 1,000 feet inside Israel near Notera, north of the Sea of Galilee. Damascus radio Feb. 19 acknowledged the death of the Syrian soldier but described his intrusion into Israeli territory as accidental.

■ A series of incidents had also broken out along the Israeli-Jordanian border. Forces of both countries exchanged gunfire briefly Jan. 15 at the northern end of the Gulf of Aqaba. The Israelis claimed that Jordanian soldiers had precipitated the skirmish by directing machinegun fire at a point between the Israeli town port of Elath and the adjacent Jordan village of Aqaba. Three Israeli soldiers were wounded. According to Jordan's version of the incident, an Israeli force had sought to invade Jordan but was repulsed.

■ An Arab terrorist group calling itself "Heroes of Repatriation" reported Jan. 23 that its armed terrorists had attacked the Israeli town of Beit Jibrin near Jerusalem Jan. 18. The group reportedly was connected with the Palestine Liberation Organization. According to the group's statement in *Al Moharrer*, a pro-Egyptian newspaper in Beirut, the terrorists had detonated 33 pounds of explosives at an Israeli ammunition depot in Beit Jibrin and then had fled back to Jordan. The statement accused Jordanian King Hussein of attempting to suppress Arab infiltration attacks against Israel. It accused the Amman government of cooperating with the U.S.' Central Intelligence Agency "in protecting Israel's security."

■ Israeli authorities reported Feb. 19 that an Arab-planned dynamite charge had exploded during the night near a water pipeline on the outskirts of Arad in the northern Negev, 7 miles south of the Jordanian border. The pipeline was undamaged. Israeli authorities said footprints of 2 infiltrators had led from the pipeline to the Jordanian frontier.

Israel announced Mar. 16 that its forces had slain 2 of 5 Arab infiltrators who had set off an explosion in an effort to blow up a water pipe and reservoir near Arad. An Israeli army spokesman said one of the infiltrators had been killed on Israeli territory, the other just across the border on Jordanian territory. According to the Israelis, one of the slain infiltrators carried papers indicating that he had crossed the Syrian-Jordanian border 7 times since Oct. 1966.

Israeli-Syrian Air & Ground Clashes

Relative calm prevailed on the Syrian-Israeli frontier from Feb. 18 until April, when there was an outbreak of heavy air and ground clashes. These clashes were the forerunners of the serious crisis that developed in May.

Israeli pilots Apr. 7 claimed the shooting down of 6 Syrian MiG-21s that day in air clashes that followed a sharp exchange of gunfire between ground troops of both countries in the border area east of the Sea of Galilee. According to the Israelis, 3 of the Syrian planes were shot down by 2 pursuing Israeli Mirage fighter pilots over Syrian territory, at least one on the outskirts of Damascus, 60 miles beyond the Syrian-Israeli border; the 3 other planes crashed in Jordan. Amman radio confirmed that 3 Syrian planes had crashed on the Jordanian side of the Yarmuk River. One Syrian pilot was said to have bailed out safely. The Israelis said the MiGs had not fired a single shot.

Damascus radio conceded the loss of 4 Syrian planes but claimed that 5 Israeli planes also were destroyed. Reporting on the ground fighting, the broadcast said that Israeli losses totaled "not less than 70 dead" and that Syrian border artillery had "completely destroyed" military emplacements in 4 Israeli settlements and knocked out 3 tractors and 2 tanks. The Damascus broadcast asserted that Syrian artillery had opened up after one of the tractors ignored a Syrian warning not to plow in a disputed area of the demilitarized zone. The Israeli-Syrian exchange of heavy automatic-weapon, tank and mortar fire continued for several hours.

According to the Israelis, the Syrians had precipitated the clash by firing on a tractor near the Israeli settlement of Haon. The Israelis said they had retaliated with air attacks on Syrian gun positions after further Syrian shelling of the nearby settlement of Tal Kazir. The Israeli settlements of Ein Gev and Gadot also came under Syrian mortar fire until Israeli planes silenced the border guns.

Syrian mortars and artillery fired on the Israeli settlement of Beit Katsir at the southern tip of the Sea of Galilee Apr. 11. Syria said the firing was aimed at armored Israeli tractors that allegedly had entered the disputed area of the demilitarized zone.

Israeli and Syrian forces clashed north of the Sea of Galilee Apr. 12. Damascus claimed that 3 soldiers of an Israeli patrol were killed and 2 others wounded when the unit crossed into Syrian territory. Israel claimed that the Israeli unit was searching for land mines when it was fired on by the Syrians. One Israeli farmer was seriously wounded, according to the Israeli report.

Israeli delegate Michael Comay in New York Apr. 7 filed with the UN Security Council a protest against the alleged Syrian attacks.

The Israeli town of Ramin in the Galilee region was shelled May 5 from Lebanese territory (one house was damaged), and a water pump was blown up near Capernaum on the western shore of the Sea of Galilee. The Syrian-based Arab terrorist group Al Asifa claimed May 6 that its commandos had shelled and damaged Israeli military installations in the Upper Galilee town of Manara the previous day.

Arab terrorists May 8 penetrated 5 miles inside Israel to plant an explosive charge that blew up an Israeli military vehicle on a highway at Ammiad. Two soldiers in the vehicle were uninjured.

In a note to the UN Security Council May 11, Gideon Rafael, Israeli delegate to the UN, warned that unless Syria altered its "unrealistic and aggressive policy," Israel "regards itself as fully entitled to act in self-defense." UN Secy. Gen. U Thant May 11 deplored the Arab raids against Israel. He said the attacks, "by their nature . . ., seem to indicate that the individuals who committed them have had more specialized training than has usually been evident in El Fatah incidents in the past." George J. Tomeh, Syria's permanent representative to the UN, met with Thant May 13 to criticize his remarks. Tomeh later told reporters he had informed Thant that the May 11 statement was interpreted by Israel "as condoning the use of force by Israel." Tomeh said he had also advised Thant of a May 13 *N.Y. Times* dispatch from Tel Aviv that said that "some Israeli authorities have decided that the use of force against Syria may be the only way to curtail increasing terrorism." Tomeh said he had also cited statements by Israeli leaders since May 11 that "contain a very clear threat of the use of force against Syria."

APPROACHING CONFLICT
May 14 - June 4

The Israeli-Syrian clashes of Apr. 1967, followed by continued fighting in early May, built up to the crisis that erupted June 5 in all-out war between Israel and the Arab states. Troops of the United Arab Republic and Syria began to mass on the borders of Israel May 14, and ultimately UAR and Syrian forces there totaled 85,000 and 12,000 troops, respectively. Cairo and Damascus said they were making these military moves because Israel was preparing to attack Syria.

Other Arab states, displaying traditional solidarity against Israel, acted immediately to aid Cairo and Damascus. Troops of Jordan, Iraq, Algeria, Saudi Arabia and Kuwait were alerted. Iraqi and Saudi troops joined Jordanian forces on the Israeli border. The UAR and Jordan signed a mutual defense pact May 30, and Iraq signed the accord June 4.

As Israel responded to the Arab show of force by deploying its own troops, the UAR increased the pressure on Israel. Cairo asked UN Secy. Gen. U Thant May 19 to withdraw UN Emergency Force troops that had been stationed for 10 years as a buffer between Israel and Egypt in the Gaza Strip and at Sharm el Sheik (some times transliterated Sharm ash-Shaykh), near the mouth of the strategic Gulf of Aqaba. Thant immediately complied. The UAR May 23 closed the gulf to Israeli shipping and enforced the blockade by announcing the mining of the entrance to the waterway.

International efforts to avert war proved unavailing. The UN Security Council met in emergency session May 24-June 3, but the meetings failed. The maritime powers, led by the U.S. and Britain, deplored the blockade of the Gulf of Aqaba and issued pronouncements upholding the international character of the gulf. But they took no definitive action to support their position.

Arabs Mass Troops on Israel's Borders

The UAR alerted its armed forces May 14 and began moving troops to Sinai Peninsula positions bordering Israel in observance of Cairo's 1966 defense pact with Syria. A state of emergency was declared throughout Egypt May 16. A Cairo broadcast announced that all military forces were "in a complete state of preparedness for war." By May 20, the number of Egyptian forces deployed along the Israeli frontier was estimated at 58,000.

A Damascus broadcast May 17 said that Syria's armed forces had been brought to "maximum preparedness" in view of "information about the Israeli build-up along the Syrian border and threatening statements by Israeli officials." It was reported that Syria had massed a force of 12,000 men along Israel's border.

The UAR May 21 mobilized its full 100,000-man army reserve and Cairo announced May 22 that Iraq had agreed to send army and air force units to Egypt to strengthen the military build-up against Israel.

The UAR-Syrian moves apparently had been coordinated at meetings held in Damascus May 14-15 by Gen. Mohammed Fawzi, UAR chief of staff, and Syria's 2 top military officials—Maj. Gen. Hafez Assad, defense minister, and Maj. Gen. Ahmed Sweidani, chief of staff. Maj. Gen. Mahmoud Chakry, Iraqi defense minister, was quoted May 18 as saying that Iraqi officials were in consultation with UAR and Syrian military leaders to coordinate "the use of military units in case of aggression." The Iraqi Defense Ministry announced that the country's armed forces were alerted and ready to support Syria. Kuwait also announced its forces had been alerted and were at the disposal of the Arab League's Cairo-based Unified Command. The UAR's military actions were supported May 20 by a resolution signed in Cairo by ambassadors of 12 Arab League nations: the UAR, Iraq, Saudi Arabia, Syria, Lebanon, Jordan, Yemen, Libya, Sudan, Morocco, Kuwait and Algeria.

Israel had announced May 18 the adoption of "appropriate measures" to cope with the UAR build-up. Israeli tanks were reported May 20 to have moved to the Sinai frontier. Premier Levi Eshkol reported May 21 that his government had "completed a partial mobilization of reserves [estimated at 230,000] and . . . taken political measures to preserve peace and assure Israel's full rights." In an address to the Israeli Knesset (parliament) May 22, Eshkol said that in the past few days Egypt had increased its forces in the Sinai Peninsula from 35,000 to 85,000 men. Because of this threat, Eshkol declared, Israel had been forced to mass its forces to meet any eventuality. Eshkol assured Cairo and Damascus that Israel had no intentions of launching aggressive moves against the UAR or Syria. He appealed for a mutual reduction of troop concentrations in the Middle East and pledged that Israel would pull back its troops from the Sinai frontier if Cairo also withdrew its forces. Eshkol asserted that Syrian-originated infiltration attacks on Israel, numbering more than 100, were largely responsible for the current tensions. Eshkol added: "On the heightening and growing effectiveness of these sabotage activities, I found it necessary to address clear and explicit warnings to Syria that we are not prepared to put up with their continuation."

Thant May 19 formally stated his reasons for halting UNEF operations. In a report to the UN Security Council, Thant said:

(A) The UNEF was introduced into the territory of the UAR on the basis of an agreement reached in Cairo [in 1956] between the Secretary General [the late Dag Hammarskjöld] and the president of Egypt, and it therefore seemed fully clear to me that since UAR consent was withdrawn, it was incumbent on the Secretary General to give orders for the withdrawal of the force. The consent of the host country is a basic principle which has applied to all UN peace-keeping operations.

(B) In practical fact, UNEF could not remain or function without the continuing consent and cooperation of the host country.

(C) I have also been influenced by my deep concern to avoid any action which would either compromise or endanger the contingents which make up the force. The UNEF is, after all, a peace-keeping, not an enforcement, operation.

(D) In the face of the request for the withdrawal of the force, there seemed to me to be no alternative course of action which could be taken by the Secretary General without putting into question the sovereign authority of the government of the UAR within its own territory.

Thant also said that a series of harassing tactics by Egyptian troops against UNEF positions May 17-18 had made it "incumbent" on him to order UNEF's withdrawal.

In a further report on the crisis, Thant told the UN Security Council May 20 that he woud leave for Cairo May 22 in an effort to ease tensions. Thant said the situation in the Middle East was "more disturbing, . . . more menacing that at any time since the fall of 1956." Thant said that the Arab raids against Israel were "the major factor" in increased tension in the area.

The UAR governor of the Gaza Strip, Maj. Gen. Abdel Moneim Hosny, had said May 19 that Cairo had found it necessary to request UNEF's withdrawal to insure the safety of the UN troops and "to discharge fully its responsibilities for the defense of the sector in the face of Israeli aggression." Troops of the UAR-supported Palestine Liberation Organization (PLO) occupied UNEF border posts in the Gaza Strip May 20. PLO Chrmn. Ahmed Shukairy declared: "We now stand face to face with our enemies. Previously there had been that international barrier between us and the enemy, and this barrier has now fallen forever." Egypt declared a state of emergency in the Gaza Strip May 20. Cairo radio reported May 21 that UNEF troops had started to evacuate Sharm el Sheik; UAR soldiers quickly moved into the strategic post.

British Foreign Secy. George Brown May 18 had criticized UNEF's withdrawal. Speaking to a dinner of the UN Association in London, Brown said: "It really makes a mockery of the peace-keeping force of the United Nations, if, as soon as tension rises, the UN Force is told to leave. Indeed, the collapse of UNEF might well have repercussions on other UN peace-keeping forces, and the credibility of the United Nations' efforts in this field are thrown into question."

U.S. Amb.-to-UN Arthur J. Goldberg said May 20 that the U.S. shared Thant's concern over the explosive situation in the Middle East. But he added that the U.S. felt it was "vital" to maintain the UN presence in the area.

In his May 22 address to the Knesset, Israeli Premier Eshkol assailed what he held was Thant's precipitate removal of UNEF. Eshkol recalled that the late Dag Hammarskjöld, as Secretary General, had informed the UN General Assembly Feb. 26, 1957 of his assurances to Israel that the proper way to decide on a request for UNEF's withdrawal would be to inform the UNEF Advisory Committee and permit it to decide whether the General Assembly should be consulted.

UNEF Ends Operations in Sinai & Gaza

The UN Emergency Force (UNEF) halted its patrols in the Gaza Strip and at Sharm el Sheik at the mouth of the Gulf of Aqaba May 19. UN Secy. Gen. U Thant had agreed to end the UNEF operations after receiving a cabled request May 18 from UAR Foreign Min. Mahmoud Riad for termination of the UN activities there. Riad recalled that UNEF had been stationed on Egyptian territory at the invitation of Cairo and that its continued presence depended on Egyptian approval. He requested that UNEF be pulled out "as soon as possible." In his reply to Riad, Thant agreed that the UAR had the right to insist on UNEF's departure. But he said he had "serious misgivings" about such a withdrawal. UNEF, Thant asserted, "has been an important factor in maintaining relative quiet in the area of its deployment during the 10 years, and its withdrawal may have grave implications for peace."

Ceremonies were held in Gaza May 19 to mark the formal ending of UNEF's operations. The UN flag was hauled down from UNEF headquarters, and the UN troops withdrew to their barracks to await repatriation to their countries. UNEF, at the time of its withdrawal, was made up of 3,393 troops supplied by India (978 men), Canada (800), Yugoslavia (580) Sweden (528), Brazil (432), Norway (72) and Denmark (3). The Gaza Strip, originally a part of Palestine, had been seized by Egypt in the 1948-49 Arab-Israeli war. Israel recaptured the 25-mile-long, 5-mile-wide area during the 1956 Suez-Sinai campaign but was forced to relinquish it under a Nov. 6, 1956 UN General Assembly resolution ordering it restored to Egyptian administration. The same resolution established UNEF and directed it to take up positions in the strip and to act as a buffer force between Israel and Egypt. Israel refused to allow UNEF troops to be stationed on its territory.

UAR Closes Gulf of Aqaba to Israel

The UAR May 23 announced the closing of the Strait of Tiran, at the entrance to the Gulf of Aqaba, to Israeli shipping. A government statement May 24 said that all entrances to the gulf had been mined as of May 23. The blockade, the statement said, was further enforced by Egyptian shore batteries on Sinai territory, armed boats and air patrols. It warned that Israeli ships attempting to enter the gulf for the Israeli port of Elath, at the head of the strategic waterway, would be fired on if they disobeyed orders to turn back. Cairo stated that other ships would be subject to search to determine whether they were carrying strategic material, including oil, to Elath.

The Gulf of Aqaba, which meets the Red Sea at its entrance, is 100 miles long, and its width varies from 10 miles to 30. It is bordered by 4 countries: Israel and Jordan, where each had a small coastline of about 6 miles and 2 major ports—Elath (Israel) and Aqaba (Jordan); Egypt on the west (Sinai) and Saudi Arabia on the east. Entrance to the gulf is restricted to an 800-1,000-yard-wide channel between the Sinai coast and 2 rocky islands—Tiran and Sanafir. The channel east of these 2 islands is impassable because of reefs and shoals. Egyptian guns commanded the western channel after UNEF's withdrawal from Sharm el Sheik May 19.

UAR Pres. Nasser announced the closing of the Gulf of Aqaba in a speech at an Egyptian air force headquarters in Sinai May 23. Justifying the gulf's closure and other Egyptian moves to counter Israel, Nasser recalled that Britain and France had supported Israel in 1956 during the Suez crisis. But, he said, the situation had become entirely different. Nasser continued:

> Israel today is not backed by Britain and France as was the case in 1956. It has the United States, which supports it and supplies it with arms. . . . We are now face to face with Israel. In recent days Israel has been making threats of aggression and has been boasting. On May 12 a very impertinent statement was made. . . . The statement said that the Israeli commanders have announced they would carry out military operations against Syria in order to occupy Damascus and overthrow the Syrian government. On the same day the Israeli premier, Eshkol, made a strongly threatening statement against Syria. . . . On May 13 we received accurate information that Israel was concentrating on the Syrian border huge armed forces of about 11 to 13 brigades. These forces were divided into 2 fronts, one south of Lake Tiberias [the Sea of Galilee] and the other north of the lake. The decision made by Israel at this time was to carry out an aggression against Syria as of May 17. On May 14 we took our measures, discussed the matter and contacted our Syrian brothers. Lt. Gen. [Mohammed] Fawzi left for Syria to co-ordinate matters. We told them that we had decided that if Syria was attacked, Egypt would enter the battle from the first minute. This was the situation at May 14. The forces began to move in the direction of Sinai to take up normal positions. . . .

> On May 16 we requested the withdrawal of the UN Emergency Force. A worldwide campaign, led by the United States, Britain and Canada, began opposing the withdrawal of UNEF from Egypt. Thus, we felt that there were attempts to turn UNEF into a force serving neo-imperialism. It is obvious that UNEF entered Egypt with our approval and therefore cannot continue to stay in Egypt except with our approval. A campaign is also being mounted against the UN Secretary General because he made a faithful and honest decision and could not surrender to the pressure brought to bear upon him by the United States, Britain, and Canada to make UNEF an instrument for implementing imperial-

ism's plans. . . . I say this quite frankly, that had UNEF ignored its basic mission and turned to achieving the aims of imperialism, we would have regarded it as a hostile force and forcibly disarmed it. . . . At the same time I say that UNEF has honorably and faithfully carried out its duties. The UN Secretary General refused to succumb to pressure [and] issued immediate orders to UNEF to withdraw. Consequently, we laud the UNEF, which stayed 10 years in one country serving peace. . . .

Our forces are now in Sinai, and we are in a state of complete mobilization in Gaza and Sinai.

We note that there is a great deal of talk about peace these days. International peace—international security—UN intervention—and so on and so forth, which appears daily in the press. Why is it that no one spoke about peace, the United Nations, and security when on May 12 the Israeli premier and the Israeli commanders made their statements that they would occupy Damascus, overthrow the Syrian regime, and occupy a part of Syrian territory? . . . If there is a true desire for peace, we say that we also work for peace. But does peace mean that we should ignore the rights of the Palestinian people because of the lapse of time? Does peace mean that we should concede our rights because of the lapse of time? They speak about a "UN presence in the region for the sake of peace." Does "UN presence in the region for peace" mean that we should close our eyes to everything? The United Nations adopted a number of resolutions in favor of the Palestinian people. Israel implemented none of these resolutions. This brought no reaction from the United States. Today U.S. Senators, members of the House of Representatives, the press, and the entire world speak in favor of Israel, of the Jews. But nothing is said in favor of the Arabs. . . . The peace talk is heard only when Israel is in danger. But when Arab rights and the rights of the Palestinian people are lost, no one speaks about peace, rights, or anything. Therefore it is clear that an alliance exists between the Western powers—chiefly represented by the United States and Britain —and Israel. There is a political alliance [which] prompts the Western powers to give military equipment to Israel. . . .

The armed forces yesterday occupied Sharm el Sheik. It is an affirmation of our rights and our sovereignty over the Gulf of Aqaba. The gulf constitutes Egyptian territorial waters. Under no circumstances will we allow the Israel flag to pass through the Gulf of Aqaba. The Jews threatened war. We tell them: You are welcome, we are ready for war. Our armed forces and our people are ready for war, but under no circumstances will we abandon any of our rights. The water is ours. War might be an opportunity for Israel and Rabin [Maj. Gen. Itzhak Rabin, the Israeli chief of staff] to test their forces against ours and see that what they wrote about the 1956 battle and the occupation of Sinai was all a lot of nonsense.

With all this there is imperialism, Israel, and reaction. Reaction casts doubt on everything, and so does the Islamic Alliance. We all know that the Islamic Alliance is represented by 3 states—Saudi Arabia, Jordan and Iran. They are saying that the purpose of the Islamic Alliance is to unite the Moslems against Israel. I would like the Islamic Alliance to serve the Palestine question in only one way—by preventing the supply of oil to Israel. The oil which now reaches Israel through

Elath comes from one of the Islamic Alliance States. It goes to Elath from Iran. Such is the Islamic Alliance. It is an imperialist alliance, and this means it sides with Zionism because Zionism is the main ally of imperialism. The Arab world, which is now mobilized to the highest degree, knows all this. It knows how to deal with the imperialist agents, the allies of Zionism, and the 5th column. They say they want to co-ordinate their plans with us. We cannot coordinate our plans in any way with Islamic Alliance members because it would mean giving our plans to the Jews and to Israel.

This is a vital battle. When we said that we were ready for the battle, we meant that we would surely fight if Syria or any other Arab state was subjected to aggression. . . .

Israeli Premier Eshkol warned May 23 that a UAR blockade of the Gulf of Aqaba would constitute "an act of aggression against Israel." Speaking in the Knesset, Eshkol said: "Any interference with freedom of shipping in the gulf and the strait" would also be "a gross violation of international law, a blow at the sovereign rights of other nations. . . . If a criminal attempt is made to impose a blockade on the shipping of a member state of the United Nations, it will be a dangerous precedent that will have grave effects on international relations and the freedom of the seas."

Pres. Johnson May 23 expressed opposition to Egypt's closing of the Gulf of Aqaba to Israeli shipping. He described it as an "illegal" act that had "brought a new and grave dimension to the crisis" in the Middle East. The president also deplored the general deterioration of the political situation in the area. Mr. Johnson said:

. . . The government of the United States is deeply concerned, in particular with 3 potentially explosive aspects of the present confronta-tion. First, we regret that the general armistice agreements have failed to prevent warlike acts from the territory of one against another govern-ment, or against civilians, or territory, under control of another government. 2d, we are dismayed at the hurried withdrawal of the UN Emergency Force from Gaza and Sinai after more than 10 years of steadfast and effective service in keeping the peace, without action by either the General Assembly or the Security Council. . . . 3d, we deplore the recent build-up of military forces and believe it a matter of urgent importance to reduce troop concentrations. . . .

The United States considers the gulf to be an international waterway and feels that a blockade of Israeli shipping is illegal and potentially disastrous to the cause of peace. The right of free, innocent passage of the international waterway is a vital interest of the international com-munity. . . . We have urged Secy. Gen. Thant to recognize the sensi-tivity of the Aqaba question and to give it the highest priority in his discussions in Cairo.

To the leaders of all the nations of the Near East, I wish to say what 3 Presidents have said before—that the United States is firmly committed to the support of the political independence and territorial integrity of all the nations of the area. The United States strongly opposes aggression by anyone in the area, in any form, overt or clandestine. This has been the policy of the United States led by 4 Presidents—Pres. Truman, Pres. Eisenhower, Pres. Kennedy and myself—as well as the policy of both of our political parties. . . . We have always opposed—and we oppose in other parts of the world at this moment—the efforts of other nations to resolve their problems with their neighbors by aggression. We shall continue to do so. And we appeal to all other peace-loving nations to do likewise.

We call upon all concerned to observe in a spirit of restraint their solemn responsibilities under the UN Charter and the general armistice agreements. These provide an honorable means of preventing hostilities until, through the efforts of the international community, a peace with justice and honor can be achieved. . . .

The Egyptian newspaper *Al Ahram* reported May 26 that UAR Foreign Min. Mahmoud Riad had rejected a 5-point peace formula by Pres. Johnson submitted May 23 by U.S. Amb.-to-UAR Richard H. Nolte. The newspaper said Mr. Johnson's formula contained these major provisions: (1) UN Emergency Force troops would remain in the Gaza Strip and in Sharm el Sheik; (2) the UAR would not send troops to Sharm el Sheik until Cairo guaranteed shipping through the strait; (3) UAR forces would be barred from entering the Gaza sector of the UAR-Israeli border; (4) the UN would administer Gaza until the crisis was settled; (5) UAR and Israeli troops would pull back from the border areas. Riad was quoted as having told Nolte that "if Israel carries out aggression against any Arab country, we shall consider you [the U.S.] as partners." (The U.S. State Department had advised U.S. citizens May 22 not to visit Israel, the UAR, Syria and Jordan in view of the growing crisis. The department also urged Americans not having "essential business" in those countries to leave. Another department directive [reported May 25] called for dependents of U.S. officials to leave Israel and the UAR. About 400 were in Egypt and 120 in Israel. 500 U.S. businessmen and tourists were said to have left Egypt.)

A British Foreign Office statement May 23 upheld the international character of the Gulf of Aqaba and said it should remain open to shipping of all nations. The statement said: "If it appeared that any attempt to interfere with ships going through the waterway was likely to be made, we should support international action through the United Nations to secure free passage."

War Preparations

The Egyptian blockade of the Gulf of Aqaba was followed by a further intensification of Arab war preparations. A force of 20,000 Saudi Arabian soldiers crossed into Jordan May 24 and took up positions near the Jordanian port of Aqaba. Syria and Iraq signed an agreement in Damascus May 24 for bilateral military cooperation against Israel. Baghdad radio reported May 26 that more Iraqi troops were being moved into Syria to reinforce Syrian troops poised on the Israeli border.

The Soviet government reportedly had informed Cairo earlier in May that Israel had massed a large number of troops on the Syrian border. Other reports received by Cairo the following 2 weeks allegedly indicated that the Israeli force on the Syrian frontier totalled 11 brigades. However, a report issued May 19 by UN Truce Supervision Organization observers said there was no evidence of a massive Israeli troop build-up on the Syrian line. The report, read the same day to the UN Security Council by UN Secy. Gen. Thant, said: UNTSO observers "have confirmed the absence of troop concentrations and significant troop movements on both sides of the line."

The Soviet government publicly expressed its support of the Arab position. In a statement issued May 23, Moscow charged that Israel was "to blame for a dangerous aggravation of tension" in the Middle East. The statement contended that the crisis stemmed from Israel's large-scale attack on Syria Apr. 7 and from a decision of the defense and policy committees of the Israeli Knesset May 9 to grant the government "powers for military operations against Syria." This decree, the Soviet statement said, led to the massing of Israeli forces on the Syrian frontier, which prompted the mobilization of Syrian forces and the deployment of the troops of the UAR and other Arab states in support of the Damascus regime. The statement said: Following the Apr. 7 attack, "the ruling circles of Israel" had continued to "inflame the atmosphere of war hysteria" and had threatened "punitive action" against Syria. Israel had received "direct and indirect encouragement" from "imperialist circles which seek to restore colonial oppression to the Arab lands." But the Arab states had aligned themselves with "the courageous struggle of the Syrian people who are upholding their independence." The UAR was "honoring its commitment of alliance for joint defense with Syria" and "had taken steps to contain aggression." Cairo's request for UNEF's withdrawal was justified because "the presence of UN troops in the Gaza area and the Sinai Peninsula would give Israel advantages for staging a military provocation against Arab countries." Israel's alleged aggressive stance stemmed from "direct and indirect encouragement . . . from certain imperialist circles which seek to bring back colonial oppression to Arab soil." "Only a handful of colonial oil monopolies and their hangers-on can be interested" in a war in the Middle East. "Only the forces of imperialism, in the wake of whose policy Israel follows, can be interested in this." Since the Middle East area "directly adjoins the frontiers of the Soviet Union," the "maintenance of peace and security in that region" "accords with the vital interests" of Moscow. The USSR would support the Arab states in their "resolute resistance" to any nation that "would venture to unleash aggression" against them.

UAR Pres. Nasser warned May 26 that an Israeli attack on the UAR or Syria could result in an all-out conflict in which the Arabs' "main objective will be the destruction of Israel." Nasser said he had ordered the deployment of Egyptian troops along the Israeli border after reconnaissance photos had shown that Israel had massed soldiers on the frontier with Syria. Nasser said that the UAR and Syria were prepared for war and that Iraq, Kuwait and Algeria were sending troops. Nasser lauded the Soviet Union for its "magnificent" support of the Arab states. At the same time, he assailed the U.S. as "the No. 1 protector of Israel" and denounced Britain as "an American coat-tail." (Nasser was reported to have advised several world leaders that Cairo had no intentions of committing aggression against Israel. His assurances were said to have been conveyed in notes sent to French Pres. Charles de Gaulle, Indian Prime Min. Indira Gandhi, Ethiopian Emperor Haile Selassie, Afghan King Mohammad Zahir, Communist chiefs of state and other Asian and African leaders. But after the Israeli victory in the June war, Israeli air force intelligence officers June 20 made public what were described as captured

Egyptian documents purporting to show that the UAR had mapped detailed plans for a surprise military strike against Israel. The documents, said to have been captured by Israeli forces at El Arish and El Ser airfields during the fighting in the Sinai desert, reportedly called for cutting off the southern Negev, capturing the Israeli port of Elath at the head of the Gulf of Aqaba and bombing Israeli airfields and radar and missile installations near Tel Aviv. The Egyptian documents were said to have been dated between May 17 and 26 but cited no specific date for launching the attack. The Israeli air force also disclosed its possession of a Syrian map and information gathered from Syrian prisoners indicating that Syria had formulated detailed plans for an attack on Israel. The Israeli report said Damascus' plan had called for shelling the Safad area in Israel and capturing Ayelet Hashahar and Kfar Hanassi north of the Sea of Galilee June 6.)

The UAR May 27 adopted a series of measures placing the country on a virtual war footing: a directive was issued cracking down on hoarding by speculators; government funds were made available for armed forces expenditures and for food purchases and production; the Economy Ministry decreed the tightening of controls on hard-currency expenditures abroad. The UAR was reported May 27 to have shifted some troops of its 35,000-man force in Yemen to the Sinai Peninsula. More Egyptian troops were reported moving into the Sinai border area May 28 to reinforce the 80,000 already there. Additional troops and equipment were said to have been deployed near El Arish (Al Arish), just outside the Gaza Strip.

Nasser May 28 ruled out a negotiated peace in the Middle East until Palestinian Arabs were returned to their homeland, part of which was in Israel. Speaking at a news conference, Nasser said, "Be patient a year or 10 years until we restore these rights." Nasser also declared: If the U.S. 6th Fleet in the Mediterranean came to the aid of Israel in the event of an Arab-Israeli military showdown, Nasser would not request the assistance of the UAR's non-Arab allies, particularly the Soviet Union; although the U.S. supported Israel, the Arabs "have always extended the hand of friendship" to Washington; the UAR had not "budged one inch" from its decision to bar Israeli shipping in the Gulf of Aqaba.

The UAR National Assembly May 29 granted Nasser full powers to govern by decree. In a report to the Assembly the same day, Nasser said Soviet Premier Aleksei N. Kosygin had promised that Moscow would support Egypt in its blockade of the Gulf of Aqaba. Nasser did not make clear what form the assistance would take. Nasser said Kosygin's promise had been transmitted to the UAR during the Soviet premier's meeting in Moscow May 26-28 with UAR War Min. Shamseddin Badran. Badran, he said, "relayed to me a message from Premier Kosygin saying that the Soviet Union stands with us in this battle and will not allow any country to interfere, so that the state of affairs prevailing before 1956 may be restored."

A Syrian delegation, headed by Pres. Nureddin al-Attassi, conferred in Moscow May 29-30 with Soviet officials. No communiqué was issued at the conclusion of the 2 days of talks, but Damascus radio said the Soviet Union had pledged full support for Syria. Soviet leaders participating in the talks included Premier Kosygin, Foreign Min. Andrei Gromyko and Defense Min. Andrei Grechko.

British Foreign Secy. George Brown had conferred in Moscow May 24 with Soviet Premier Kosygin and Foreign Min. Gromyko. Brown urged the Soviet leaders to follow a policy of "restraint and creative imagination" in helping to resolve the Middle East crisis. A Soviet government spokesman, Leonid Zamyatin, said May 26, the day Brown left Moscow, that the British foreign secretary's position had shown "that the British government actually supports" Israel.

The UAR and Jordan signed a mutual defense pact in Cairo May 30. The document was signed by Nasser and Jordanian King Hussein. Previously, Nasser had accused Hussein of being in league with Israel. But Nasser said to Hussein after signing the agreement: "The initiative you have taken today affirms that Arabs, no matter how divided they may be, forget everything when the issue is that of the Arab destiny." The agreement added Jordan's 55,000-man army to the UAR's 300,000 soldiers and Syria's 60,000 in the force being mustered against Israel. Under the agreement, Jordan and the UAR pledged to "use all means at their disposal, including . . . armed forces, to repulse" an attack on either nation. In the event of joint military operations, the combined UAR-Jordanian force (as well as Syria's troops) were to come under the command of Gen. Mohammed Fawzi, UAR chief of staff. The treaty provided for the creation of a joint defense council (composed of UAR and Jordanian ministers of foreign affairs, defense and war) and a joint command (made up of a chiefs-of-staff council and a joint general staff). The treaty was to run for 5 years; it was automatically renewable for subsequent 5-year periods, but either nation could terminate it on notification within one year of its expiration.

Hussein June 4 announced the extension of the UAR-Jordan pact to include Iraq. A protocol extending the defense agreement to Iraq had been signed in Cairo earlier that day by Nasser and Iraqi Vice Premier Taher Yehia. An Iraqi delegation simultaneously initialed the accord in Amman. Iraq had stepped up its military efforts May 30 by moving troops and armored units into Jordan to bolster Jordanian soldiers on the Israeli border. Iraqi jets June 1 took off from Habbaniyah for what was described as "front line" positions in an undisclosed Arab country—actually, Jordan.

The atmosphere of crisis was further evidenced by reports of movements of British, U.S. and Soviet warships in the Middle East area. The British Admiralty in London announced May 24 that British warships passing through the Mediterranean were being "held over" there "in readiness against any eventuality." The U.S. 6th Fleet, consisting of 50 ships, was reported to have been deployed in the Eastern Mediterranean. The flotilla included 3 aircraft carriers with several hundred planes, 25,000 sailors and 2,000 Marines. It was disclosed in Washington May 30 that a major portion of the ships of the 6th Fleet was concentrated between Greece and Crete and that they were being shadowed by a Soviet destroyer escort and a trawler. Reinforcement of the Soviet Union's permanent Mediterranean naval force was disclosed by the Turkish government May 30. An Ankara announcement said Moscow had informed Turkey the previous week that 10 Soviet warships would pass through the Bosporus and the Dardenelle Straits between May 30 and June 7. (The 1936 Montreux Convention permitted warships of the Soviet Union and of other Black Sea powers to pass through the straits in peace-time after giving the Turkish government one week's notice.) The London *Times* reported that the Soviet ships moving into the Mediterranean included a cruiser, 5 modern destroyers armed with guided missiles, 2 minesweepers and some submarines.

UN Security Council Fails to Resolve Crisis

The UN Security Council convened in emergency session May 24 to take up the Middle East crisis. Meetings were held almost continuously through June 3 but failed to head off the war that ultimately erupted June 5. Canada and Denmark had requested the Council meeting May 23. They called "the grave situation in the Middle East" a threat to "international peace and security."

At the opening session May 24, U.S. Amb. Arthur J. Goldberg proposed joint U.S., British, French and Soviet action "both within and outside the United Nations" "to restore and maintain peace" in the Middle East. Goldberg appealed to all nations "to avoid any action which might exacerbate the already tense situation" in the area.

Soviet delegate Nikolai T. Fedorenko May 24 voiced strong backing for the Arab cause. He repeated the accusation made May 23 in a Soviet government statement in which Moscow blamed Israel for fomenting the tension. Charging Israeli provocation, Fedorenko asserted that "it is quite clear that Israel could not act in this way if not for the direct and indirect encouragement it had for its position from certain imperialist circles." Fedorenko pledged that his government would "continue to do everything in its power to prevent a violation of peace and security in the Near East and safeguard the legitimate rights of the peoples."

A 3-point Canadian-Danish resolution introduced by George Ignatieff of Canada (1) expressed "full support" for UN Secy. Gen. U Thant's efforts "to pacify the situation," (2) urged all nations "to refrain from any steps which might worsen the situation" and (3) invited Thant to report to the Council on his return from a peace mission he was making to Cairo.

After adjourning, Council members received a report May 27 on Thant's meeting in Cairo May 23-25 with Pres. Nasser and other UAR officials. Thant said "a peaceful outcome to the present crisis will depend upon a breathing spell which will allow tensions to subside. . . . I therefore urge all the parties concerned to exercise restraint, to forego belligerence and to avoid all other actions which could increase tension, to allow the Council to deal with the underlying causes of the present crisis and seek solutions." Thant suggested that the situation could be eased if Israel rejoined the Egyptian-Israeli Mixed Armistice Commission, which it had boycotted since 1956, and if Israel and Syria resumed meetings of the Israeli-Syrian Mixed Armistice Commission. Thant said that in his meeting with Egyptian leaders he had expressed concern over Cairo's decision to restrict shipping in the Gulf of Aqaba. He said that in response to his plea against "precipitate action," Nasser and UAR Foreign Min. Mahmoud Riad had assured him that the UAR "would not initiate offensive action against Israel. Their general aim . . . was for a return to the conditions prior to 1956 and to full observance by both parties of the . . . General Armistice Agreement between Egypt and Israel." The other factors besides the blockade of the Gulf of Aqaba that could "lead to serious fighting" were "sabotage and terrorist activities" against Israel and "rights of cultivation in disputed areas in the demilitarized zone between Israel and Syria," Thant said.

Thant's appeal for a "breathing spell" in the Middle East crisis received strong support in the Security Council when it reconvened May 29. Leading the movement for such action was U.S. Amb. Goldberg, backed by the representatives of Argentina, Brazil, Britain, Canada, Ethiopia and India. Goldberg stated that Thant's plea to all sides "to forego belligerence" "must mean foregoing any blockade of the Gulf of Aqaba during the breathing spell requested by the Secretary General and permitting free and innocent passage of all nations through the Strait of Tiran as it has during the last 10 years."

Israeli delegate-to-UN Gideon Rafael, assailing the blockade of the Gulf of Aqaba as "an act of aggression against Israel," demanded May 29 that the waterway be open to all shipping. Rafael recalled "that the international character of the Strait of Tiran" had been acknowledged in UN General Assembly debates in Mar. 1957 following the 1956 Suez crisis. Rafael called for 4 steps to ease the situation: (1) A halt to "all inflammatory statements and threats against the territorial integrity and political independence of any state"; (2) compliance with the UN Charter's "obligation of non-belligerence"; (3) withdrawal of Arab and Israeli armed forces "to their position as at the beginning of this month";

(4) free passage for all ships through the Strait of Tiran and a cessation of all acts of sabotage along Israel's borders.

UAR delegate Mohamed Awad El Kony upheld Cairo's right to bar Israeli shipping in the Gulf of Aqaba on the ground that the Strait of Tiran "was situated in the joint territorial waters" of the UAR and Saudi Arabia. The Gulf of Aqaba, El Kony insisted, "always had been a national waterway subject to absolute Arab sovereignty. It does not belong to the class of international waterways." El Kony charged that Israel had illegally occupied 7 miles of coastline of the gulf, including Elath (formerly Om Ramrash), Israel's only port at the head of the gulf. El Kony said UN authorities who had arranged the 1949 truce in the region contended that Israel had taken control of the area after the cease-fire had been negotiated and signed. Accusing Israel of constant violations of the armistice, El Kony urged the Council to call on Israel to honor its "obligations and responsibilities as stipulated by the Egyptian-Israeli General Armistice Agreement" and to advise the UN Truce Supervision Organization (UNTSO) to re-establish the headquarters of the defunct Egyptian-Israeli Mixed Armistice Commission at El Auja (Al Awja) in the Sinai Peninsula within 2 weeks. In Council debate May 30, El Kony reiterated that the Strait of Tiran was in UAR territorial waters and that Cairo had the right to control passage through the waterway.

At the Council's May 31 meeting, draft resolutions were presented by the U.S. and the UAR. The U.S. resolution called on all parties to the dispute to comply with Secy. Gen. Thant's May 27 appeal for a "breathing spell" to allow, in the words of the resolution, "the immediate pursuit of international diplomacy in the interests of pacifying the situation and seeking reasonable, peaceful and just solutions." The resolution also called for "continuous review" of the situation by the Council. Presenting the resolution, U.S. Amb. Goldberg said it was an "interim" measure designed to provide the time for more "deliberate disposition of the underlying issues" "without prejudice to the ultimate rights or claims of any party" involved in the dispute. He said its purpose was to "gain time and to create a climate" in which solutions to the crisis could be sought "under more favorable conditions."

The UAR draft resolution, submitted by Amb. El Kony and supported by India, called on the Council to note the "grave situation" in the Middle East and to express its "grave concern" at the fact that UN enforcement of the 1949 General Armistice Agreement between Egypt and Israel "became particularly inoperative due to the attitude of Israel authorities." Asserting that Israel's "unilateral denunciation" of the armistice agreement was something that "cannot be tolerated," the resolution called for the full restoration of its provisions. It also called on the Council "to bolster additional measures necessary for the full implementation of this resolution in case of . . . noncompliance" by Israel.

At the proposal of French delegate Roger Seydoux, the Council agreed to adjourn until June 2 to study the resolutions. The reconvening of the Council was later postponed to June 3 to allow additional time for consultation. The Council meeting of June 3 was the last before war broke out 2 days later. The June 3 session was no more successful than the previous ones in easing the situation and preventing a military showdown between Israel and the Arab states.

An Israeli letter submitted to the Council stated that 2 members of an Israeli patrol had been killed and 2 wounded June 2 in an exchange of fire with Syrian "armed marauders" near the Syrian border. One Syrian was killed and 3 escaped towards the Syrian border, the Israelis said. The UAR delegation submitted a letter in which Foreign Min. Riad warned that any attempts by maritime powers to break the blockade of the Gulf of Aqaba would be regarded by Cairo as an infringement on its territorial sovereignty. Riad said Egypt would take all necessary measures to resist what he called any act of aggression against its territorial waters.

(Thant June 4 again defended his decision to withdraw UNEF from its position along the Egyptian-Israeli border. He asserted that withdrawal of UNEF was not "a primary cause of the present crisis." Rather, the crisis was due to "the continuing Arab-Israeli conflict, which has been present all along, and of which the crisis situation created by the unexpected request for the withdrawal of UNEF is the latest expression." The withdrawal of UNEF had been dictated by "legal and practical considerations of an overriding nature," Thant said. Egypt had the right, unilaterally, to terminate the UNEF presence, Thant declared. This right had been agreed to before the force arrived in 1956. Thant further asserted that at the time of the UAR's request, Egyptian troops had already placed themselves in confrontation with Israel so that "UNEF had, in fact, no further useful function." Since the force was no longer officially welcome, Thant added, any attempt to keep it there "would have made the situation of the force both humiliating and untenable.")

Israel Defers Action as West Opposes Blockade

Premier Levi Eshkol announced in a nationwide radio address May 28 that the Israeli cabinet had decided earlier that day to continue to employ political means for the time being in its efforts to get the Gulf of Aqaba reopened to Israeli shipping. Israel would continue "political action in the world arena" to encourage "international factors to take effective measures to insure free international passage" through the Strait of Tiran, Eshkol said. Eshkol, however, did not rule out eventual military action. Charging that the closing of the strait was "equivalent to an act of aggression," Eshkol said Israel would "oppose it at the hour of need." As for the massing of Egyptian troops in the Sinai Peninsula, Eshkol said, "lines of policy have also been laid down to secure the removal of military concentrations from Israel's southern border as well as for safeguarding of our rights and our security on the border and forestalling foreign aggression so as to obviate the necessity of Israel having to use her armed forces for her defense."

Eshkol told the Knesset May 30 that the U.S., Britain and other countries had embarked on joint action to restore freedom of navigation in the Straits of Tiran. He added: "It is our duty to put the pledges to the test. Very shortly it will be clear if this prospect materializes. Pres. Nasser is driving this region to the brink of war through his blockade, his threats of guerrilla war, the massing of his troops. . . . As long as the armies of Egypt and her allies are massed on Israel's borders there is the danger of a conflagration."

Israeli Foreign Min. Abba Eban had taken up the question of the Egyptian blockade of the Gulf of Aqaba with French, British and U.S. officials in Paris, London and Washington May 24-26. Eban met with French Pres. Charles de Gaulle May 24 and with U.S. State Secy. Dean Rusk and Pres. Johnson May 25-26. Reporting on his diplomatic endeavors at a news conference in

Jerusalem May 30, Eban declared that Israel would continue the policy of attempting to open the Strait of Tiran, "alone if we must, with others if we can." Eban said: "It was natural for Israel to invest a little time in an effort to clarify whether its task of insuring the opening of this waterway was one it must confront alone, or whether there would be others who would concert their efforts. Now it is clear from the contacts we have made with the major powers that there are others in the world who are prepared to make common cause for the restoration of the legal question in the Gulf of Aqaba." Eban had declared in a TV interview in London May 24 that the hasty withdrawal of the UN Emergency Force from the Gaza Strip and Sharm el Sheik "is why the world is in a state of tension now."

During a stop-over in Paris May 27, before returning to Israel, Eban said at a news conference: "I have made an exploratory trip to be informed of the viewpoint of the 3 friendly governments about the illegal measures taken by Egypt in the Strait of Tiran. . . . It is self-evident that peace cannot co-exist with an illegal blockade. I have explained this thesis to the eminent British, French and American leaders. They represent the 3 governments which 10 years ago pledged solemnly to insist on the international character of this waterway and to practice there their right of free and innocent passage."

British Foreign Secy. Brown announced in the House of Commons May 30 that Britain had consulted with other maritime powers on the possible issuance of a joint declaration that the Gulf of Aqaba was an international waterway and that all nations were entitled to free passage. The British move was strongly endorsed by the U.S. May 31. A State Department statement said: "The focus of the Middle East crisis without hostilities is in the United Nations. We regard its responsibilities as essential and fundamental, and we are doing everything in our power to seek a fair and just outcome of the crisis in that form. As part of that effort, . . . we are supporting the British initiative which was announced by . . . Brown yesterday. We are consulting other maritime powers as to their views on the international character of the Straits of Tiran and the Gulf of Aqaba in the light of the President's statement of May 23."

The question of a declaration by the maritime powers on the maintenance of freedom of navigation in the Gulf of Aqaba was said to have been the principle topic of discussion in Washington June 2 by British Prime Min. Harold Wilson and Pres. Johnson. Wilson had arrived that day from Ottawa, where he had discussed the Middle East crisis with Canadian Prime Min. Lester B. Pearson. After meeting with the President, Wilson declared at a news conference that freedom of shipping in the gulf was the key to the crisis. Asserting that "time is not on our side" and that "we must use every minute," Wilson warned that if the Egyptian blockade were not ended peacefully a major war could erupt within hours. Wilson conferred again with Mr. Johnson June 3. Before returning to London, he stopped in New York and met with UN Secy. Gen. U Thant. Wilson said he had reached "complete agreement" with Pres. Johnson that the U.S. and Britain should seek a "multilateral solution" of the Middle East crisis through the UN.

According to news reports, a U.S.-British declaration calling for freedom of passage through the Gulf of Aqaba had been presented to 20 maritime powers. The declaration was in the form of a statement of principles and was said to contain no provisions for enforcement. The text had not been made public, but the London *Times* said it contained these 3 points: (1) the gulf was an international waterway open to shipping of all nations; (2) the signatories were ready to pursue their right of free and innocent passage; (3) this right applied to all nations.

Acceptance of the plan was announced by the Israeli embassy in Washington and by Australia, New Zealand and the Netherlands. The Soviet Union and France expressed opposition to the plan.

Following a French cabinet meeting presided over by Pres. Charles de Gaulle, Information Min. Georges Gorse June 2 issued a statement saying that a declaration by the maritime powers on the Gulf of Aqaba would "not fit into the framework of the 4-power contacts which we wish for and would not help matters forward." De Gaulle, according to Gorse, had stated at the cabinet meeting that: (1) Israel and the Arab states had "the right to live." (2) An outbreak of conflict in the Middle East would be the worst thing that could happen. (3) If war broke out, "the country which was the first to use arms will have neither our support nor our aid." (4) The problems of navigation in the gulf,

Arab refugees and Arab-Israeli relations should be "settled by international decision"; only Britain, the U.S., France and the USSR should participate in such decisions. De Gaulle May 24 had proposed a conference of the U.S., Britain, France and the Soviet Union to resolve the crisis. Information Min. Gorse said France regarded the 1950 tripartite declaration as unrealistic since no cooperative international action could be taken in the Middle East without Soviet participation. Under the tripartite pact, the U.S., Britain and France had pledged joint action to prevent violation of the truce that had ended the 1948-49 war between Israel and the Arab states. The USSR later rejected the French proposal of a 4-power conference. The French cabinet declaration said that France was not "committed in any way and on any subject" on the side of "any of the states involved" in the Middle East dispute. The statement reaffirmed de Gaulle's assertions that: France supported the policy that all nations had a "right to live" but that the "worst thing" that could occur "would be the opening of hostilities"; the nation that "used arms first" would have neither French "approval, nor . . . her support."

Dayan Becomes Israeli Defense Minister

Gen. Moshe Dayan, 52, was appointed Israeli defense minister June 1 in a cabinet reshuffle announced as a broadening of the government coalition (from 5 to 7 parties) to cope with the mounting crisis. The defense portfolio had been previously held by Premier Eshkol. Eshkol, who had been pressured to adopt a more militant policy against the UAR, had been empowered to broaden the cabinet at a meeting of the secretariat of the ruling Mapai party. Dayan was a member of ex-Premier David Ben-Gurion's more militant Rafi party. The 2d party brought into the cabinet was the rightwing Gahal (a combination of the nationalist Herut and the independent Liberals), represented by Menahem Begin and Joseph Saphir, both serving as ministers without portfolio. Dayan was a member of the Knesset.

Dayan declared June 2 that Israel needed no military allies to fight its battles: "If, somehow, it comes to real fighting, I would not like American or British boys to get killed here in order to secure Israel, and I don't think we need it. I think we can win."

(The son of Russian-born parents, Dayan was born in 1915 in Degania, near the Sea of Galilee in Palestine. He was trained as a farmer. At the age of 14 he joined the Haganah, the Jewish fighting force in Palestine. Eight years later Dayan joined one of the commando units formed by British Capt. Orde Wingate to defend Jewish farm settlements against Arab raids. During his service with British forces in Syria in World War II, Dayan suffered the loss of his left eye when a bullet struck the binoculars through which he was looking. He was later transferred to Jerusalem, where he was assigned as liaison officer with the British. At the end of the war Dayan returned to farming. But he was recalled to military service after the state of Israel, established in 1948, was attacked by Arab armies. Dayan commanded Israeli forces in the Jerusalem area and was one of the signers of the armistice agreement with Jordan that ended the fighting in 1949. Dayan was appointed chief of staff of the Israeli army in 1953 and was largely responsible for the Israeli victory in 1956 over Egyptian forces in the Sinai Peninsula during the Suez crisis. Dayan relinquished his military post after Israeli forces were forced to withdraw from the Sinai Peninsula. Dayan studied political science and was appointed to Premier David Ben-Gurion's cabinet in 1959 as agriculture minister. Dayan resigned in 1964 following a political dispute with Levi Eshkol, who became Ben-Gurion's successor.)

Eshkol's Peace Appeals to USSR

Israeli Premier Eshkol appealed June 3 to Soviet Premier Aleksei N. Kosygin to use the USSR's "great political powers" and influence with the Arab states to ease the crisis. Eshkol said Israel's conditions for peace were Arab acceptance of Israel's territorial integrity and the lifting of the blockade of the Gulf of Aqaba. In a message to the Israeli government May 26 (made public June 3), Kosygin had warned that it would be a "tremendous error if arms began talking" instead of "serious political thought."

Eshkol sent a more urgent plea to Kosygin June 5 as the Arab states and Israel approached the brink of war. Eshkol called on Kosygin to join efforts to bring peace to the Middle East. In a message delivered to the Soviet ambassador in Tel Aviv, Premier Eshkol said that Israel, "surrounded by enemy armies on all sides," was "engaged in a mortal struggle to defend our existence. . . ." He cited recent grave developments: the Egyptians' "provocative troop concentrations" in Sinai, the massing of more than 900 tanks on Israel's southern frontier and opposite Elath. The message continued: "The acts of sabotage and terrorism from Syria and Gaza, this morning's engagement and the bombardment of the Israeli villages . . . , all of this amounts to an extra-ordinary catalogue of aggression that must be abhorred and condemned by world opinion."

THE WAR
June 5 - 11

Large-scale warfare erupted in the early hours of June 5 with Israel pitted against 3 Arab neighbors—the UAR, Syria and Jordan. Lebanon, the 4th Arab state bordering Israel, stayed out of the conflict. Each side accused the other of starting the fighting.

According to the Israeli version of events: Radar screens indicated early June 5 that Egyptian planes were headed toward Israel's Mediterranean coast and the Negev Desert. As Israeli aircraft were sent up to intercept the UAR force, Egyptian artillery in the Gaza Strip opened fire on the Israeli border settlements of Nahal Oz, Kissufim and Ein Haselosh (Hashelosha). Israeli tanks returned the fire, and Israeli forces began counter-attacking across the Israeli-UAR border into the Sinai Peninsula. Firing started almost simultaneously along the Jordanian and Syrian frontiers with Israel.

The Cairo government charged June 5 that the Israeli air force had launched an unprovoked surprise attack against the UAR earlier that day by carrying out raids in the Cairo area and near the Suez Canal, El Arish, and Sharm el Sheik. Israeli troops also were accused by Cairo of launching surprise attacks on Egyptian positions in Sinai. Cairo claimed that an Israeli pilot shot down and captured by the Egyptians had confessed that his unit had been ordered to carry out surprise raids against UAR strongpoints in the early hours of June 5.

Rapidly advancing on all fronts, Israeli forces scored a smashing victory over the combined Arab armies by the time all hostilities halted June 10 in response to repeated cease-fire appeals by the UN Security Council. On the first day of fighting, Israel gained control of the air on all fronts by virtually destroying the air forces of the UAR, Jordan and Syria. In quick thrusts Israeli troops: (1) overran the entire Sinai Peninsula, including Sharm el

Sheik, and advanced to the east bank of the Suez Canal; (2) captured the Gaza Strip; (3) captured Jordanian Jerusalem, occupied by Jordan since the 1948-49 Arab-Israeli war; (4) seized all Jordanian territory adjoining Israel west of the Jordan River and took control of the major west-bank cities of Bethlehem, Hebron, Jericho, Nablus, Ramallah and Jenin; (5) drove 12 miles into Syria, seized the high strategic ground on the border (the Golan Heights) and captured the Syrian garrison town of El Quneitra (sometimes transliterated Al Qunaytirah), 40 miles from Damascus.

Of the 3 Arab armies involved in the war, the armed forces of the UAR bore the major brunt of losses at the hands of the Israelis. But Jordanian and Syrian troop losses were also heavy. Although Iraq, Algeria, Kuwait and Saudi Arabia pledged to join the fighting against Israel, their mobilized forces were never committed to combat. Iraqi troops moved into Jordan, and some Iraqi planes carried out a few minor raids against Israel.

The reported combat strength of Israeli and Arab forces prior to outbreak of fighting (asterisk indicates figures from the Institute of Strategic Studies in London): Israel—264,000 troops, 800 tanks, 300 planes*; Egypt—240,000 troops, 1,200 tanks, 450 planes*; Jordan—50,000 troops, 200 tanks, 40 planes; Syria—50,000 troops, 400 tanks, 120 planes*; Iraq—70,000 troops, 400 tanks, 200 planes*; Lebanon—12,000 troops, 80 tanks, 18 planes*; Saudi Arabia—50,000 troops, 100 tanks, 20 planes; Kuwait—5,000 troops, 24 tanks, 9 planes; Algeria—60,000 troops, 100 tanks, 100 planes.

The Arabs asserted in the early hours of the fighting that they were winning decisively, and they reported inflicting heavy losses on the Israelis. As their defeat became more obvious, however, Arab spokesmen stopped repeating their exaggerated claims—but did not retract them.

The Egyptian army in the Sinai suffered staggering losses in men and matériel: 7 divisions totaling 80,000-100,000 men were routed and destroyed as a fighting force; an estimated 600-700 Soviet-supplied tanks, constituting virtually the entire UAR armored force in the Sinai, were wrecked. More than 100 undamaged tanks fell into Israeli hands. The Israelis also reported destroying or capturing huge quantities of other Soviet-made

Before and after: Light shading shows area seized by Israel in 6-day conflict—all of Sinai Peninsula and Gaza Strip, the Jordan bulge west of the Jordan River (the west bank) and Syria's Golan Heights on Israel's northern border. By comparison, dark shading shows Israeli territory before the fighting.

UAR equipment, including 400 field guns, 50 self-propelled guns and thousands of vehicles. A large amount of ammunition and provisions of all kinds was captured. The Israelis claimed the destruction of 444 Arab planes, most of them on the ground during the first day of fighting.

The destruction of the Egyptian army was regarded a major political set-back for the Soviet Union in the Middle East. The UAR's armed forces, including planes and tanks, had been supplied almost exclusively by the USSR, which had provided Cairo with several billion dollars worth of military equipment since 1955.

Arabs Unite for War

UAR Pres. Nasser had declared at the outbreak of hostilities that all Arab states were fighting to "eliminate the shadow of Zionism from Palestine and to restore it to Arabism." Nasser made a similar statement in response to a message from Saudi Arabian King Faisal in support of the UAR. The UAR declared a nationwide state of emergency but did not issue a declaration of war against Israel. Such a declaration apparently was unnecessary since the UAR regarded itself as technically already at war with Israel.

King Hussein informed Jordanians in a broadcast June 5 that they were at war with Israel. He said that the defense pact he had signed with Nasser May 30 had gone into effect and that the Jordanian army was under the command of Lt. Gen. Abdel Moneim Rivad, deputy chief of staff of the Unified Arab Command.

Israeli Premier Eshkol had appealed to Hussein earlier June 5 to stay out of the conflict. In a message sent to the king through Lt. Gen. Odd Bull, commander of the UN Truce Supervision Organization, Eshkol said: "We shall not initiate any action whatsoever against Jordan. However, should Jordan open hostilities, we shall react with all our might, and she will have to bear the full responsibility for all the consequences." Jordan's reply to Eshkol's appeal was a call to arms by Amman radio later that morning. It said: "Free citizens of Jordan. The hoped-for moment has arrived. . . . Forward to arms, to battle, to new pages of glory. To regain our rights, to smash the aggressor, to revenge."

Five other Arab states announced June 5 that they were in a state of war with Israel: Algeria, Iraq, Syria, Sudan and Kuwait. All 5 pledged to send troops to the UAR to assist in the struggle against Israel. Lebanon declared a state of emergency. Saudi Arabia reported that its forces were operating against Israel from bases in Jordan. Morocco announced that it was sending troops to the UAR. Libya was reported to have moved troops to the western frontier of the UAR and to have pledged all-out support for Cairo. Tunisia announced that it would permit its territory to be used for passage of North African troops to Egypt.

Algerian Pres. Houari Boumedienne denounced the West and "certain powers" for having aligned themselves with Israel. Demanding that the U.S. and Britain quit the Arab world, Boumedienne declared: "Today we say that Arab riches and Arab oil must be restored to the Arabs."

Syrian Pres. Nureddin el-Attassi asserted that the Israelis had "dug their graves with their own hands." "Israeli aggression," he charged, had been fomented by "international imperialism."

Tunisian Pres. Habib Bourguiba said that despite his friendship for Britain and the U.S. he could not "remain silent when the right of the people to take back their homeland is at stake."

Israeli Foreign Min. Abba Eban June 5 blamed the Arab states for starting the war. Speaking at a news conference in Tel Aviv, Eban said Israel had informed the Security Council that Israel had invoked Article 51 of the UN Charter, permitting the right of member states to act in self-defense. He said Israel was fighting "to frustrate the attempt of Arab armies to capture our land, to break their wall of encirclement and the siege of aggression that has been established around us." Eban said the hostilities against Israel actually had begun with UAR Pres. Nasser's announcement of his plans to bar Israeli shipping from the Gulf of Aqaba.

Gen. Moshe Dayan, newly-appointed Israeli defense minister, declared in a radio message to Israeli troops June 5 that "we have no aim of territorial conquest. Our sole aim is to bring to nought the attempt of the Arab armies to conquer our country, and to destroy the encircling blockade and aggression."

The U.S. and Britain expressed determination June 5 to pursue a neutral course in the conflict. (The U.S., however, later qualified its stand.) A similar position had been outlined by France June 2. Paris reinforced its non-aligned stance June 5 by announcing a suspension of shipments of military equipment and spare parts to the Middle East.

The first American reaction to the outbreak of hostilities came in a State Department statement that said: the U.S. would "steer an even-handed course"; "our position is neutral in thought, word and deed." A qualifying statement issued later June 5 by White House Press Secy. George Christian said that the earlier State Department remark was "not a formal declaration of neutrality." Christian recalled that Pres. Johnson, in his May 23 declaration against the Aqaba blockade, had reaffirmed that the U.S. was "firmly committed to the support of the political independence and territorial integrity of all nations of the area." (The President's statement was in reference to the 1950 declaration in which the U.S., Britain and France had pledged that "should they find that any of these states [Arab or Israeli] was preparing to violate frontiers or armistice lines, [they] would . . . immediately take action, both within and outside the United Nations, to prevent such violation.")

British Foreign Secy. George Brown declared in the House of Commons June 5 that Britain was "not to take sides" in the Arab-Israeli war. British forces in the Middle East, he disclosed, had been ordered "to avoid any involvement in the conflict." "We shall serve the cause of peace better by not now pronouncing on the merits of the case as seen by Israel or the Arabs," Brown said.

The French arms embargo was announced June 5 after a meeting of de Gaulle with Premier Georges Pompidou and Foreign Min. Maurice Couve de Murville. Although the ban applied equally to both sides, Israel was most affected since it was the only country in the area largely dependent on French arms. Israel's air force was equipped mostly with French jets of the Mirage, Mystère and Ouragan types.

The Arab-Israel conflict had additional international repercussions. Charging that U.S. and British planes had intervened in the war on the side of Israel, UAR Pres. Nasser June 6 closed the

Suez Canal to all shipping and severed diplomatic relations with the U.S. The Arabs refused to accept U.S. and British offers to prove that their aircraft had not intervened. In another act of retaliation for the fictitious aerial intervention, Iraq and Kuwait, major oil producers in the Middle East, cut off all oil supplies to the U.S. and Britain. The USSR, declaring anew its support for the Arabs, denounced Israel as an aggressor and demanded that its forces be withdrawn from Arab territory. The Soviet position was enunciated in government statements and during UN Security Council debate on the Middle East crisis June 5-12. In further support of the Arab position, the Soviet Union and several other European Communist states severed diplomatic relations with Israel June 10-13.

Israeli Jets Hit Arab Airfields

The fighting got under way at about 7:30 a.m. June 5 when Israeli air force planes launched widespread attacks on airfields in Egypt, Jordan, Syria and Iraq.

Taking off from airbases that ringed Tel Aviv, the Israeli aircraft directed their main thrust at Egypt toward the west. To avoid Egyptian radar detection, the Israeli attackers flew at altitudes as low as 150 feet in a wide curve over the Mediterranean beyond Alexandria. They then hooked inland toward the east and carried out devastating attacks on UAR airbases extending from the Cairo area to the Suez Canal Zone and the Red Sea coast. Catching the Egyptians by surprise, the Israeli jets wreaked heavy destruction on Soviet-supplied UAR warplanes, many of them MiG-21s and MiG-19s, lined up in neat rows on the fields. About 16 Egyptian airfields were put out of action in the first wave of attack. Ten of them were hit almost simultaneously: El Arish, Jebel Libni, Bir Gifgafa, Bir Thamada, Abu Sueir, Kabrit, Inchas, Cairo West, Beni Sueif and Fayid. The remaining 9 Egyptian airfields struck June 5 were: Mansura, Helwan, El Minya, Almaza, Luxor, Deversoir, Hurghada, Ras Banas and Cairo International. Twenty-six Egyptian radar screens were put out of action, 16 in Sinai. The Israelis encountered some resistance in the air and on the ground. Only 2 flights of 4 MiG-21s managed to take to the air during the raids. The defending MiGs shot down 2 Israeli aircraft but then were downed by the Israelis. UAR antiaircraft was light and inaccurate. The Egyptians fired several Soviet-made SA-2 surface-to-air missiles at the Israeli raiders, but none found their targets. The Israelis claimed that their jets, French-made Mirages, had shot down 50 UAR MiGs in 64 dogfights with no Israeli losses. It was believed that 100 of the Egyptian air force's 350 pilots were killed on the ground in the first Israeli air strike.

While the bulk of the 400-plane Israeli air force concentrated on targets in the UAR, the remaining Israeli jets made simultaneous strikes in Jordan, Syria and Iraq. They bombed ground installations and knocked out planes on fields near the Syrian capital of Damascus and put out of action Jordanian airbases at Mafraq and Amman and a radar station at Ajlun. The Israeli attack on Syria was in retaliation for a Syrian air raid earlier June 5 near the oil refinery in Haifa Bay and at an airfield near Megiddo. The Jordanian air force also had bombed Israel earlier in the day, attacking an airfield at Kfar Sirkin and destroying a transport on the ground. Israeli planes June 6 ranged as far east as 500 miles to attack the Iraqi airbase at Habbaniyah, where they reportedly destroyed 6 planes on the ground. The raid was in retaliation for an Iraqi air strike June 5 against the Israeli city of Natanya.

The Israeli raids against Arab targets continued throughout June 5, and by nightfall Israel had complete mastery of the sky. The intensity of the Israeli air offensive was evidenced by the fact that some planes flew as many as 8 single missions between quick stops to refuel and rearm and that the attack waves were spaced at 10-minute intervals.

In a preliminary report on the number of planes downed in the first day's fighting, Brig. Gen. Mordecai Hod, commander of the Israeli air force, said in Tel Aviv the evening of June 5 that 387 Arab aircraft had been lost: 280 Egyptian MiGs on the ground and 20 in the air; 52 Syrian, 20 Jordanian and 15 Iraqi planes. Hod, who later revised these figures upwards, said 19 Israeli planes had been lost.

According to Egyptian counter-claims June 5, the UAR, Syrian and Jordanian air forces that day had destroyed 161 Israeli planes. Cairo said only 2 Egyptian planes had been lost.

One of 2 Lebanese Hawker Hunter jets was shot down June 6

just north of the Sea of Galilee. The appearance of the 2 jets was Lebanon's only display of belligerency during the war.

In a further report on plane losses, Gen. Hod reported June 7 that 441 Arab planes had been destroyed—410 June 5, 17 June 6 and 14 June 7. Hod said Israeli planes had delivered a fatal blow to the air forces of the UAR, Syria and Jordan in the first 3 hours of fighting June 5 by carrying out destructive raids against 25 airbases.

An additional 3 Arab planes were reported by Tel Aviv June 8 to have been destroyed. The total Arab loss: 444.

Israeli plane losses totaled 40. Twenty-one Israeli pilots were lost, about ½ of them being taken prisoner in Egypt or Syria. (Two pilots were returned by Iraq and 2 by Jordan before the end of 1967.)

The Arabs eventually discontinued — but did not quickly retract—their charges that U.S. and British aircraft had aided the Israelis.

SINAI CAMPAIGN

Israelis Launch 3-Pronged Drive

At 8:15 a.m. June 5, 45 minutes after the launching of the Israeli air offensive, Israeli troops started their crushing ground offensive against the forces of the United Arab Republic in the Sinai Peninsula.

Egyptian commanders, anticipating a main Israeli thrust down the coast of the Gulf of Aqaba toward Sharm el Sheik, had deployed the bulk of their troops in the southern sector of the Sinai several days before the outbreak of hostilities. The Israelis, therefore, decided to deliver their main blow at Egypt's weakest point, the northern Sinai coast.

The Israeli drive began with 3 principal thrusts, each supported by a division of about 15,000 men. The first column, led by Brig. Gen. Israel Tal, attacked with tanks at Khan Yunis, at the southern end of the Gaza Strip, and from there headed west on the northern coastal road toward El Arish, the UAR's main military base in the northern Sinai. The 2d Israeli column, under the command of Brig. Gen. Ariel Sharon, moved on the heavily fortified Egyptian stronghold of Abu Agweigila, about 25 miles southeast of El Arish. The 3d Israeli force, headed by Brig. Gen. Avraham Yoffe, penetrated Egyptian territory between the 2 other Israeli columns and came around behind the Egyptian force under attack by Gen. Tal's troops to prevent their escape to the west.

The first UAR stronghold to come under attack was the Gaza Strip. Its borders had been heavily mined and lined with a complex system of trenches armed with dug-in antitank guns. The immediate target of the attack was Khan Yunis, at the southern end of the strip, and the neighboring town of Rafah. After a preliminary bombardment of the border strip, Israeli tanks and troops crashed the Egyptian defenses and reached the coastal road. The Israeli force then split, one column heading north toward the city of Gaza and the other turning southwest toward El Arish. Khan Yunis was quickly captured, and Rafah fell shortly thereafter. The entire strip was thus sealed off.

El Arish was captured the night of June 5, but the Israelis encountered stiff resistance in their advance into the Gaza Strip. They launched an all-out assault against the city of Gaza June 6. Aided by an air strike, the Israelis took control of the city by nightfall after bitter fighting. During the battle, Israeli artillery shells and planes hit the UN headquarters in Gaza city and caused the death of 14 Indian soldiers and one Brazilian soldier of the disbanded UN Emergency Force (UNEF), who were awaiting evacuation from the area. Twenty-five Indian soldiers were wounded.

Thousands of Egyptian prisoners were taken by the Israelis in the battle for Gaza. Their captives included Gen. Abdul Monam Husseini, military governor of the Gaza Strip.

The fight for the Gaza Strip was the first land battle of the war. Gen. Tal said afterward: "My men knew that on this battle depended the outcome of the war—possibly the fate of Israel. More than 10 years had passed since we had clashed with the Egyptians. We could not tell what effect the Russian training, the modern Russian equipment and the new morale of the Egyptian army would have on their fighting capacity. We knew that we would be fighting forces whose equipment was superior both in quality and quantity to our own. We knew that the first break-through would actually be a trial between us and the Egyptian

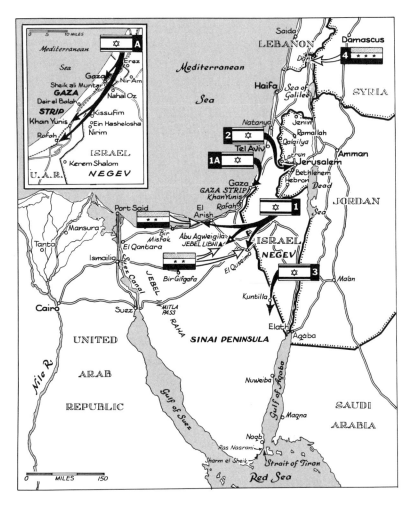

In first 2 days of conflict June 5-6, Israeli forces seized Gaza Strip (1A on main map, A on inset map), scored quick initial victories over UAR forces in thrusts into Sinai Peninsula (1) in direction of Suez Canal, surrounded Jerusalem (2) and fought Jordanian forces in Old City, advanced south past Kuntilla (3) down Sinai Peninsula in direction of Sharm el Sheik, where UAR forces had blockaded Gulf of Aqaba, and fought off Syrians attacking from north (4).

army. It was clear to all our soldiers that the attack would be carried out regardless of losses."

Gen. Sharon's forces encountered strong resistance in attacking Abu Agweigila June 6. The Egyptian position was heavily defended by an infantry brigade, about 90 tanks and some regiments of artillery. The Israelis assaulted the strongpoint in a 3-pronged attack. Paratroopers stormed the artillery positions from the rear; infantry and armored troops smashed into the front line positions; the northern side was attacked with tanks and troops. After 20 hours of savage fighting the Israelis finally captured Abu Agweigila.

Abu Agweigila's capture was vital to the Israeli advance to the west. The Egyptian strongpoint commanded the junction of the roads from El Arish, Jebel Libni and El Quseima and had held up the main movement of Israeli troops in the Nitsana area to the central part of Sinai. Failure to take the Egyptian stronghold would have enabled the UAR troops there to block fuel and ammunition supplies that were necessary to maintain the Israeli offensive.

Following the capture of El Arish, the forces of Gen. Tal split in 2 again: part of one Israeli column continued west in the direction of El Mazar and El Quantara, on the east bank of the Suez Canal, about 30 miles south of the entrance from the Mediterranean; the other column turned south to join Gen. Yoffe's forces, which were preparing to assault the UAR army's 2d defense line, stretching from Jebel Libni south to Bar Hasana. The remaining troops of the Tal-Yoffe force stayed behind to attack from the rear a strong Egyptian concentration at El Quseima. The Israeli pincer movement was aimed at crushing a heavy force of Egyptian tanks that were dug in at El Quseima with their guns pointing east.

Meanwhile, another Israeli force to the south pushed out from the Negev, captured the Egyptian stronghold of Kuntilla, just over the border, seized El Thamada further south and made its way to the strategic Mitla Pass, which commanded all access to the Suez Canal from the central Sinai. This force carried out its 140-mile advance in 36 hours.

By June 7 the Israelis were ready for the final onslaught against the Egyptians. Israeli troops were at the Mitla Pass; they had penetrated Egypt's 2d defense line at Jebel Libni-Bar Hasana, and they had reached Bir Gifgafa. Thus, they were in control of 3 routes to the Suez Canal—one leading to El Qantara in the north, a 2d to Ismailia in the center and a 3d to Port Taufiq (opposite the city of Suez) in the south.

Israeli forces earlier June 7 had moved into Sharm el Sheik without firing a shot and had thereby lifted the blockade of the Gulf of Aqaba. The Egyptians had abandoned the base before it was taken, and a Cairo communiqué said UAR troops at Sharm el Sheik had been pulled back for "regrouping." Sharm el Sheik had been the object of 3 Israeli drives: one column was speeding south from Kuntilla; paratroopers were dropped on Sharm el Sheik from helicopters, and troops went ashore from patrol boats that had come down from Elath, the Israeli port at the head of the gulf. Israeli navy officials reported after the taking of Sharm el Sheik that they had found that the Strait of Tiran had not been mined as claimed by the Egyptians.

A Tel Aviv communiqué issued June 7 claimed total victory for Israeli forces in the Sinai campaign. The report said Israeli troops had captured the entire peninsula, sweeping to the east bank of the Suez Canal. A victory proclamation issued June 7 by Maj. Gen. Itzhak Rabin, Israeli chief of staff, declared: "The Egyptians are defeated. All their efforts are aimed at withdrawing behind the Suez Canal, and we are taking care of that. The whole area is in our hands. The main effort of the Egyptians is to save themselves."

The Israeli military successes were confirmed by an Egyptian military communiqué June 7. It conceded that UAR troops in Sinai had withdrawn from first-line positions and were engaged in heavy fighting from secondary positions. A UAR high command communiqué later June 7 reported that Israeli paratroopers had been "completely wiped out" after landing on the "2d-line Egyptian front." The command did not locate the fighting. The withdrawal of Egyptian forces from some areas, the communiqué said, was necessary because of the activities of "the Zionist enemy, supported by foreign sources." (The latter phrase was a reference to Arab charges that U.S. and British planes had provided air cover for advancing Israeli troops.) The command also reported the downing of 6 Israeli jets in the Suez area June 7.

Battle of Mitla Pass

Some Israeli tanks reached the east bank of the Suez Canal by the early hours of June 7. The main force of Israeli armor and troops arrived there June 8 following a total Egyptian collapse that resulted from the final battle of the Sinai, fought at the Mitla Pass, 30 miles from the canal.

The battle for the Mitla Pass started late June 7. An estimated 1,000 tanks on both sides were committed to the engagement, which raged for 24 hours. The Egyptians also threw their few remaining planes into the battle, bombing Israeli positions at Bir Gifgafa to the northeast. Finally overcoming Egyptian resistance, Israeli tanks began to move through the pass. An Israeli force was deployed at the western end to bottle up retreating Egyptians who were trying to make their way to the canal through the pass. Escaping UAR troops, thus entrapped in the pass, became easy targets for Israeli air attacks and suffered heavy casualties. The Egyptians launched a powerful counterattack between Bir Gifgafa and the Mitla Pass to clear a path for other retreating UAR soldiers, but the Israelis threw back the assault after some of the fiercest fighting of the war. The Israelis then carried out a large-scale mopping-up operation in the west and north-west sections of the Sinai Peninsula where the remnants of 7 Egyptian divisions were stranded.

The road to the canal was now open to the Israelis. One tank column reached the east bank opposite Ismailia early June 8, while another, 2 hours later, pulled up to a point just north of the town of Suez. All Sinai fighting came to a halt later June 8 as Egypt and Israel accepted a UN Security Council call for a cease-fire.

The Egyptian high command earlier June 8 had again charged U.S. and British intervention on the side of the Israelis. It said Egyptian troops in the Sinai were engaged in "battles unprecedented in fierceness and ferocity" against "an enemy supported by 2 great powers who are attempting to camouflage their collusion by vile means." The communiqué said that Israeli ground troops were supported by an air force that "greatly surpasses our own potential." Other Cairo communiqués told of British warplanes allegedly escorting Israeli jets in the Sinai and of U.S. planes flying reconnaissance missions over the Suez Canal for Israeli tank columns. Arab leaders ignored U.S. and British offers to provide proof that their charges of U.S. and British aerial intervention were false.

The UAR high command and other Egyptian sources gave this fictitious account of military developments June 8: Egyptian planes had shot down 25 Israeli jets over the Sinai, Sharm el Sheik and Suez areas. Seven of the planes had been downed in the Suez Canal Zone and 2 near Cairo. Some areas of Cairo had been bombed, but there was little damage. 3,500 Israeli prisoners had been brought to Cairo June 7. Several Israeli armored columns were "locked in between El Arish and the coast." Israeli armored units attempting to infiltrate behind El Arish and drive along the coastal road toward Cairo were destroyed by Egyptian planes. "Our gallant forces are still resisting with matchless courage inside El Arish itself," despite Israeli claims that the stronghold had been taken.

Following the UAR's acceptance of a UN cease-fire order June 8, a Cairo broadcast June 9 informed the Egyptian people of the government's decision and announced that the war with Israel was over. Several hours before the announcement, an Egyptian military communiqué had charged that "Israeli enemy forces supported by the forces of imperialism are continuing the attacks against our forces westward toward the Suez Canal" despite the UAR's observance of the cease-fire. The Israeli truce violations, according to the Egyptians, included air strikes against ships in the Suez Canal that resulted in the obstruction of the waterway.

Further details on the blockage of the Suez Canal was provided by the Cairo newspaper *Al Gomhouria* June 18. The newspaper said 3 Egyptian ships and 2 dredges had been sunk in the waterway during the fighting. Fifteen foreign ships of 8 nations, including the U.S. and Britain, were trapped in the waterway, according to the newspaper.

Israelis Attack U.S.S. Liberty off Sinai

Israeli planes and torpedo boats June 8 attacked a lightly-armed U.S. electronic reconnaissance ship, the U.S.S. *Liberty,* in international waters about 15 miles north of the Sinai Peninsula during the height of the Israeli-Egyptian fighting. Thirty-four American crewmen were killed and 75 wounded. The ship, heavily damaged, made its way to Malta June 13.

U.S. Asst. Defense Secy. (for public affairs) Phil Goulding said June 8 that the *Liberty* had left its base in Rota, Spain June 2 to "assure communications between United States government posts in the Middle East and to assist in relaying information concerning the evacuation of American dependents and other American citizens" in the area.

Pres. Lyndon B. Johnson informed Senate Majority Leader Mike Mansfield (D., Mont.) in a letter June 8 that the U.S. had "found it necessary to make a prompt and firm protest to the Israel government which, to its credit, had already acknowledged its responsibility and had apologized." The Israeli apology, sent to Mr. Johnson by Premier Levi Eshkol (made public June 9), expressed grief at the "tragic loss of life" in the incident. An Israeli note June 10 again expressed deep regret and offered to pay compensation for the loss of American lives and for damage to the ship.

A U.S. Navy board of inquiry conducted an investigation June 11-17 into the attack on the *Liberty*. The board, headed by Rear Adm. I. C. Kidd, met in London and in Valletta, Malta, where the *Liberty* was undergoing repairs. According to a summary of the board's findings, released June 28 by the Defense Department, the Joint Chiefs of Staff had ordered the *Liberty* (before the attack) "to move farther from the coast, even though such a move would partially degrade her mission. The message was misrouted, delayed and not received until after the attack." The summary did not say how far from the coast the Joint Chiefs had ordered the *Liberty* to withdraw. The *Liberty's* commanding officer, William L. McGonagle, said the ship had been under orders not to approach closer than 12½ nautical miles from shore.

Other conclusions reached by the board of inquiry: The attack on the *Liberty* had been "unprovoked"; the Israeli armed forces had had "ample opportunity to identify the *Liberty* correctly"; the vessel had "a right to be where she was"; neutral nations had a right to send ships into war zones, and as long as the vessels maintained "the impartial attitude of neutrality, each belligerent has a duty to refrain from attacking her."

Although the board of inquiry did not explain the *Liberty's* mission, Defense Department officials June 28 denied that the ship was gathering intelligence information. Department officials reiterated a statement they had issued immediately after the incident: The *Liberty* had been stationed off the Sinai coast "to assist in relaying information concerning the evacuation of American citizens from countries of the Middle East."

Israeli authorities conducted an inquiry of their own into the attack on the *Liberty*. Although the findings were never officially made public, Israeli sources were said to have disclosed June 29 that, according to Tel Aviv's version of the incident, an Israeli torpedo boat, sighting the *Liberty,* had challenged it to identify itself. The U.S. vessel signalled back "A-A," meaning "identify yourself." Suspecting that this signal indicated that it was an Egyptian ship, Israeli planes and torpedo boats went into action against the vessel. Israeli suspicions were said to have been based on an incident during the 1956 Sinai war when an Egyptian destroyer had transmitted a similar "A-A" signal as it moved into position to shell the port of Haifa.

A U.S. Defense Department spokesman said June 29 that the *Liberty's* alleged failure to respond properly to the Israeli torpedo boat's query "could not . . . be the reason for making the attack" since the *Liberty* had not received any signal from the Israelis until after an initial air attack on the ship. The *Liberty's* captain, the department said, was unable to decipher the Israeli signal lights because of the smoke and flames resulting from the air attacks.

An Israeli official in Washington was reported to have quoted the Israeli Defense Department as saying that an Israeli aerial reconnaissance mission had identified the *Liberty* the morning of June 8 but that this information had not been transmitted to local Israeli commanders in time to prevent the attack.

U.S. Defense Department sources had confirmed June 13 that 2 Israeli jets had flown over the *Liberty* 30 minutes before the vessel was bombed.

The eruption of fighting in the Middle East June 5 and the Israeli attack on the *Liberty* resulted in the first operational use of the "Hot Line" emergency communications link installed between Washington and Moscow in Aug. 1963. After being informed of the outbreak of war June 5, Pres. Johnson received an urgent message from Soviet Premier Aleksei N. Kosygin on the Hot Line teletype at the Pentagon. Kosygin's message informed Mr. Johnson that the Soviet Union had no intention of intervening in the Middle East conflict and would do so only if the U.S. stepped in. An immediate reply from Pres. Johnson assured Kosygin that the U.S. had no plans to enter the conflict. Mr. Johnson used the Hot Line again June 8 after the Israeli attack on the *Liberty*. White House Press Secy. George Christian said Mr. Johnson had informed Soviet leaders of the incident and told them that American 6th Fleet planes, then taking to the air, were only going to the aid of the stricken ship.

UAR Closes Suez Canal, Charges U.S.-UK Air Role

The UAR closed the Suez Canal to all shipping June 6 after charging that U.S. and British planes had joined Israeli forces in the war against the Arabs. In a further act of retaliation, the UAR severed diplomatic relations with the U.S. (The UAR had broken with Britain in 1966 in the Rhodesia dispute.) Syria, Iraq and Sudan followed Cairo's lead and cut diplomatic relations with the U.S. and Britain; Algeria, Yemen and Mauritania severed ties with the U.S.

A Cairo communiqué charged that there was "conclusive evidence" to prove that U.S. and British carrier planes had flown cover for advancing Israeli troops in the Jordanian and Sinai Peninsula sectors and that planes with British markings had bombed UAR positions in the Sinai Peninsula June 5. The UAR called the alleged intervention "an actual aggressive action against the Arab nation as a whole and against its security and territorial integrity." Cairo claimed that 32 U.S. bombers had left Wheelus Air Force Base in Libya for Israel. The UAR contended that it was necessary to close Suez because Israeli attacks against shipping in the canal threatened to obstruct the vital waterway.

The U.S. June 6 rebuked Cairo for charging that American planes had participated in the fighting. A protest handed to the UAR embassy in Washington called the accusation "wholly false" and "malicious." The note demanded that Cairo cease its "hostile and provocative" statements. State Secy. Dean Rusk said he believed the UAR charges were "invented" for the purpose of creating "difficulties for Americans" in the Middle East.

British Foreign Secy. George Brown June 7 also denied the Arab charges of British air intervention. Cairo had lied, Brown said, because the UAR "is trying to give itself an alibi for its own military failures and the extent to which its failures have let down its allies." (Brown June 8 reported the lifting of a British arms embargo imposed on the Middle East June 6 by Prime Min. Harold Wilson. Brown said Britain had been compelled to decide to "honor" its weapons contracts with undisclosed Middle East nations after other major suppliers, including the Soviet Union and the U.S., had displayed no interest in a British suggestion for a general arms ban in the region.)

The Arab charges of Anglo-American air intervention was reported by Israel June 8 to have been fabricated in a radio-telephone conversation June 5 between UAR Pres. Nasser and Jordanian King Hussein. The Israelis said they had intercepted and taped the conversation, and the recording was made public by the Defense Ministry June 8.

In the recording, a voice identified as Nasser's was heard saying: "I will make an announcement and you will make an announcement and we will see to it that the Syrians will make an announcement that American and British airplanes are taking part against us from aircraft carriers. . . . We will stress the matter and drive the point home." In the recording, Nasser asked Hussein: "Will we say the U.S. and England or just the U.S.?" Hussein replied: "The U.S. and England." Nasser then asked: "Does Britain have aircraft carriers?" Hussein's answer was unintelligible on the recording.

The Hussein-Nasser conversation was said by the Israelis to have taken place early June 5, after most of the Arab air forces had been knocked out by Israeli attacks. Cairo radio had reported later June 5 that Hussein had phoned Nasser to inform Nasser that he had observed on radar British planes taking off from carriers. The Israeli announcement accompanying the release of the recorded conversation said: "When the extent of the military defeat was finally clear to Nasser, he began to act to save his prestige . . . by claiming that Egyptian forces in the Sinai retreated not as a result of a clear and sharp military defeat in his war with Israel but because of imaginary foreign forces." Arabic experts differed on the authenticity of the recording.

Hussein, in his statements made after the start of the war, never explicitly supported the charges of U.S. and British aerial intervention. Commenting on the matter at an Amman news conference June 19, he said: "We are not accusing any particular nation," but "we are not saying categorically that this is beyond the possibility of having happened." Hussein said Jordanian radar information had been sent to the UN to allow other nations to decide on the validity of the charges.

Hussein charged June 27 that Israel had altered the tape recordings of his radio-telephone conversation with Nasser to make it appear that he and Nasser had fabricated the report that U.S. and British aircraft had intervened on the side of Israel. A spokesman for the king said the Israelis had taken phrases out of context and then had retaped the altered text. The spokesman said the Hussein-Nasser radio-telephone talks had dealt only with an exchange of "information" on the outbreak of hostilities June 5.

The UAR charges against Britain and the U.S. were followed by widespread anti-American and anti-British demonstrations in capitals throughout the Middle East. U.S. and British embassies and consulates were the object of demonstrations and stone-throwing attacks in Alexandria and Cairo, UAR; Benghazi and Tripoli, Libya; Baghdad; Damascus; Kuwait; Khartoum, Sudan; Sana, Yemen; Tunis.

(Because of rising anti-American sentiment and the increasing crisis in the Middle East, the U.S. government June 6 took steps to evacuate 40,000 Americans in the area. The Defense Department reported that 20 military transport planes were being flown from Western Europe to Wheelus Air Force Base for possible evacuation duty. An earlier Washington directive had brought the evacuation of 10,000 Americans from Israel, Jordan, Syria and the UAR.)

Arabs Ban Oil to U.S. & Britain

In further retaliation against London and Washington for their alleged military support of Israel, Kuwait and Iraq June 6 announced the suspension of all oil shipments to the U.S. and Britain. Algeria also announced a halt of oil supplies to the U.S. and Britain and said that all American and British oil companies in Algeria were "placed under state control." Officials of 11 Arab nations meeting in Baghdad June 5 had agreed to stop the flow of Arab oil to nations that attacked Arab states or their territorial waters, "particularly the Gulf of Aqaba." The Baghdad meeting had started June 4. Participating nations were Iraq, Saudi Arabia, Qatar, Bahrein, Kuwait, Libya, Algeria, Abu Dhabi, the UAR, Syria and Lebanon.

A Shell Oil Co. storage tank exploded near Beirut June 6 and burned for an hour before the fire was brought under control. The blast followed an appeal by Damascus radio June 5 for workers to "blow up oil pipelines all over the Arab world." Cairo radio appealed to oil workers to "stop exporting oil to enemy countries" and to "call on your governments to expel nationals or aggressors working for oil companies."

British Prime Min. Harold Wilson June 6 assailed the Arab oil embargo as "blackmail" and denied UAR charges that British planes had taken part in the fighting on behalf of Israel. Speaking to the House of Commons, Wilson warned that the oil ban could be more detrimental to the Arab states than to the West. (About 75% of Britain's oil supplies came from Arab states.)

JORDAN-JERUSALEM CAMPAIGN

Fighting Centers on Old City

Fighting on the Jordanian front started at 11:20 a.m. June 5 as Israeli and Jordanian forces exchanged machinegun and mortar fire across the border dividing the city of Jerusalem. Jordanian artillery then opened fire on Israeli positions from high points along the ridge that overlooked the Israeli-Jordanian border, and the battle spread quickly along the entire frontier. Jordanian guns north of Latrun fired across Israel's so-called narrow waist to Tel Aviv, 12 miles away. At least 15 civilians in the city were killed and 500 wounded.

Israeli strategy called for seizing the hills to the north and south of Jordanian Jerusalem and thus encircling the Old City, which adjoined Israeli Jerusalem. Before the Israeli troops could carry out this operation, Jordanian troops in the Old City captured the UN headquarters building on a hill that commanded the city from the south. Israeli troops penetrated into Old Jerusalem and recaptured the UN headquarters later June 5. Lt. Gen. Odd Bull,

UN Truce Supervision Organization commander, was in the building with his staff at the time, but all escaped injury. Intensive shelling continued through the night and into June 6 as Israeli and Jordanian troops fought in Jerusalem, block by block and house by house.

The northern Jordanian front collapsed June 6 as Israeli forces closed a pincer movement on Jenin and then captured the city, which was located on a vital road junction southwest of the Sea of Galilee. Driving to capture the entire west bank of the Jordan River, Israeli troops the same day pushed out from Jerusalem to take Ramallah, 25 miles to the north. The Israelis also captured Qalqilya, where Jordanian territory jutted to within 12 miles of Tel Aviv, Latrun, which overlooks the Tel Aviv-Jerusalem highway, and Hebron and Bethlehem to the south of the Old City. The entire west bank was secured by the Israelis June 7 with the capture of Nablus, north of Ramallah, and Hebron, Bethlehem and Jericho to the south.

Israeli forces had virtually encircled the Old City June 6 by linking up with a number of small Israeli units holding Mt. Scopus, an Israeli enclave inside the Old City. Mt. Scopus, site of Hebrew University, had been recognized as a demilitarized zone administered by Israel and had been supplied by UN-escorted convoys. Jordanian forces had seized Mt. Scopus June 5, but it was recaptured by Israeli forces the following day.

A Jordanian communiqué June 6 said that fighting had broken out between Israeli and Jordanian troops in Bethlehem and that the Israelis had been repulsed with heavy losses. The communiqué said Jordanian troops had penetrated into Israeli Jerusalem. Amman said 6 of 35 Israeli planes had been shot down during raids over the Jordan Valley.

The battle for Jordanian Jerusalem entered its final phase June 7 when an Israeli column broke through St. Stephen's gate at the eastern end of the Old City. The occupation of the Old City followed a night of intensive shelling and bombing of Jordanian positions. The Israeli firing was centered on the Mount of Olives and the Garden of Gethsemane, and Jordanian artillery and mortar positions had shelled the Israeli sector of Jerusalem, hitting the Yemin Moshe and Musrara quarters and Mount Zion.

The Old City was officially surrendered June 7 to the Israeli commander, Brig. Gen. Uzzi Narkiss, head of the central command, by a group of Arab civilians outside the Mosque of Omar. Despite the fierce fighting in Jerusalem, the mosque and other Moslem and Christian shrines in the city were unscathed. Israeli forces were under strict orders to take every precaution not to inflict damage to the holy places. (Pope Paul VI had appealed for Jerusalem to be declared an open city to spare its shrines from the war. The pope's first plea was made June 5 to UN Secy. Gen. U Thant and the governments of Egypt, Syria and Jordan. The pope also called on Thant to "make every effort" to halt the conflict. In an address to a group of pilgrims in the Vatican June 7, Pope Paul expressed hope that the belligerents would make Jerusalem "a refuge for the unarmed and the wounded [and] a symbol for all men of hope and peace.")

The fighting finally halted on all fronts in Jordan as Israeli and Jordanian commanders accepted a UN call for a cease-fire at 8 p.m. June 7. The halt in fighting found the Israelis in complete control of the Old City and the entire west bank of the Jordan River.

Amman radio had announced ½ hour before the truce went into effect that King Hussein had called on the Jordanian people to "fight to the last breath and the last drop of blood."

As the fighting ended in Jerusalem June 7, Israeli soldiers made an emotional pilgrimage to the Wailing (West) Wall, one of the most revered Jewish shrines in the city. The wall was believed to have been part of the First Temple, built by Solomon in the 10th Century B.C., rebuilt in the 6th Century B.C. and destroyed by the Romans in 70 A.D. The soldiers sang hymns, prayed and wept as Brig. Shlomo Goren, chief chaplain of the Israeli army, blew the *shofar,* a ram's horn used to usher in Jewish religious festivals and holidays.

Addressing Israeli troops at the wall, Gen. Dayan declared: "The Israeli defense forces liberated Jerusalem. We have reunited the city, the capital of Israel, never to part from it again. To our Arab neighbors we offer even now—and with added emphasis at this hour—our hands in peace."

Other prominent Israelis who visited the Wailing Wall June 7-8 included Premier Levi Eshkol, ex-Premier David Ben-Gurion and Maj. Gen. Rabin.

King Hussein June 8 attributed Jordan's defeat to overwhelming Israeli air superiority. Hussein said: "Our losses were tremendous. . . . The battle was waged against us almost exclusively from the air with overwhelming strength. . . ." The king complained that Jordan had been "left alone by our many friends all over the world."

(Israeli army intelligence June 28 made public what it said were detailed, explicit Jordanian army operational orders to kill all civilians in Israel's border settlements after the anticipated Jordanian victory. One of the alleged orders, said to have been captured at the Jordanian army headquarters in Ramallah, assigned a reserve battalion to destroy the Israeli village of Motza [population about 800], 3 miles west of Jerusalem on the highway to Tel Aviv.)

SYRIAN CAMPAIGN

Border Heights Captured, Syrians Defeated

Military activity on the Syrian front June 5-8 was principally confined to Syrian shelling of Israeli border settlements north of the Sea of Galilee. The Syrians, shooting from the protection of strongly fortified positions high on the Golan Heights overlooking Israeli territory, inflicted heavy damage on the towns of Kfar Szold, Shamir, Gadot Gonen and Notera in the Hula Valley. The Syrians, however, claimed June 8 that their forces had entered Israel and were advancing toward Nazareth. Israeli officials said the Syrian claims were fictitious. The Damascus report said Syrian forces had destroyed many Israeli tanks and battered artillery units and troops observed moving "in the northern sector of the front across from the Azulia."

Heavy fighting between Israeli and Syrian forces began June 9, the day Syria announced its acceptance of the UN cease-fire order. (Israel had agreed to the truce June 6 on condition that Syria, the UAR, and Jordan accepted it.) Following an Israeli charge that Syria had violated the cease-fire by shelling 16 settlements on the border, Israeli troops and armored forces smashed deep into Syria that day. The Israeli column, attacking north of the Sea of Galilee, forced the Syrians to abandon bunkers and well-entrenched artillery and mortar positions near the border. The initial Israeli thrust thus shattered the Syrian defense line in the area that extended from Mount Hermon to the northern end of the Sea of Galilee (Lake Tiberias). Many of the Syrian positions were stormed in hand-to-hand fighting. By the morning of June 10 Israeli troops were in complete control of Syria's Golan Heights overlooking the Israeli border.

After the capture of the Syrian heights, the Israeli army set the stage for the final onslaught June 10 with a powerful aerial attack on Syrian positions. The Israeli troops then plunged further into Syrian territory. But the fighting halted by the day's end as Syria and Israel agreed to comply with the UN Security Council's cease-fire call.

The halt in the fighting found Israeli troops occupying the Syrian towns of Moussadiye (Masadah), Butmiyah and El Quneitra (Al Qunaytirah). El Quneitra represented the deepest Israeli advance, about 12 miles inside Syria and 40 miles from Damascus. The entire southwestern corner of Syria was thus in Israeli hands, including the great Golan plateau, which dominated Israeli territory in the Jordan Valley and around the Sea of Galilee.

A Syrian military broadcast June 9 had said that "a wide-scale Israeli invasion of the Syrian frontier" had been launched. Damascus reported initial successes that day, claiming the destruction of 2 Israeli tank columns attempting to advance on the villages of Bahriyat, near the demilitarized zone north of the Sea of Galilee, and on Nasiryah. But a Damascus report June 10 conceded the fall of El Quneitra. This admission was followed by a Syrian dispatch asserting that fighting was still in progress in the town. Syria charged that Israeli planes had bombed Damascus 5 minutes after the latest cease-fire was to have gone into effect. The Syrians reported that 2 Israeli planes had been shot down in the raid. The Syrian radio charged that Israeli planes had flown 500-600 sorties over the Syrian capital June 9.

Israeli and Syrian representatives signed the cease-fire agreement in El Quneitra June 11 at a meeting with UN military personnel. Gen. Moshe Dayan, Israeli defense minister, had arranged for the truce in a meeting June 10 with Gen. Odd Bull, head of the UN Truce Supervision Organization.

The presence of Soviet military advisers on the Syrian front assisting Syrian troops was reported in an AP dispatch June 12. It quoted Israeli military sources as saying that their forces had captured 5 Soviet officers. But the AP said the report was later denied by an Israeli army spokesman. Russian-speaking foreign correspondents on the Syrian front were reported June 10 to have overheard Russian-language transmissions on Syrian military radio wavelengths, and other sources also said that evidence had been found of Soviet advisers aiding Syrian combat forces. Brig. Gen. I. Elazar, the Israeli northern commander, confirmed that radio signals in Russian had been intercepted during the fighting. He said some of the radio messages dealt with instructions relating to the direction of artillery fire. Syrian forces were equipped largely with Soviet arms, and Soviet officers were believed to have advised and trained the Syrians, particularly in the use of tanks and artillery.

CASUALTIES & PRISONERS

As in all wars, initial reports of casualties were confused and conflicting.

Brig. Gen. Yeshayahu Gavish, Israeli commander of the southern front, said June 12 that Israeli forces in the Sinai campaign had destroyed 500-600 Egyptian tanks and captured 100 others in working order. About 3,000 prisoners had been taken, but "10s of thousands" of other UAR troops were still wandering in the Sinai, Gavish said. Gavish estimated that of 150,000 UAR troops in the Sinai campaign, 7,000-10,000 had been killed. But a week later Israeli authorities estimated that 20,000 Egyptians had been killed in the Sinai campaign. (The Cairo semi-official newspaper *Al Ahram* estimated June 30 that UAR casualties in the war totaled 5,000.) Israeli losses in the Sinai operation, according to Gavish, were 275 killed, about 800 wounded and 61 tanks destroyed or damaged. Gavish disclosed that Israeli forces had captured a UAR rocket site with 9 Soviet-made surface-to-air missiles intact in an area between the Mitla Pass and the Suez Canal.

Subsequent Israeli reports revised the number of Arab captives upward. Brig. Gen. Shmuel Eyal, personnel chief of the Israeli chief of staff, said June 14 that Israeli forces had captured 5,499 Arab soldiers on the Sinai, Jordanian and Syrian fronts, and the figure was later raised to about 5,950. Of this number, about 4,980 were Egyptians. The prisoners included 600 officers, 9 of them generals. All were imprisoned in Israel at a camp near the coastal town of Atlit, about 10 miles south of Haifa. Thousands of other defeated Arab troops had been permitted to return to the Arab side of the truce lines after the fighting halted. Eighteen Israelis were known to be prisoners of the Arabs—11 in the UAR (at least 3 pilots and 6 navy frogmen); 7 in Syria, Jordan, Iraq, and Lebanon. Among the prisoners held by the Israelis were hundreds of commandos of the Palestine Liberation Army who for years had carried out raids against Israel from the Gaza Strip. Trucks carrying 800 Palestinian and Egyptian captives from the strip had arrived June 7 at an Israeli camp 10 miles north of Beersheba in the Negev Desert.

UAR Pres. Nasser confirmed Nov. 23 that 80% of Egypt's military equipment had been destroyed in the Sinai campaign. 10,000 soldiers and 1,500 officers had been killed and 5,000 soldiers and 500 officers had been captured, Nasser said.

Jordan issued conflicting reports on the casualties its forces had suffered in the war. Amman reported June 9 that 15,000 Jordanians—soldiers and civilians—had been killed. A report from Beirut June 10 quoted Jordanian military sources as saying that 25,000 Jordanian soldiers—about half the army's strength—had been killed, wounded and captured. And Premier Saad Jumaa said July 5 that Jordanian casualties had totaled 6,094 killed and missing on the Jerusalem-Jordan front June 5-7.

Syrian Information Min. Mohamed Zohbi announced June 24 that 145 Syrian troops had been killed and 1,598 wounded in the fighting. Zohbi charged that Israeli forces had perpetrated "indescribable atrocities" against Syrian civilians and that thus far 40,000 had been expelled from their homes.

The commander of Indian troops of the UN Emergency Force (UNEF), Col. M. S. Brar, reported June 13 that 14 of his men had been killed and 24 wounded by Israeli action in the Sinai campaign. (The Indian death toll previously had been listed as 9.) Brar said 3 of the Indians had been killed when Israeli artillery shelled UN headquarters in the town of Gaza. Brar made the statement in Nicosia, Cyprus, where he and 243 other Indian UNEF troops had arrived after their departure from Egypt.

Two Israeli prisoners of war were exchanged June 27 for 425 Jordanian captives. The prisoners were repatriated at the Allenby Bridge near Jericho. Three Iraqi consular officials who had been captured by Israeli forces in the battle for Jerusalem also were returned to the Arab side. The Israeli prisoners were 2 pilots who had been shot down during an attack on an Iraqi airfield near Kirkuk June 5. The PW agreement had been announced June 25 by Israeli Defense Min. Moshe Dayan. The International Committee of the Red Cross supervised the prisoner exchange.

In the aftermath of the Sinai fighting, thousands of Egyptian troops whose escape routes had been cut off by advancing Israeli forces were left stranded in the desert. Most of them sought to make their way on foot back to Egyptian-held areas. Many of these stragglers were reported June 14 to have reached the Suez Canal-side cities of Suez, Ismailia and Port Said in a state of near-collapse from thirst, hunger and fatigue. Israel had launched a ground and air mission to rescue Egyptians wandering in the Sinai desert, and by June 16 Israeli officials reported that most of them had been collected and returned to Egypt. The search continued for isolated survivors. About 6,000 UAR troops had been returned to Egyptian hands since the conclusion of the Sinai fighting, Israeli authorities reported June 16. The Israelis had accelerated their search procedures under an agreement with the International Red Cross (announced by IRC officials in Geneva June 15). The IRC had allocated $58,000 for the relief of the Sinai victims June 14. The IRC also said that at its request Egypt had reopened a pipeline running under the Suez Canal to Qantara, an Israeli-held town on the east bank of the canal, to make water available for UAR soldiers collected in Sinai. A previous Israeli request for the re-opening of the pipeline had been rejected by Cairo. As a result, the Israelis were forced to truck water to the vicinity of the canal from El Arish, 100 miles to the east. An Egyptian representative to UN organizations in Geneva, Hussein Khallaf, charged June 15 that Israel had permitted "tens of thousands" of UAR soldiers to die in the Sinai Peninsula without water or treatment of their wounds, but IRC representatives indicated that the charge was untrue.

UN Security Council

The UN Security Council met nearly continuously June 5-12 in an effort to stop the fighting in the Middle East. In the course of debate, the Council unanimously adopted 4 cease-fire resolutions June 6, 7, 9 and 12. The latter 3 were accepted by the belligerents, and the hostilities were thereby ended. The June 6 and 7 resolutions called for an immediate truce by all combatants. The June 9 resolution urged a prompt cease-fire by Israel and Syria. The June 12 resolution called for an immediate withdrawal of all Syrian and Israeli forces to the lines held at the time of the acceptance of the cease-fire.

Council Pres. Hans Tabor of Denmark had called the emergency session the morning of June 5 after being informed by Israel and Egypt of the outbreak of hostilities. The Israeli delegation advised Tabor at 3:10 a.m. June 5 that Israel had come under Egyptian attack and that its forces were throwing back the assault. The Egyptian delegation reported to Tabor 20 minutes later that Israeli forces had attacked his country.

The Council debates were marked by bitter attacks on Israel by Soviet delegate Nikolai T. Fedorenko and by unsuccessful Soviet efforts to have Israel condemned as an aggressor. Adding to the heat of Council debate were vigorous U.S. and British denials of Arab charges that American and British planes had intervened in the conflict on the side of Israeli forces. The urgency of the Council meetings was heightened by receipt from UN Secy. Gen. U Thant of detailed reports of the fighting that had been transmitted to him by UN observers on the scene.

U Thant Reports on Fighting

At its opening emergency session June 5, the Security Council heard a report on the outbreak of hostilities. Secy. Gen. Thant, who delivered the report, submitted supplemental reports later June 5 and June 6-10. He noted June 5 that much of the initial information, transmitted by the UNEF commander, Maj. Gen. Indar Jit Rikhye, of India, had come from the Egyptian-staffed UAR liaison service in Gaza. Thant added that the UNEF had been confined to its camps and had "no means of ascertaining how the fighting started."

Details of the reports:

First report (early June 5)—At 8:00 a.m. local time (LT) 4 Israeli planes violated UAR air space over Gaza and El Arish, and the UAR reported that 2 were shot down. UNEF personnel in Rafah reported heavy fighting between UAR and Israeli forces across the frontier at 8:00 a.m. LT. Rikhye was informed by UAR authorities that Israeli planes had made bombing raids throughout the UAR, including Cairo; Israel denied the Cairo charge.

UAR artillery started firing into Israel at 9:15 a.m. LT.

The UNTSO chief of staff, Gen. Odd Bull, reported that firing in Jerusalem had started at 11:25 a.m. LT. Cease-fires were called for at noon and and 12:30 p.m. LT, but light firing continued from the Jordanian side.

UN observers on the Syrian border reported air battles between Israeli and Syrian planes beginning at 11:55 a.m. LT. Israel announced a state of war with Syria at 12:18 p.m. LT. The chairman of the Israel-Syria Mixed Armistice Commission reported that Israeli planes had bombed Damascus airport at 11:10 a.m. LT.

Gen. Rikhye reported that Israel had opened fire on 2 camps of the Indian UNEF contingent at 12:45 p.m. LT and had strafed a UNEF convoy south of Khan Yunis. Three Indians were reported killed in the strafing.

Jordanian soldiers occupied the garden of Government House, UN headquarters in Jerusalem, at 1:30 p.m. LT. They refused UN demands to withdraw, and at 8:52 (N.Y. time) they occupied the headquarters proper and ended communications with New York. King Hussein was asked to remove his troops.

June 5 (afternoon) — Firing continued around Government House in Jerusalem despite a cease-fire called for at 3:00 p.m. LT.

In the Rafah UNEF camp one Brazilian soldier and 2 local civilians were reported wounded. A later report on the firing on the Indian contingent's main camp said that one Indian officer and one soldier were killed and one officer and 9 soldiers were wounded.

Rikhye said that at 4:30 p.m. LT Israeli aircraft had attacked and destroyed the Wadi Gaza Bridge on the main road south from Gaza.

The UN radio in Amman reported that it was under air attack at 5:48 p.m. LT.

The UN Secretary General protested to Israel against the attacks on UNEF contingents.

Gen. Bull reported that Israeli troops had occupied Government House at 12:30 p.m. Greenwich Mean Time (GMT) and that he had then been escorted into Israel, where he attempted to set up temporary headquarters.

June 6 (afternoon)—Israel reported to the Jordan-Israel Mixed Armistice Commission that Jordan was shelling Tel Aviv and Lydda. Israel threatened retaliation on Amman and Ramallah if the shelling was not stopped.

Firing continued in Jerusalem the night of June 5-6, and Israeli units attacked Mt. Scopus at dawn.

The UNTSO Tiberias Control Center reported that fighting raged June 6 along the entire Israel-Syria Armistice Demarcation Line. Attempts at a cease-fire were unsuccessful.

Israel reported capturing Latrun and Jenin in Jordan.

UNEF headquarters in Gaza were reportedly under artillery fire June 5. Arrangements were made to evacuate UN personnel the following day. Israeli artillery fired on the camp for 2½ hours during the night of June 5-6. During that time 3 Indian soldiers were killed and 3 wounded. A protest was sent to Israel.

UNEF headquarters was moved to the Tre Kroner camp on Gaza beach early June 6. Fighting was reported in the city of Gaza and El Arish. Israeli troops entered Gaza at 11:00 a.m. GMT, and fighting stopped at 11:45 a.m. GMT. El Arish was quiet by noon.

June 7 (Jordan front)—Gen. Odd Bull reported at 10 a.m. GMT from Jerusalem that during the night of June 6-7 fighting had continued in many parts of the city. Mount Scopus, UN headquarters and the Mandelbaum Gate area suffered heavy artillery bombardment. The Jordan-Israel Mixed Armistice Commission chairman reported that at 10:00 a.m. GMT the area was quiet. The commission's headquarters then was occupied by Israeli troops. Thant advised the commission chairman to remain at headquarters.

Bull reported that all was quiet in Jerusalem at 10:45 a.m. GMT and that UNTSO observers at Jenin and Latrun had "returned under UNTSO control under Israeli forces' escort." Observers at Tulkarm and Hebron were reported safe.

At 10:30 a.m. GMT Israeli mortars began bombarding the vicinity of Bethlehem.

June 7 (UN casualties)—Commandant Wickham of the Irish army, a UNTSO observer in Syria, was killed early June 7 on the road between El Quneitra and Damascus. The death of one Brazilian soldier in the Rafah camp (Gaza Strip) June 5 was confirmed. Total casualties suffered by the Indian UNEF contingent were reported to be 9 killed, 20 wounded and 12 missing.

The remaining contingents of UNEF in Gaza reported that they were not in danger and that means for their evacuation were being sought. Thant appealed to Israeli forces occupying headquarters of UNEF in Gaza and UNTSO in Jerusalem to safeguard all UN records and documents. Thant said that he believed fighting was continuing at numerous points.

June 8 (morning)—Jordan reported that, in spite of the cease-fire ordered by the Security Council, Israel was bombing Mafraq and Israeli troops were massing on the west side of the Jordan River south of the Damiya Bridge; some Israeli troops were reported to have crossed to the eastern bank. Israeli sources claimed that Jordan had massed troops and aircraft in the Mafraq area.

No response to the cease-fire appeal had been received from the Iraqi government.

UN observers in Tiberias reported heavy air and ground fire near the Israel-Syria central demilitarized zone.

The UNEF commander reported that one evacuation ship was in the Gaza area and 2 more were on their way. (A Swedish freighter removing UNEF troops arrived in Famagusta, Cyprus June 10 carrying 334 Swedes, 58 Norwegians and 138 Indians. More than 500 Indian and 400 Brazilian troops were reported still in Gaza awaiting evacuation.)

June 9—The Israel-Syria Mixed Armistice Commission reported that artillery and air bombardment had taken place in the central demilitarized zone at 7:45-7:55 a.m. GMT. Further bombing in the area was reported by the Tiberias Control Center ½ hour later. The commission confirmed later that Israeli aircraft had bombed north and east of Lake Tiberias (the Sea of Galilee) at 7:46 a.m. GMT.

The commission confirmed bombing in the vicinity of Damascus at 12:46 p.m. GMT and observed Israeli bombing far to the north of Tiberias at 12:48 p.m. GMT. Syria claimed that 200 Israeli planes were in the area and that ground fighting had moved as far east as El Quneitra. The commission reported an air raid on Mount Damascus at 2:01 p.m. GMT.

Gen. Bull reported that Israeli sources had informed him of heavy shelling near Syria and in the town of Safad and that earlier about 16 Israeli villages and towns had come under heavy artillery fire.

June 10 (6 reports on Syrian fighting)—At 11:33 p.m. New York time (NYT) June 9, the Israel-Syria Mixed Armistice Commission chairman had reported that the Syrians claimed fighting had broken out in the northern area near Baniyas. The Syrians said at 2:54 a.m. GMT that full-scale Israeli attacks had been launched near Baniyas and Moussadiye [Masadah] and that air strikes had been directed against El Quneitra.

The Tiberias Control Center reported hearing explosions and fighting to the north and east from 1:10 to 4:50 a.m. GMT.

Syria said at 6:16 a.m. GMT that Israel had launched 2 attacks on El Quneitra and at 6:30 a.m. GMT that Israeli forces had taken control of the city.

Gen. Bull reported that at 7:35 a.m. GMT the Damascus airport area had suffered an air attack. The Israeli Foreign Office had assured Bull ½ hour earlier that Israeli troops were not in El Quneitra nor on the way to Damascus. Tiberias reported that air attacks were continuing in the valley and on the shore of the lake; at 7:44 a.m. GMT Tiberias reported that the air attack had ended. The commission chairman said that an air attack on Damascus was taking place at 9:23 a.m. GMT.

Gen. Bull reported that 10:10 a.m. GMT Damascus had been bombed. Bull said at 10:16 a.m. GMT that the Israeli Foreign Office had denied mounting an air attack on Damascus. The Israelis said that planes over the city were providing cover for Israeli troops in the area.

The commission chairman confirmed that there were air attacks outside Damascus or near Damascus airport at 7:35 a.m., 8:55 a.m. and 9:19 a.m. GMT.

A meeting of Bull and Israeli Defense Min. Moshe Dayan was arranged for 12:15 p.m. GMT in Tel Aviv to discuss implementing the cease-fire. Israel was reported ready to arrange for the cease-fire. The Israeli Foreign Office said at 11:30 a.m. GMT that Israeli aircraft were taking protective measures over the Syrian border area.

Council Seeks Cease-Fire

The Security Council sought without success at the June 5 session to adopt a cease-fire resolution that would be acceptable both to the members of the Council and to the parties engaged in the fighting. The UAR, supported by the Soviet Union and India, indicated that it would not comply with any resolution calling for withdrawal of UAR forces beyond the positions they had held before the fighting began June 5. This stand was taken before it became obvious that the UAR was being pushed back. The U.S. and Britain rejected the UAR position because it would appear to condone Egypt's May 22 blockade of the Gulf of Aqaba. In speeches to the Council, Israeli delegate Gideon Rafael and UAR delegate Mohammed El Kony each asserted that his country had acted in self-defense under Article 51 of the UN Charter.

Rafael read an Israeli Defense Ministry statement that said: "We have no aim of conquest. Our sole objectives are to put an end to the Arab attempt to plunder our land and to suppress the blockade the belligerents mounted against us. Egypt has recruited and taken command of the armed forces of Syria, Jordan and Iraq. Later, units from Kuwait to Algeria have joined them. Their numbers are greater than ours, but we will prevail over them. . . . We want peace, but we are ready to fight for our land and our lives."

El Kony charged that Israel had once again "committed a cowardly and treacherous aggression" against the UAR. The fact that the Israeli offensive began in the early hours of the day (June 5) "indicate beyond doubt that the Israelis had as usual engineered and planned this aggression," he asserted. El Kony demanded that the Israeli "aggression" be "vigorously condemned" by the Council.

A resolution calling for an immediate cease-fire was finally adopted by the Council June 6. The resolution, presented by Hans Tabor of Denmark in his capacity of Council president and adopted unanimously without debate, did not call for the withdrawal of Israeli and Arab forces to the positions held before the outbreak of fighting. The resolution said:

The Security Council,

Noting the oral report of the Secretary General in this situation,

Having heard the statements made in the Council,

Concerned at the outbreak of fighting and with the menacing situation in the Near East,

1. Calls upon the governments concerned as a first step to take forthwith all measures for an immediate cease-fire and for a cessation of all military activities in the area,

2. Requests the Secretary General to keep the Council promptly and currently informed on the situation.

(Pres. Johnson said the resolution "opens a hopeful path away from danger" and "toward what we all must hope will be a new time of settled peace and progress for all the peoples of the Middle East." The resolution, he said, reflected the "responsible concern for peace" on the part of all who had voted for it, and he urged that "the parties directly concerned . . . promptly act upon it.")

In an address to the Council after the adoption of the resolution, Israeli Foreign Min. Abba Eban said that his country welcomed the cease-fire resolution. However, he said, its implementation "depends on . . . acceptance and cooperation of the other parties," who were "responsible for the situation." Eban declared that the fighting had destroyed the *status quo* existing in the area since the 1948-49 Arab-Israeli war. He made it clear that Israel would not accept a return to the system of armistice agreements on which the Middle East's stability had rested precariously for the past 20 years. He declared that Israel now would demand formal recognition by the Arab states and direct negotiation of the political differences that had led to the outbreak of hostilities. A new Middle East settlement, he said, must "be constructed after the cease-fire [and] must depend upon certain principles: The first of these principles surely must be the acceptance of Israel's statehood and the total elimination of the fiction of her non-existence. . . . The 2d principle must be that of a peaceful settlement of disputes . . . [through] direct contact."

Eban asserted that Israel would not tolerate the blockade of the Gulf of Aqaba. Israel "cannot be expected to return to a dwarf stature with our face on the Mediterranean only," he declared. Eban criticized the precipitate withdrawal of the UN Emergency Force and asserted that "future arrangements for peacekeeping [in the Middle East] must depend more on the agreement and the implementation of the parties themselves than on machinery which is totally at the mercy of the host country. . . ." He asked: "What is the use of the United Nations presence if it is in effect an umbrella which is taken away as soon as it begins to rain?" Eban concluded by saying that, in the face of overt aggression from the UAR, Israel had "proved her steadfastness and vigor." However, Israel was "now willing to demonstrate her instinct for peace." "Let us build a new system of relationships from the wreckage of the old," he declared.

U.S. Amb.-to-UN Arthur J. Goldberg hailed the resolution as "a first step on the road back toward peace." He added: "It is now the duty of all the parties concerned to comply fully and promptly with the terms of this resolution. It is equally the duty of every member of the United Nations to support the implementation of the resolution by the full weight of its influence." Goldberg added that the U.S. was "ready to join in efforts to bring a lasting peace to the [Middle East] area. . . ." Goldberg rejected as "totally without foundation in fact" Arab charges that U.S. aircraft had provided air cover for Israeli ground and air operations and had bombed Arab cities. In order "to prevent the further spread of these dangerous falsehoods," Goldberg announced that the U.S. (1) would cooperate in an "immediate impartial investigation" of the charges by UN personnel and (2) invited UN personnel to board U.S. aircraft carriers in the Mediterranean "today, tomorrow or at the convenience of the UN" to question pilots and verify past activities of the fleet and its aircraft. Goldberg said the presence of the UN observers on the carriers would be "welcomed throughout the period of this crisis and so long as these ships are in the eastern waters of the Mediterranean."

Syrian Amb. George J. Tomeh called on the Council to "condemn aggression" and "apply sanctions" against Israel. He asserted that, "right from the beginning, . . . the Israelis were the ones who started the aggression against the United Arab Republic." He said that Israel had attacked "after premeditation." Tomeh repeated Arab charges that U.S. and British aircraft had engaged in the hostilities on the side of Israel. He said that his government had "decisive, irrefutable proof" at its disposal that U.S. and UK planes had participated from "the very first moment of the Israeli attack on Cairo, Damascus and Amman."

Soviet delegate Nikolai T. Fedorenko said it was the Council's "duty" to adopt another resolution calling for the "immediate and unconditional withdrawal" of Israeli forces.

Soviet Resolution Adopted

The Security Council met again June 7 on Soviet request and unanimously adopted a Soviet-sponsored resolution calling for an immediate cessation of all military activities in the area of conflict. Presenting the resolution, Soviet Amb. Fedorenko charged that "the forces of the aggressor [Israel] continue to engage in military operations, paying no heed to the . . . [June 6] resolution of the Security Council concerning an immediate cease-fire." It was therefore "essential" that the Council act "without any delay" in reaffirming its call for a "cease-fire of all military activities on June 7 at 2000 hours Greenwich Mean Time." The Soviet resolution said:

The Security Council,

Noting that despite its appeal to the governments concerned as the first step to take forthwith all measures for an immediate cease-fire and for a cessation of all military activities in the Near East, the military activities in the area continue,

Concerned that the continuation of the military activities can create an even more menacing situation in the area,

1. Demands that the governments concerned as a first step cease fire and all military activities on June 7, 1967, at 2000 hours GMT;

2. Requests the Secretary General to keep the Council promptly and currently informed on the situation.

Secy. Gen. Thant reported to the Council that he had received from Israeli Amb. Gideon Rafael June 7 a letter informing him that Israel welcomed the call for a cease-fire and would observe it if the Arabs did. Thant also reported that he had received from Jordanian Foreign Min. Ahmed Toukan June 7 a cable stating that Jordan had agreed to accept the June 6 cease-fire resolution. The cable said that Jordanian forces would "observe the cease-fire resolution except in self-defense."

In Council debate during the June 7 session, UAR Amb. Mohammed El Kony repeated the charge that the U.S. and Britain had intervened in the hostilities on Israel's side. "It was proved beyond doubt," he asserted, "that both the U.S. and the United Kingdom have participated in the air operations of the Israeli aggression, assisting Israel on a large scale in its attack against the Egyptian, Jordanian and Syrian fronts. They, moreover, provided an air umbrella over Israel." El Kony charged that while Jordan had accepted the cease-fire, Israel "continued its aggression and is still occupying territories in Jordan." Israel was also "continuing its aggression on United Arab [Republic] territory." El Kony demanded that the Council "condemn Israel, order her to cease fire immediately and . . . withdraw to positions prior to the outbreak of hostilities."

Jordanian Amb. Muhammad H. El Farra accused Israel of ignoring the cease-fire resolution to capture more territory. "This is another well-planned maneuver by the Israelis, aimed at accomplishing another part of their expansionist designs," he declared.

Israeli Foreign Min. Abba Eban told the Council that Israel accepted the cease-fire resolution. But he noted that the UAR, Syria and Iraq "have rejected or at the very least have neglected an opportunity to accept" the same call for a cease-fire. In addition, he said, Jordan's acceptance was conditioned by the fact that its forces were under UAR command. "UAR acceptance [of the cease-fire] is crucial not only for what happens on the Egyptian-Israeli front but also for what happens on the Jordan-Israeli front," he declared. Eban said Israeli aims in the war were: "[1] to repel the attempt that was mounted 3 weeks ago to procure our encirclement and strangulation and [2] thereafter to work with our neighbors to build a better and more stable system of relationships."

U.S. Amb. Goldberg welcomed the implementation of a cease-fire resolution as a "necessary first step" toward building a stable peace in the Middle East. Goldberg again rejected the UAR charges that the U.S. had participated in the conflict. "They are false charges," he declared, and "the authors of these charges know full well that they are false." He repeated his June 6 proposal that UN personnel investigate the allegations "to give an objective report about their truth or falsity."

Canadian Amb. George Ignatieff proposed in a draft resolution submitted to the Council that the Secretary General and the Council president "take all necessary measures to bring about full and effective compliance" with the Council resolutions. The Council adjourned without voting on the resolution.

UAR Accepts Cease-Fire

Secy. Gen. Thant announced June 8 that the UAR had agreed to a cease-fire, and the fighting in the Sinai Peninsula ended the same day. Since a cease-fire had gone into effect June 7 in Jerusalem and on the Jordanian front, the only remaining hostilities were in the Syrian sector. Thant said he had received word from Amb. El Kony that the UAR had "decided to accept the cease-fire call" as formulated in the 2 Council resolutions "on the condition that the other party ceases the fire." Thant had announced earlier that Kuwait had refused to accept the call for a cease-fire because it did "not condemn the Israeli aggressors" and "ignored the just rights of the Palestinians in their homeland."

Thant made his announcements at a Security Council session held June 8 at the request of the U.S. to consider a draft resolution presented by Amb. Goldberg. The resolution said:

> The Security Council,
>
> Recalling its resolutions 233 and 234,
>
> Recalling that in the latter resolution the Council demanded that the governments concerned should as a first step cease fire and discontinue military operations at 2000 hours GMT on 7 June 1967,
>
> Noting that Israel and Jordan have indicated their mutual acceptance of the Council's demands for a cease-fire, and that Israel has expressed with respect to all parties its acceptance of the cease-fire provided the other parties accept;
>
> Noting further with deep concern that other parties to the conflict have not yet agreed to cease fire,
>
> 1. Calls for scrupulous compliance by Israel and Jordan with the agreement they have reached on a cease-fire;
>
> 2. Insists that all the other parties concerned immediately comply with the Council's repeated demands for a cease-fire and cessation of all military activity as a first urgent step toward the establishment of a stable peace in the Middle east;
>
> 3. Calls for discussions promptly thereafter among the parties concerned, using such 3d party or UN assistance they may wish, looking toward the establishment of viable arrangements encompassing the withdrawal and disengagement of armed personnel, the renunciation of force regardless of its nature, the maintenance of vital international rights, and the establishment of a stable and durable peace in the Middle East;
>
> 4. Requests the President of the Security Council and the Secretary General to take immediate steps to seek to assure compliance with the cease-fire and to report to the Council thereon within 24 hours;
>
> 5. Also requests the Secretary General to provide such assistance as may be required in facilitating the discussion called for in paragraph 3.

Goldberg asserted that the purpose of the U.S. resolution was to "provide for movement toward the final settlement of all outstanding questions between the parties. . . . No outstanding question should be excluded. The objective must be a decision by the warring powers to live in peace and to establish normal relations as contemplated and pledged by the UN Charter."

Soviet Amb. Fedorenko declared that there was not "the shadow of a doubt" that Israel had "planned in advance and carried out a treacherous attack against the United Arab Republic and other Arab states." Fedorenko demanded that the Council "severely condemn Israel as the aggressor and as the state which has flagrantly violated the decisions of the Security Council." Above all, he asserted, it was the Council's task "to demand the withdrawal of the aggressor from territory it has taken from the Arab countries without any further delay." Fedorenko then presented a draft resolution that said:

> Noting that Israel has disregarded the Security Council decisions calling for the cessation of military activities,
>
> Considering that Israel not only has not halted military activities but has made use of the time elapsed since the adoption of the aforementioned resolutions in order to seize additional territory of the UAR and Jordan,
>
> Noting that even now Israel is continuing military activities instead of halting its aggression, thus defying the United Nations and all peace-loving states,
>
> 1. Vigorously condemns Israel's aggressive activities and its violation of the aforementioned Security Council resolutions, of the United Nations Charter and of United Nations principles;
>
> 2. Demands that Israel should immediately halt its military activities against neighboring Arab countries and should remove all its troops from the territory of these states and withdraw them behind the armistice lines.

Jordanian Amb. El Farra joined Fedorenko and Bulgarian Amb. Milko Tarabanov in branding the Israelis "aggressors." He charged that the Israeli aggression had been made possible by "generous U.S. help" in the form of money and arms and by "aerial cover" during the fighting.

British Amb. Lord Caradon said that the tasks facing the UN after a cessation of hostilities were "to insure and secure disengagement, to bring relief and succor to the wounded and the homeless and then to move on to the greater tasks of conciliation and the establishment of order and justice."

Israeli Foreign Min. Eban welcomed the UAR acceptance of the cease-fire and said that a cessation of Israeli-Egyptian hostilities was now "possible." He noted, however, that Syria and Iraq had not yet acknowledged the cease-fire calls and that Kuwait had indicated its rejection of them. As to the U.S. resolution's call for "agreed measures of disengagement," Eban said his government would reserve comment until the resolution had been thoroughly examined. He declared that the "major responsibility" for developing a stable peace in the Middle East fell to "the governments in the area." They should establish "direct, bilateral contacts," he said, in order to work out the "elements of coexistence."

Council Ends Syrian-Israeli Fighting

The Security Council encountered more difficulty in trying to end the fighting on the Syrian-Israeli front than it had found in halting the hostilities on either of the 2 other fronts. Syria accepted the UN cease-fire resolution June 9 but requested a meeting of the Council later that day to press charges that Israel was violating the truce. The Council adopted a cease-fire resolution June 9 but continued to meet in virtually continuous session through June 12 to consider Soviet and Syrian charges of new Israeli violations of the cease-fire. The June 12 session finally produced a resolution that brought the fighting to a permanent halt in the Israeli-Syrian sector.

After the Council adopted the cease-fire resolution June 9, Israeli Amb. Rafael announced that Israel accepted it "provided that Syria accepts and will implement the cease-fire."

The June 9 session was marked by contradictory reports of violations of the truce by both Israel and Syria. Thant announced at the beginning of the session that, at 7:14 a.m. New York time, he had received through the chairman of the Israel-Syria Mixed Armistice Commission this message from Syria: "In spite of our observation of the cease-fire which was communicated to you at 0400 hours this morning, we are now being subjected to an Israeli attack on the whole length of the armistice demarcation line and against our towns and villages which began this morning and continues at this moment. Different arms are being employed, aircraft, tanks, artillery and infantry. . . . We demand immediately the convocation of the Security Council, the immediate cessation of the aggression and the punishment of the aggressors."

Thant also announced that Gen. Odd Bull had reported to him at 7:45 a.m. New York time that, according to Israeli authorities, Syrian artillery was shelling northern Israel.

At 10:32 a.m. New York time, Thant received a further report from the Syrian foreign minister, transmitted through the Mixed Armistice Commission. The report charged: "Israeli attack still going on inside our territory. All enemy air and ground arms assaulting our country. Israel lying. Did not for a moment respect Security Council resolutions."

In Council debate, Syrian Amb. Tomeh charged that one hour

after Syrian acceptance of the cease-fire "Israeli military forces unleashed and are still doing so with increasing intensity vast air and land operations, . . . leaving no doubt that their aim is a total invasion of Syria." Tomeh asserted that Israeli aircraft were "indiscriminately bombarding military positions, towns, villages and civilians" and that "heavy armor" was advancing into Syria.

Israeli Amb. Rafael asserted that Syria's acceptance of the cease-fire was "nothing else but a camouflage for a premeditated . . . attack against Israel." He said that Syrian mortars had opened fire on Israeli hilltop positions on the border 18 miles north of Tiberias and that "Israeli artillery responded promptly." The shelling, "confirmed" by Thant's report to the Council, had caused "heavy damage" to Israeli villages and was "still going on," he said. Rafael asked the Council president to take whatever steps might be necessary to insure Syrian compliance with the cease-fire order.

Amb. Goldberg urged the Council to grant Thant powers to enforce the cease-fire.

Amb. Fedorenko demanded again that the Council condemn Israel for "ignoring" the cease-fire resolutions and issue a warning that "non-compliance will have the gravest consequences for the Israeli state." Indian Amb. Gopalaswami Parthasarathi asserted that Israel should not be permitted "to enjoy the fruits of aggression." Morocco, Jordan and Mali made similar declarations.

UAR Amb. El Kony accused Israel of carrying out bombing raids June 9 on Cairo and other points in Egypt. He read these charges: "Cairo was bombed for one hour beginning at 8 p.m. local time. Ein Shatt had 2 air raids, Ismailia had one air raid at 10:40 p.m. local time. The Suez Canal area in general had more than 8 air raids beginning at 12:35 until 8 p.m. Between Ismailia and the delta road 2 civilian buses were strafed with the result of 12 killed and 30 wounded, all civilians, including women and children. One Israeli plane was shot down over Ismailia." (The AP reported from Cairo June 9 that the city had not been bombed up to 11:30 p.m. local time.)

The Council was called into session at 4:30 a.m. June 10 to hear new Syrian charges of Israeli land and air attacks in the Baniyas-El Quneitra area of Syria. The Council adjourned in mid-afternoon after Thant announced that Israel and Syria had again agreed to a cease-fire, effective at 1630 GMT (12:30 p.m. New York time) June 10. The debate was marked by repeated UAR and Syrian charges of Israeli aggression against Syria, and assertions by Israel that it had complied with the cease-fire and was only acting in self-defense.

Syrian Amb. Tomeh charged that Israeli planes had bombed Damascus and other towns and that Syrians were being killed "by the hundreds" in the manner of "Nazi atrocities." Tomeh disclosed that UN observers in Damascus had been "confined" as a safety precaution. (Presumably this confinement was the reason they could not verify or deny reports of air attacks in Syria.)

Israeli Amb. Rafael dismissed the Syrian charges as "malicious fabrications." He reaffirmed his government's intention to abide by the cease-fire.

Jordanian Amb. El Farra told the Council that thousands of Jordanians from the Israeli-occupied areas of Jordan were arriving in Amman "hungry and emaciated." The remarks prompted a draft resolution, sponsored by Argentina, Brazil and Ethiopia, calling on the governments concerned to insure "the safety, welfare and security of the area" where fighting had taken place. It called for "scrupulous respect" of the 1949 Geneva Convention on treatment of war prisoners and protection of civilians.

Earlier June 10 Thant had re-activated the UN Observer Corps in the Middle East to check on charges of cease-fire violations. The Council called on the parties concerned to "extend all possible cooperation to UN observers in discharge of their responsibilities." (Gen. Bull reported June 12 that 9 UNTSO observer teams had taken up positions in Tiberias [Israel], while others had been stationed in the Syrian areas of Rafid and El Quneitra.)

Thant presented the Syrian-Israeli cease-fire arrangement, worked out through the offices of Gen. Bull and transmitted by him to the chairman of the Israel-Syria Mixed Armistice Commission. It called for cessation of hostilities by 1630 hours GMT and for deployment of UN cease-fire observers on both sides of the truce line. UN observers were to operate from headquarters in Tiberias and El Quneitra.

A UN spokesman in Jerusalem reported later June 10 that the

cease-fire had become effective at 1830 GMT. He said the chairman of the Israel-Syria Mixed Armistice Commission reported that firing had ceased on both sides.

Soviet Amb. Fedorenko called the Council into session again in the evening of June 10 to hear charges that Israel was violating the cease-fire. Israel denied the charges and asserted that all hostilities had ceased.

Thant read reports from UN observers alleging that some military action had occurred on both sides after the deadline of 12:30 p.m. EDT (1630 GMT) agreed to by Syria and Israel. A cable to Thant from Israeli Foreign Min. Eban stated, however, that the cease-fire had gone "effectively into force" at 6:30 p.m. local time (1630 GMT) and had continued without interruption.

Amb. Goldberg submitted a draft resolution condemning all violations of the truce and calling on the Secretary General to investigate all charges of violations.

The Council was called into session again late June 11 to consider new Syrian charges of Israeli truce violations. It adjourned at 3:10 a.m. June 12 after unanimously adopting a resolution calling for a return of Israeli and Syrian forces to the lines established by the June 10 truce.

Syrian Amb. Tomeh charged that Israeli armor was advancing toward the headwaters of the Yarmuk River, one of the tributaries of the Jordan River, in an effort to secure "all points" in the area. He asserted that the Israeli forces had begun advancing at 6:00 p.m. local time June 10 (½ hour before the truce was to go into effect) from Rafid (12 miles southeast of El Quneitra) toward the east and south. He said there had been further attacks June 11.

Thant confirmed that UN observers had reported movement of Israeli tanks in the Rafid area during the day June 11. He noted that the reports were limited to June 11 because the observers had not been able to proceed to Rafid until that morning. He said the main question to be answered was whether the Israeli troops "were in Rafid and environs before 1630 hours GMT [6:30 p.m. Syrian time] on June 10, or whether they have advanced to that sector after the time fixed for the cease-fire to go into effect."

Israeli Amb. Rafael acknowledged that tank movements had

occurred, but he asserted that they had been confined to areas on Israel's side of the cease-fire lines.

The resolution unanimously adopted June 12 called on Syria and Israel to prohibit any "forward military movement" beyond the June 10 truce lines. It condemned "any and all violations" of the cease-fire.

Council Rejects Soviet Demand to Condemn Israel

The Security Council reconvened June 14, at the request of the Soviet Union, to consider a USSR draft resolution calling for the condemnation of Israel and the withdrawal of its forces behind the 1949 armistice lines. The resolution was rejected. Text of the Soviet draft:

The Security Council,

Noting that Israel in defiance of the Security Council resolutions on the cessation of military activities and a cease-fire has seized additional territory of the UAR, Jordan and Syria,

Noting that though at present the military activities are stopped, Israel continues to occupy the territory of the above mentioned states, thus continuing its aggression and defying the United Nations and all peace loving states,

Considering inadmissible and unlawful the laying by Israel of territorial claims to the Arab states,

1. Vigorously condemns Israel's aggressive actions and its continuing occupation of part of the territory of the UAR, Syria and Jordan, considering it as an act of aggression and the most flagrant violation of the UN Charter and of generally recognized principles of international law;

2. Demands that Israel should immediately and without any conditions withdraw all its troops from the territory of the above mentioned states behind the armistice lines and respect the status of the demilitarized zones as prescribed in the general armistice agreements.

In debate after the presentation of the resolution, U.S. Amb. Goldberg rejected the Soviet draft as "a prescription for renewed hostilities." He declared that the UN should develop "a new foundation for peace" in the Middle East rather than "run the film backwards" to the morning of June 5 and thereby reestablish all the conditions that had led to the outbreak of war.

The Council voted on the 2 operative paragraphs of the resolution at its first session June 14. The Soviet Union, Bulgaria, India and Mali voted in favor of the first paragraph, while the U.S., Britain, France, China, Argentina, Brazil, Canada, Japan, Ethiopia, Nigeria and Denmark abstained. (9 affirmative votes were required for adoption.) On the 2d paragraph, the Soviet Union, Bulgaria, Ethiopia, India, Mali and Nigeria voted in favor, while the U.S., Britain, France, China, Denmark, Argentina, Brazil, Canada and Japan abstained.

At its 2d session June 14, the Council unanimously adopted a resolution calling on Israel to "facilitate the return" of Arab refugees who had fled from areas occupied by Israeli forces. The resolution was sponsored by Argentina, Brazil and Ethiopia.

AFTERMATH

Israel's security appeared assured, at least temporarily, by its decisive victory in June. But the manifold problems that victory left in its wake defied resolution and left the Middle East in a characteristic state of turmoil and uncertainty.

The UN General Assembly and Security Council held emergency hearings from June through Nov. 1967 in attempts to cope with the problems created by the war. Their efforts to prescribe a formula acceptable to both Israel and the Arabs, however, proved futile.

The Israelis, detailing their position in government pronouncements and in bitter UN debate, insisted that Israel must hold the Arab areas captured during the war until the question of secure and agreed boundaries could be settled in direct Arab-Israeli negotiations. Israel was unyielding on the status of the Old City of Jerusalem, captured from Jordan. By administratively merging the Old City with the Israeli section of Jerusalem, Israel reinforced its assertion that it intended to retain the Old City permanently.

The Arabs demanded the unconditional withdrawal of Israeli forces from Arab areas and held out little hope of mitigating their antagonistic attitude toward the existence of Israel as a state. The Arabs' cause was championed staunchly by the Soviet Union and other members of the Communist bloc in UN debate and in other diplomatic forums. In the months following the hostilities, Moscow reportedly replaced most of the Soviet-made Arab arms destroyed or captured by the Israelis in the war. The Soviet Union thus concretely manifested its intention to continue to back the Arab struggle against Israel and to pursue its goal of expanding its influence in the Middle East. The Soviet replenishment of the Egyptian and Syrian arsenals stiffened Arab resolve not to reach a compromise with Israel and raised the specter of another round of conflict in the Middle East. Jordan, which had traditionally bought its weapons from the West, sought to rebuild its armed forces with equipment from Western sources.

In contrast to the demands by the Soviet Union and other pro-

Arab states that Israel be condemned for aggression and that it unconditionally withdraw its forces from conquered areas, the U.S. advocated linking the principle of Israeli relinquishment of the Arab territories with an end to Arab belligerency against Israel. Western sympathy for Israel as spearheaded by the U.S., however, was not unanimous. A notable exception was France, which joined the chorus of those condemning Israel as an aggressor.

Further contributing to post-war tensions were the emergence of a new Arab refugee problem, sporadic but bloody clashes between Arab and Israeli forces along the new war-created frontiers, on the shores of the Suez Canal and in the west bank of the Jordan River, and Arab passive and armed resistance to Israeli occupation of the west bank.

About 200,000 Arabs on the west bank, home of thousands of Arab refugees of the 1948 Arab-Israeli war, fled to Jordan in the wake of the latest conflict. By the end of 1967, only 14,000 of these newly-displaced Arabs had returned to their homes on the west bank.

Nasser's Brief Resignation

Gamal Abdel Nasser June 9 announced his resignation as president of the United Arab Republic, but he withdrew his resignation June 10 after the Egyptian cabinet and the legislative National Assembly voted not to accept it. Nasser June 11 then made major changes in the UAR's military command.

Nasser's announcement that he was relinquishing his post was made in a TV broadcast June 9, less than 24 hours after the UAR-Israeli cease-fire had gone into effect. Nasser announced that he had called on Vice Pres. Zakariya Mohieddine (premier in 1965-66) to replace him as president so that he could "return to the ranks of the public and do my duty with them like every citizen." Conceding that Egypt's military forces had suffered "a grave setback," Nasser reiterated the charge that British and American planes had entered the war on the side of the Israelis at the start of fighting June 5. Nasser said in his speech:

> Brothers, we have been accustomed . . . to speak with open hearts and to tell each other the facts, confident that through this means alone we can always find our sound direction, however critical the circumstances and however low the light. We cannot hide from ourselves the fact that we have met with a grave setback in the last few days. But I

am confident that all of us can in a short time overcome our difficult situation. To do this we shall need much patience, much wisdom and moral courage, and ability for devoted work. . . .

We all know how the crisis began in the first half of May. There was an enemy plan to invade Syria, and the statements by his politicians and his military commanders declared that frankly. The evidence was ample. The sources of our Syrian brothers and our own reliable information were categorical on this. Even our friends in the Soviet Union told a parliamentary delegation which was visiting Moscow early last month that there was a calculated intention. It was our duty not to accept this in silence. In addition to it being a question of Arab brotherhood, it was also a matter of national security. Who starts with Syria will finish with Egypt. So our armed forces moved to our frontiers. Following this came the withdrawal of the United Nations Force, then the return of our forces to the Sharm el Sheik position which commands the Tiran Strait, which the Israeli enemy used as one of the results of the tripartite aggression on us in 1956. . . .

Our estimates of the enemy's strength were precise. . . . . Our armed forces had reached a level of equipment and training at which they were capable of deterring and repelling the enemy. We realized that the possibility of an armed clash existed, and we accepted the risk.

There were several factors before us—nationalist, Arab, and international. These included a message from Pres. Lyndon Johnson of the United States, which was handed to our ambassador in Washington on May 26, asking us for restraint and not to be the first to open fire; otherwise we would face serious consequences. The same night the Soviet ambassador asked to see me urgently at 3:30 and told me that the Soviet Government strongly requested we should not be first to open fire.

On the morning of last Monday, June 5, the enemy struck. If we say it was a stronger blow than we had expected we must say at the same time, and with assurance, that it was much stronger than his resources allowed. It was clear from the very first there were other forces behind him which came to settle their accounts with the Arab nationalist movement.

There were significant surprises: (1) the enemy we expected to come from the east and north came from the west. This showed he had facilities beyond his own resources and exceeding the estimate of his strength. (2) The enemy attacked at one go all the military and civil airfields in the United Arab Republic. This meant he was relying on something more than his normal strength to protect his skies from any retaliation from us. The enemy was also fighting on other Arab fronts with other assistance. (3) The evidence of imperialist collusion with the enemy is clear. It sought to benefit from the lesson of the former open collusion of 1956, this time concealing itself cunningly.

What is now established is that American and British aircraft carriers were off the enemy's shores, helping his war effort. Also, British aircraft raided in broad daylight positions on the Syrian and Egyptian fronts, in addition to operations by a number of American aircraft reconnoitering some of our positions. The inevitable result was that our land forces, fighting a most violent and brave battle in the open desert, found their air cover was inadequate in face of decisive superiority. It can be said without fear of exaggeration that the enemy was operating an air force 3 times its normal strength.

This was also faced by the forces of the Jordanian army which fought a valiant battle under the command of King Hussein, who, to be just and honest to him, adopted a fine attitude. I confess that my heart bled as I followed the battles of his gallant army in Jerusalem and other positions on a night in which the enemy and the powers plotting with him massed at least 400 aircraft to operate over the Jordanian army. . . .

The Algerian people and their great leader, Houari Boumedienne, gave without reservation to the battle. The Iraqi people and their loyal leader, Abdel Rahman Arif, also gave without reservation. The Syrian army fought heroically. . . . The peoples and governments of Sudan, Kuwait, Yemen, Lebanon, Tunisia, and Morocco adopted honorable attitudes. The peoples of the entire Arab nation, without exception, . . . struck an attitude of manhood, dignity, and determination, an attitude of insistence that Arab rights will not be lost nor will they dwindle, and that the war in defense of them continues whatever the sacrifices and setbacks along the road of inevitable and definite victory.

There were great nations outside the Arab world which gave us moral support which cannot be estimated, but the conspiracy was bigger and stronger. . . .

I realize that the development of the armed battle may not be favorable to us. I tried with others to use all resources of Arab strength. Arab petroleum played its part. The Suez Canal played its part. And there is still a major role required of Arabs everywhere, and I am fully confident they will be able to perform it. . . .

We responded to the cease-fire resolution following assurances in the Soviet draft resolution to the Security Council and following declarations by the French government that no one could achieve a territorial expansion as a result of the recent aggression. . . .

We now have several urgent tasks before us. The first task is to remove the remnants of this aggression against us and adopt, with the Arab nation, an attitude of firmness and steadfastness. In spite of the setback, the Arab nation, with all its energies and resources, is able to insist on removing the remnants of the aggression.

The 2d task is for us to learn the lesson of the setback. In this connection there are 3 vital facts: (1) The destruction of imperialism in the Arab world leaves Israel with its own strength alone. Whatever the conditions and however long they may last, the abilities of the Arabs are greater and more effective. (2) The reorientation of Arab interests in the service of Arab rights is a primary safeguard. The U.S. 6th Fleet was moving with Arab petroleum. There are Arab bases which were forcibly, and despite the will of the peoples, placed at the service of aggression. (3) What is now needed is a unified voice by the entire Arab nation. . . .

We now reach an important point in this soul-searching by asking ourselves: Does this mean we do not assume responsibility for the consequences of this setback? I tell you truthfully that I am ready to assume the entire responsibility. I have taken a decision with which I want you all to help me. I have decided to give up completely and finally every official post and every political role and to return to the ranks of the public to do my duty with them like every other citizen.

The forces of imperialism imagine that Abdel Nasser is their enemy. I want it to be clear to them that it is the entire Arab nation and not Gamal Abdel Nasser. The forces hostile to the Arab nationalist movement always try to picture it as Abdel Nasser's empire. That is not true, for the hope of Arab unity began before Gamal Abdel Nasser. It will remain after Gamal Abdel Nasser. I have always told you that it is the nation which survives. Whatever his [Nasser's] contribution to the causes of his homeland, he is but an expression of a popular will and is not the creator of that will.

In accordance with Article 110 of the Provisional Constitution promulgated in March 1964, I have asked my colleague, friend, and brother, Zakariya Mohieddine, to take over the post of president of the republic and to carry out the constitutional provisions. Consequently, and after this decision, I place all I have at his disposal. . . .

I am not thereby liquidating the Revolution. The Revolution is not the monopoly of one generation of revolutionaries. I am proud of the contribution by this generation of revolutionaries. It has brought about the evacuation of British imperialism and the independence of Egypt. It has defined [Egypt's] Arab character, fought the policy of zones of influence in the Arab world, led the Socialist revolution, and brought about a profound change in the Arab way of life. It has affirmed the people's control of their resources and the product of their national action. It recovered the Suez Canal and laid down the bases of industrial build-up in Egypt; built the [Aswan] High Dam to turn the arid desert green; extended generating power networks all over the northern Nine Valley; and extracted petroleum resources. . . .

Canceling his resignation June 10, Nasser said in a broadcast: "I wished, if the nation had helped me, to stand by my decision to resign. [But] no one can imagine my feelings at this moment in view of the people's determination to refuse my resignation. I feel that the people's will cannot be refused; therefore I have decided to stay where the people want me to stay until all traces of aggression are erased. Afterward there should be a plebiscite."

Vice Pres. Mohieddine, who had declined June 9 to replace Nasser as president, explained in a radio address June 10 that "like other citizens of this nation, I accept no leadership but his leadership"; "as for myself I do not accept the presidency."

The military shake-up carried out June 11 had been approved June 10 by the National Assembly, which had empowered the president "to mobilize all the popular forces and rebuild the country politically and militarily." Nasser replaced 11 senior Egyptian commanders, who resigned or who were retired. Two top military leaders had resigned June 9: Field Marshal Abdel Hahim Amer, commander of the UAR's armed forces, and Defense Min. Shamseddin Badran. Amer was replaced by Gen. Mohammed Fawzi, 52, former chief of staff, who was given the new title of commander-in-chief. Amer's title had been deputy supreme commander; Nasser retained the title of supreme commander. The service chiefs who resigned were Adm. Soleiman Ezzat, navy commander, Gen. Abdul Mohsen Mortaga, army commander, who had led the ill-fated Sinai campaign, and Gen. Sidky Mahmud, air force commander. Their replacements: Gen. Madkour Mabulzz, air; Vice Adm. Mohammed Ahmed Fikri, navy; Gen. Salah Eddin Mohsen, assistant commander-in-chief.

The presidential decree announcing the military shake-up was accompanied by a government statement that said: "We will not rest until Israel evacuates the land she now occupies. Israel will not gain any privileges through her cheap victory." (A proclamation issued by Nasser June 11 called on Egyptians to "fight the battle of production from which we shall emerge victorious to finance our military battles.")

Nasser expanded his political powers June 19 by assuming the additional post of premier, by naming a 28-member cabinet and by taking control of the Arab Socialist Union, Egypt's only political party. Vice Pres. Aly Sabry, who was replaced by Nasser as secretary of the Arab Socialist Union, was named a deputy premier in the new cabinet. Two other vice presidents also were appointed deputy premiers: Zakariya Mohieddine and Hussein Mamoud el-Shafei. The 4th deputy premier was Mohamed Sidky Soliman, premier in the outgoing cabinet. Shamseddin Badran, who had resigned as defense minister June 9, was replaced by Abdel Wahab al-Bishri. Bishri was replaced as defense minister July 21 by Amin Howeidi, a longtime associate of Nasser's.

USSR Leads Red Split with Israel

The Soviet Union severed diplomatic relations with Israel June 10 "in view of continued Israeli aggression against Arab states" and Israel's "gross violation of the Security Council decision" calling for a cease-fire. These 5 other East European Communist states followed Moscow's lead and broke diplomatic relations with Israel: Bulgaria and Czechoslovakia June 10; Poland and Hungary

June 12; Yugoslavia June 13. Rumania, however, refused to discontinue relations with Israel or to condemn Israel.

The Soviet decision, communicated in a note handed to Israeli Amb.-to-USSR Katriel Katz, warned that "unless Israel halts immediately its military actions" against Syria, the Soviet Union, "jointly with other peace-loving states, will undertake sanctions against Israel, with all the consequences flowing therefrom." On receipt of the Soviet note, the Israeli embassy staff in Moscow was ordered by Soviet authorities to leave the USSR "as soon as possible." (Katz, and his aides, and the 80-member Soviet embassy staff in Israel left their respective posts in Moscow and Tel Aviv June 18. Dov Sattath, Israeli ambassador to Poland, left his post in Warsaw June 18. The Polish government permitted Israeli 1st Secy. Joshua Pratt and Zeev Golan, an attaché, to remain at their posts in Warsaw.)

The rupture of relations followed a condemnation of Israeli military action issued by representatives of the Soviet Union, Poland, Yugoslavia, East Germany, Hungary, Czechoslovakia and Bulgaria at a meeting in Moscow June 9. A statement issued at the conclusion of the 7-nation conference (as reported by Tass) promised "everything necessary to help the peoples of the Arab countries to administer a resolute rebuff" to Israel if it "does not stop the aggression and withdraw its troops behind the truce line." The statement added: "It is the duty of the United Nations to condemn the aggressors. If the Security Council does not take the proper measures, grave responsibility will rest with those states that fail to fulfill their duty as members of the Security Council." The statement assured the Arab states that the East European Communist nations were "fully and completely in solidarity with their just struggle and will render them aid in the cause of repelling aggression and defending national independence and territorial integrity." The document charged that "Israel's aggression" was "the result of a collusion of certain imperialist forces and first of all the United States against Arab countries."

The statement was signed by Pres. Tito of Yugoslavia; Polish Communist Party First Secy. Wladyslaw Gomulka and Premier Jozef Cyrankiewicz; East German CP First Secy. Walter Ulbricht and Premier Willi Stoph; Hungarian CP First Secy. János Kádár; Czech CP First Secy. Antonin Novotny; Bulgarian CP First Secy.

Todor Zhivkov; Soviet CP First Secy. Leonid I. Brezhnev, Premier Aleksei N. Kosygin and Pres. Nikolai V. Podgorny. Rumanian CP Gen. Secy. Nicolae Ceausescu and Premier Ion Gheorghe Maurer also attended the Moscow conference but were reported to have refused to sign the statement because it condemned Israel as an aggressor. The Rumanian leaders were said to have argued that the question of aggression was one that should be decided by the UN.

Moscow's severance of diplomatic relations with Israel followed a Soviet demand June 6 for the immediate and unconditional cessation of hostilities by Israel's armed forces and the withdrawal of Israeli troops from Egyptian territory. The Soviet statement assailed Israel as the aggressor and warned that the USSR reserved the "right to take all steps that may be necessitated by the situation." The statement asserted that the UN "must discharge its direct duty" by condemning Israel's "actions and promptly take steps to restore peace in the Middle East." Reiterating support for the Arab cause, Moscow charged that Israel, "encouraged by covert and overt action of certain imperialist circles," was entirely to blame for the outbreak of war.

Statements issued by individual Communist governments were equally vehement in assailing Israel and expressing support for the Arab states. Among the Communist reactions:

■ East German Premier Willi Stoph June 5 scored Israel's "imperial aggression" and pledged his government's "total solidarity" with the Arabs.

■ Yugoslav Pres. Tito June 5 pledged the Arabs full support in their "just confrontation with Israel."

■ A statement issued by the Polish government June 6 condemned with the "most profound indignation" Israel's "aggression" against the Arab states.

■ A Communist Chinese government statement June 6 accused "the Soviet revisionist clique" of plotting "at the aggression committed by Israel." 100,000 demonstrators marched through the streets of Peking June 7 and shouted support of the Arab cause. The Chinese CP newspaper *Jenmin Jih Pao* charged June 9 and 11 that the Soviet Union had betrayed the Arab cause by cooperating with the U.S. in promoting a cease-fire in the Security Council. The newspaper asserted that the USSR and the U.S. were "plotting further aggression" by supporting plans for guaranteeing the passage of Israeli ships through the Suez Canal and the Gulf of Aqaba and for establishing a UN-supervised Arab-Israeli demilitarized zone. These proposals, Peking asserted, would amount to "giving Israel a free hand to commit expansion and aggression in the Arab region." *Jenmin Jih Pao* charged that the Soviet Union had "stabbed the Arab people in the back."

■ A Cuban government announcement June 7 assailed the Soviet-supported

UN Security Council cease-fire resolution as "scandalous capitulation." The Havana statement pledged assistance for "any kind of resistance adopted" by the UAR.

■ In South Vietnam, the Viet Cong's National Liberation Front radio June 8 promised to support the Arabs in their struggle "against imperialism" by escalating the war against American forces. North Vietnamese Pres. Ho Chi Minh vowed support for the Arabs the same day and assailed the U.S. and Britain for their role in the Middle East.

A Soviet note delivered to Israel June 16 supported Arab allegations that Arab civilians had been driven out of the Gaza Strip, Jerusalem and Israeli-held areas of Jordan. The Soviet message said that this "all seems to indicate the same practice has been adopted that the Hitlerite invaders followed in those regions which were the victims of oppression during the 2d World War. The Israeli government shall have no illusions: Israel will be made entirely responsible for the criminal acts which she commits."

An Israeli reply June 16 expressed "revulsion" at the Soviet note for comparing Israeli administration of conquered Arab territories to the Nazi occupation of Europe. It denied mistreatment of Arab civilians. The note said: "The Arab population in all the areas under Israeli control is resuming its normal life. All public services are already operating. Certain numbers of civilians and soldiers who have discarded their arms and uniforms have crossed to the east bank [of the Jordan River], returning to their families. Others have moved to the opposite direction to cross into Israeli-controlled territory. Israel's authorities have not prevented this movement." The Israeli note said it was "regrettable" that the Arab charges "should be given further currency by the Soviet Union." It reminded the USSR that Hitler had launched World War II only after the signing by the USSR of the Aug. 1939 Nazi-Soviet non-intervention pact.

Polish Communist Party First Secy. Wladyslaw Gomulka warned Polish Jews June 19 against supporting Israel. Speaking at a trade union congress in Warsaw, Gomulka said: "We do not want a 5th column in our country." "We have made no difficulty for Polish citizens of Jewish nationality in emigrating to Israel if they wished to do so. But we maintain that all Polish citizens should have only one fatherland—People's Poland."

UN Peace Moves

The UN General Assembly convened in emergency session at UN headquarters in New York June 17, 1967 to consider the problems created by the Arab-Israeli conflict. The meeting had been requested by the Soviet Union June 13 after it had become apparent that the Security Council, at its emergency session, would not adopt the USSR's resolution calling for condemnation of Israel and withdrawal of its forces behind the 1949 armistice lines.

Like the Council, the Assembly was unable to find an acceptable solution. The Assembly received 7 resolutions between June 19 and July 3. Only 2 were adopted—a Pakistani resolution declaring Israel's June 28 reunification of Jerusalem invalid, and a Swedish resolution urging assistance to the war's victims. The Assembly adjourned temporarily July 21 and returned the discussion of the crisis to the Security Council. The emergency Assembly reconvened Sept. 18, but only to vote the same day to place the Middle East crisis on the agenda of the 22d regular General Assembly session, which opened Sept. 19. The Assembly ended debate on the Arab-Israeli impasse Oct. 13 after inconclusive discussion and adjourned Oct. 25.

When the Assembly debate ended, the Security Council resumed closed-door efforts to find a formula to resolve the crisis. The Council then convened a public emergency session Oct. 25 to act on a fresh outbreak of heavy fighting between Israeli and Egyptian forces along the Suez Canal. After appealing to both sides to observe the cease-fire, the Council adjourned Oct. 25. In private consultation through the rest of October, and following public debate in November, the Council finally agreed to a British-sponsored plan, which it approved Nov. 22. The plan coupled (a) Israeli withdrawal from captured Arab territories with (b) an end to Arab belligerency; but neither item was accepted by the Israelis or the Arabs. The British resolution also suggested the dispatch of a UN representative to the Middle East to help promote peace. UN Secy. Gen. U Thant complied and sent a Swedish diplomat, Dr. Gunnar V. Jarring, to Israel and the Arab capitals. Jarring sounded out the interested parties, but as 1967 ended, it appeared that his mission was no more successful than previous UN attempts to solve the Middle Eastern riddle.

Assembly Action

The General Assembly was convened June 17 after Moscow's request for an emergency session was transmitted by Soviet Foreign Min. Andrei A. Gromyko in a letter to UN Secy. Gen. Thant June 13. Gromyko's letter cited Article 11 of the UN Charter, which said the Assembly could "discuss any questions relating to the maintenance of international peace and security brought before it by any [UN] member." The article also stipulated that "any such question on which action is necessary shall be referred to the Security Council by the General Assembly either before or after discussion."

Thant began polling the Assembly's 122 delegates, and by June 15 he had received the concurrence of 61 members, the required majority for the calling of an emergency session.

The U.S. June 15 had refused to concur with the Soviet request. U.S. Amb. Arthur J. Goldberg stated in a letter to Thant that the "Uniting for Peace" resolution and rules 8B and 9B of the Assembly's rules of procedure governing the convening of a special session constituted "the only source of authority and the basis for the holding of an emergency session." (The "Uniting for Peace" resolution, adopted in 1950, stipulated that an emergency session of the Assembly could be called "if the Security Council . . . fails to exercise its primary responsibility for the maintenance of international peace and security in any case where there appears to be a threat to the peace, breach of the peace or act of aggression.") Goldberg contended that the "Uniting for Peace" resolution was not applicable in the current case since the Security Council was still engaged in consultation on the issue and had not voted on all the resolutions before it. Despite his opposition to the Soviet request, Goldberg said he would attend the session if it were called. Israel and Botswana expressed similar views.

On confirming that the session would be held, the Soviet Foreign Ministry announced June 15 that Premier Aleksei N. Kosygin would head the Soviet delegation. Kosygin, accompanied by about 50 Soviet officials, flew June 16 from Moscow to Paris, where he conferred for more than 2 hours with Pres. Charles de Gaulle. Kosygin then flew on to New York, where he arrived early June 17.

Other heads of state who attended the session were: Premiers Jens Otto Krag of Denmark, Todor Zhivkov of Bulgaria, Jozef Lenárt of Czechoslovakia, Jenö Fock of Hungary, Yumzhagin Tsedenbal of Mongolia, Josef Cyrankiewicz of Poland, Ion Gheorghe Maurer of Rumania and Mika Spiljak of Yugoslavia and Pres. Nureddin el-Attassi of Syria.

The Assembly met briefly June 17 to approve, without dissent, an agenda presented by Secy. Gen. Thant.

The Assembly's first substantive meeting was held June 19. Leading the list of speakers was Soviet Premier Kosygin, who delivered a harsh denunciation of Israel and demanded, in a resolution, that the Jewish state (1) be condemned for its "agression," (2) withdraw its forces from Arab territory and (3) pay war reparations to the Arab states. Kosygin warned that as long as Israeli forces continued "to occupy the seized territories and urgent measures are not taken to eliminate the consequences of the aggression, a military conflagration can flare up any minute with a new intensity."

Kosygin asserted that "increasing tension and the mounting scale of attacks by Israeli troops against one or another of its neighbors" had characterized the latter part of 1966 and 1967. "The facts irrefutably prove that Israel bears responsibility for unleashing the war, and for its victims and for its consequences," Kosygin declared. Kosygin referred to "atrocities and violence committed by the Israeli invaders on the territories they have seized" and declared that such actions reminded one of the "heinous crimes" committed by the Fascists in World War II. "In the same way as Hitler's Germany used to appoint *gauleiters* in the occupied regions," he declared, "the Israeli government is establishing an occupation administration on the seized territories and appointing its military governors there."

Kosygin asserted that Israel had been aided in its aggression by "outside support from certain imperialist circles" whose statements and actions "might have been interpreted by Israeli extremists solely as direct encouragement to commit acts of aggression."

Declaring that "the task is to clear all territories of Arab countries occupied by the Israeli forces from the invaders," Kosygin asserted that recognition of territorial conquests "would only lead to new and perhaps larger conflicts." The Soviet Union, therefore, "voices a categoric demand that the Israeli forces should be immediately removed from the shores of the Suez Canal and from all occupied Arab territories," Kosygin said.

Kosygin submitted the following Soviet draft resolution to the Assembly:

The General Assembly,

Stating that Israel, by grossly violating the United Nations Charter and the universally accepted principles of international law, has committed a premeditated and previously prepared aggression against the United Arab Republic, Syria and Jordan, and has occupied a part of their territory and inflicted great material damage upon them,

Noting that in contravention of the resolutions of the Security Council on the immediate cessation of all hostilities and a cease-fire on June 6, June 7 and June 8, 1967, Israel continued to conduct offensive military operations against the aforesaid states and expanded its territorial seizures,

Noting further that although at the present time hostilities have ceased, Israel continues the occupation of the territory of the UAR, Syria, and Jordan, thus failing to cease the aggression and challenging the United Nations and all peace-loving states,

Regarding as inadmissible and illegitimate the presenting by Israel of territorial claims to the Arab states, which prevents the restoration of peace in the area,

1. Resolutely condemns the aggressive actions of Israel and the continuing occupation by Israel of a part of the territory of the UAR, Syria and Jordan, which constitutes an act of aggression;

2. Demands that Israel immediately and without any condition withdraw all its forces from the territory of those states to positions beyond the armistice demarcation lines, as stipulated in the general armistice agreements, and should respect the status of the demilitarized zones, as prescribed in those armistice agreements;

3. Also demands that Israel should restitute in full and within the shortest possible period of time all the damage inflicted by its aggression upon the UAR, Syria and Jordan, and their nationals, and should return to them all seized property and other material assets;

4. Appeals to the Security Council to undertake on its part immediate effective measures in order to eliminate all consequences of the aggression committed by Israel.

Kosygin's address was answered by Israeli Foreign Min. Abba Eban, who accused the Soviet Union of a major share of responsibility for the conflict by (1) spreading war fever among the Arab states, (2) escalating the arms race in the Middle East and (3) blocking the efforts of the Security Council to resolve the crisis. Eban charged that between May 14 and June 5 the Arab states, "led and directed by Pres. Nasser, methodically prepared and mounted an aggressive assault designed to bring about Israel's immediate and total destruction." Eban denounced as a "monstrous fiction" charges that Israel had massed its forces in mid-May for an invasion of Syria. Damascus authorities, Eban said, had twice refused suggestions by UN representatives, accepted by Israel, for "simultaneous and reciprocal inspection of the Israeli-Syrian frontier."

Eban again criticized UN Secy. Gen. Thant's hasty compliance with the Egyptian request to remove UN Emergency Force troops from the Gaza Strip and the Sinai Peninsula. Thant's decision, Eban complained, had been taken "without reference to the Security Council or the General Assembly; without carrying out the procedures indicated by [the late] Secy. Gen. Hammarskjöld in the event of a request for a withdrawal being made; without heeding the protesting voices of some of the permanent members of the Security Council and of the government at whose initiative the force had been established; without consulting Israel . . .; and without seeking such delay as would enable alternative measures" to ease the threat of war.

The Soviet Union had contributed to Middle East tensions, Eban asserted, by providing massive military assistance to the Arab states since 1955 and by using its veto 5 times in the UN Security Council to block "a just and constructive judgment" on the Middle East.

The emergency Assembly session was marked June 20-30 by the submission of 4 peace resolutions by the U.S., Albania, Yugoslavia and a group of 18 Latin American nations. There were also major policy statements delivered by Britain and France. Interest centered on a Rumanian statement calling for direct Arab-Israeli negotiations. The Rumanian suggestion departed sharply from the Soviet bloc position on the Middle East crisis.

U.S. Amb. Goldberg proposed at the June 20 session that a 3d party assist in Middle East negotiations. Goldberg's suggestion was incorporated in a draft resolution, which also included the 5 conditions for peace that Pres. Johnson had outlined June 19. Goldberg opposed the Soviet resolution submitted June 19 as "a one-sided condemnation" of Israel. The Soviet proposal, in effect, would ask Israel to withdraw its troops and "let everything go back to exactly where it was before the fighting began June 5,"

Goldberg said. He declared that the Middle East needed "new steps toward real peace—not just a cease-fire, which is what we have today; not just a fragile . . . armistice, which is what we have had for 18 years; not just withdrawal, which is necessary but insufficient." Goldberg then read this U.S. draft resolution:

The General Assembly,

Bearing in mind the achievement of a cease-fire in the Middle East as called for by the Security Council in its Resolutions 233, 234, 235 and 236 (1967),

Having regard to the purpose of the United Nations to be a center for harmonizing the actions of nations,

1. Endorses the cease-fire achieved pursuant to the resolutions of the Security Council and calls for its scrupulous respect by the parties concerned;

2. Decides that its objective must be a stable and durable peace in the Middle East;

3. Considers that this objective should be achieved through negotiated arrangements with appropriate 3d-party assistance based on:

a. Mutual recognition of the political independence and territorial integrity of all countries in the area, encompassing recognized boundaries and other arrangements, including disengagement and withdrawal of forces, that will give them security against terror, destruction and war;

b. Freedom of innocent maritime passage;

c. Just and equitable solution of the refugee problem;

d. Registration and limitation of arms shipments into the area;

e. Recognition of the right of all sovereign nations to exist in peace and security;

4. Requests the Security Council to keep the situation under careful review.

The U.S. resolution was later withdrawn without a vote.

The other major speeches June 20 were delivered by Secy. Gen. Thant and Syrian Pres. Nureddin el-Attassi.

Thant sought to refute Israeli Foreign Min. Eban's critical remarks of June 19 of the rapid withdrawal of UNEF troops. Thant reminded Eban that UNEF troops had been posted on Egyptian territory only because of the UAR's "voluntary decision" "to keep its troops away from the line with only United Nations troops in the buffer zone on the UAR side of the line." Israel, on the other hand, had "extended no such cooperation" to UNEF, Thant pointed out. "Despite the intent of the General Assembly resolution, that United Nations troops should be stationed on both sides of the line, Israel always and firmly refused to accept them on

Israel territory on the valid grounds of national sovereignty," Thant asserted. Thant insisted that he "did engage in consultations before taking my decision, to the full extent required of me, and even somewhat more."

Supporting the Soviet Union's draft resolution, Syrian Pres. Attassi called on the Assembly to "condemn aggression and immediately liquidate its traces." He charged that Arab countries had been "ravaged, their energies wasted in self-defense against the moving tentacles of Israeli aggression." Attassi contended that Israeli forces had invaded Syria June 9 after Damascus had advised Thant that Syria had accepted the UN cease-fire order. "The Israeli invasion," Attassi asserted, "was coupled with a deliberate delaying tactic" of the U.S. and Britain in the UN Security Council debate on the cease-fire resolution. "While the invasion was progressing, the Israeli representative was submitting to the Security Council false information categorically denying the occupation of Syrian territory as well as the bombing of Damascus," Attassi said.

British Foreign Secy. George Brown proposed at the June 21 session that Thant appoint a representative to go to the Middle East to promote peace between Israel and the Arab states. Under Brown's proposal: the Thant aide would "advise the Secretary General on the whole conduct of relations arising from the cease-fire and the subsequent keeping of the peace and the frontiers"; "play an active part in relations with all parties in the area itself"; advise the UN "on the form which a future UN presence should take" in the Middle East. Brown suggested an expansion of the UN Truce Supervisory Organization (UNTSO) in men and material as another means of insuring peace in the Middle East.

The basic provisions of the Soviet resolution calling for the withdrawal of Israeli troops were upheld June 21 in addresses by UAR Deputy Premier Mahmoud Fawzi, Yugoslav Premier Mika Spiljak and Indian Foreign Min. M. C. Chagla.

The French policy statement was delivered at the June 22 session by Foreign Min. Maurice Couve de Murville, who questioned Israel's demand for direct negotiations with the Arab states. Couve de Murville said that serious obstacles to direct Arab-Israeli peace talks existed. The most important of these, he said were Israel's conquest and retention of large Arab territories, its refusal to consider mediation by the UN or other 3d parties and its failure to define its terms for settlement, which, he said, "seem to go far beyond the freedom of navigation through the Gulf of Aqaba." Under these conditions, the foreign minister asked, "how can it be expected that these Arab countries, which for 20 years have refused to negotiate with Israel—however great a shock they may have suffered and possibly even because of this shock—will be any more ready to negotiate today than they were yesterday?"

Speaking at the Assembly's June 23 session, Rumanian Premier Ion Gheorghe Maurer supported Israel's call for direct Arab-Israeli negotiations and refrained from asking for condemnation of Israel as an aggressor. The Rumanian Communist leader's position (previously stated by the Bucharest government) was thus in complete disagreement with the views expressed by the USSR and other Communist delegations to the Assembly. Maurer listed 3 basic conditions for bringing peace to the Middle East: "respect for the independence and sovereignty of states"; refraining from the use of force; negotitaions and agreements based on "a spirit of realism and mutual respect."

The Albanian resolution, submitted June 26 in an address by Foreign Min. Nesti Nase, (1) assailed "the criminal aggression" of Israel, (2) charged that the U.S. and Britain had intervened on the side of Israel in the early stages of the war "by bombing with their own aircraft Arab bases and forces" and (3) scored the Soviet Union for having given "no assistance to the Arab countries" following the outbreak of hostilities. Nase then introduced this resolution:

> The General Assembly, considering that Israel, instigated by and with the direct assistance and participation by the United States of America and the United Kingdom, has perpetrated an act of aggression long premeditated and prepared long in advance against the United Arab Republic, the Syrian Arab Republic and Jordan,
>
> Noting that Israel, following its illegal and absurd territorial pretensions and in line with its expansionist designs at the expense of the Arab countries, endeavors to maintain under its occupation parts of the territories of the United Arab Republic, the Syrian Arab Republic and Jordan which it has conquered by force,
>
> Taking into account that the aggression against the Arab states constitutes a flagrant violation of the United Nations Charter, the fundamental principles of international law and a serious threat to international peace and security,
>
> Noting that Israel has committed 2 armed aggressions against the

Arab countries in a single decade, that it has become a stongpoint of American imperialism in the Middle East and is a dangerous instrument of continuous imperialist conspiracy against the freedom, independence and national sovereignty of the Arab peoples,

Taking into account the legal rights of the United Arab Republic with regards to the Suez Canal and the Strait of Tiran,

1. Resolutely condemns the government of Israel for its armed aggression against the United Arab Republic, the Syrian Arab Republic and Jordan, and for the continuance of the aggression by keeping under its occupation parts of the territory of these countries;

2. Firmly condemns the governments of the United States of America and the United Kingdom for inciting, assisting and participating directly in that aggression as well as for their continued support to the aggression and to the annexationist designs of Israel;

3. Demands instantly the immediate and unconditional withdrawal of the Israeli forces from all occupied territories in the United Arab Republic, the Syrian Arab Republic and Jordan;

4. Declares that the government of Israel is responsible for all the consequences of the aggression and demands from it complete and immediate reparations for all the damage that was caused to the United Arab Republic, the Syrian Arab Republic and Jordan, as well as the restitution of the seized property;

5. Confirms that it is for the government of the United Arab Republic alone to decide whether it can permit the passage of ships belonging to the Israeli aggressors through the Suez Canal and the Strait of Tiran.

Following Nase to the speaker's rostrum was Jordanian King Hussein. He demanded that the UN "condemn" Israel and force the withdrawal of its troops to the positions they held prior to the outbreak of fighting June 5. Anything less, he asserted, would allow the "aggressor to use the fruits of his aggression to gain the ends for which he went to war." Hussein especially condemned Israel's occupation of the west bank of the Jordan as a "completely unacceptable and intolerable situation." Hussein charged that Israel had started the war as part of its "deliberate . . . expansionist policy." Israel's "master aggression" launched June 5 had been planned for many years, he asserted, and was "an act of war as vicious as the blitzkrieg of Holland or as stunning as the sneak attack on Pearl Harbor." Hussein declared that the only peace acceptable to the Arabs was a "peace with justice" for the refugees of the 1948 Arab-Israeli war. This required, he asserted, that the "Arabs of Palestine should be permitted to return to their homes or else be compensated for their losses."

Speaking in reply to Hussein, Israeli Foreign Min. Eban charged that Jordan had launched an "intensive and destructive war on

Israel on June 5 without Israel having fired a single shot against Jordanian citizens or touched an inch of Jordan territory." He said that when Israel tried to keep Jordan out of a war "provoked by Egypt," Jordan had responded with an attack on Jerusalem and thereby "squandered an opportunity of peace."

Yugoslavia June 28 presented a draft resolution calling for the unconditional withdrawal of Israeli forces from Egyptian, Jordanian and Syrian terirtory. The draft, co-sponsored by 14 nations, was presented by Yugoslav Amb. Danilo Lekic. The co-sponsors were Afghanistan, Burundi, Ceylon, the Congo (Brazzaville), Cyprus, Guinea, India, Indonesia, Malaysia, Mali, Pakistan, Somalia, Tanzania and Zambia. Kenya and Senegal became co-sponsors June 30; Cambodia joined the list July 3. The text of the Yugoslav draft:

The General Assembly,

Having discussed the grave situation in the Middle East,

Noting that the armed forces of Israel occupy areas including territories belonging to Jordan, Syria and the United Arab Republic,

1. Calls upon Israel immediately to withdraw all its forces behind the armistice lines established by the general armistice agreements between Israel and the Arab countries;

2. Requests the Secretary General to secure compliance with the present resolution and with the assistance of the United Nations Truce Supervision Organization in Palestine established by the Security Council to secure strict observance by all parties of the provisions of the general armistice agreements between Israel and the Arab countries;

3. Calls upon all states to render every assistance to the Secretary General in the implementation of the present resolution;

4. Requests the Secretary General to report urgently to the General Assembly and to the Security Council on Israel's compliance with the terms of the present resolution;

5. Requests further the Security Council, after the withdrawal of Israel's armed forces behind the armistice lines has been completed, to give consideration to questions pertaining to the situation in the area.

The draft resolution of the 18 Latin American nations was submitted June 30 by P. V. J. Solomon, head of the Trinidad & Tobago delegation. It called for the withdrawal of Israeli forces from all Arab territories and for an end to the state of belligerency between Israel and the Arab states. The resolution also (1) requested Security Council action to resolve the other issues associated with the conflict and (2) urged the internationalization of Jerusalem. The sponsors of the resolution were: Argentina,

Bolivia, Brazil, Chile, Colombia, Costa Rica, Ecuador, El Salvador, Guatemala, Guyana, Honduras, Jamaica, Mexico, Nicaragua, Panama, Paraguay, Trinidad & Tobago and Venezuela. Barbados and the Dominican Republic became sponsors July 4. The text of the Latin American draft:

The General Assembly,

Considering that all Member States have an inescapable obligation to preserve peace and, consequently, to avoid the use of force in the international sphere,

Considering further that the cease-fire ordered by the Security Council and accepted by the State of Israel and the States of Jordan, Syria and the United Arab Republic is a first step towards the achievement of a just peace in the Middle East, a step which must be reinforced by other measures to be adopted by the Organization and complied with by the parties,

1. Urgently requests:

(a) Israel to withdraw all its forces from all the territories occupied by it as a result of the recent conflict;

(b) The parties in conflict to end the state of belligerency, to endeavor to establish conditions of coexistence based on good neighborliness and to have recourse in all cases to the procedures for peaceful settlement indicated in the Charter of the United Nations;

2. Reaffirms its conviction that no stable international order can be based on the threat or use of force, and declares that the validity of the occupation or acquisition of territories brought about by such means should not be recognized;

3. Requests the Security Council to continue examining the situation in the Middle East with a sense of urgency, working directly with the parties and relying on the presence of the United Nations to:

(a) Carry out the provisions of operative paragraph 1 (a) above;

(b) Guarantee freedom of transit on the international waterways in the region;

(c) Achieve an appropriate and full solution of the problem of the refugees and guarantee the territorial inviolability and political independence of the States of the region, through measures including the establishment of demilitarized zones;

4. Reaffirms, as in earlier recommendations, the desirability of establishing an international regime for the city of Jerusalem, to be considered by the General Assembly at its 22d session.

The Assembly adjourned June 28, and 2 more draft resolutions were submitted July 1 before it reconvened July 3.

The first draft, sponsored by Pakistan and co-sponsored July 3 by Guinea, Iran, Mali and Turkey, dealt with the measures taken by Israel to alter the status of Jerusalem. The text:

The General Assembly,

Deeply concerned at the situation prevailing in Jerusalem as a result of the measures taken by Israel to change the status of the city,

1. Declares that these measures are invalid;

2. Calls upon Israel to rescind all measures already taken and to desist forthwith from taking any action which would alter the status of Jerusalem;

3. Requests the Secretary General to report to the General Assembly and the Security Council on the situation and the implementation of the present resolution not later than one week from its adoption.

The 2d draft, sponsored by Sweden, called for humanitarian assistance to the war's victims. It was co-sponsored by these 18 nations: Argentina, Austria, Belgium, Brazil, Chile, Denmark, Ethiopia, Finland, Iceland, India, Iran, Ireland, Japan, Nigeria, Norway, Pakistan, Rwanda and Yugoslavia. Afghanistan, Canada, Italy, Liberia, Niger, Singapore and Turkey joined the list July 3. The text:

The General Assembly,

Considering the urgent need to alleviate the suffering inflicted on civilians and on prisoners of war as a result of the recent hostilities in the Middle East,

1. Welcomes with great satisfaction Security Council resolution 237 (1967) of June 1967, whereby the Council:

(a) Considered the urgent need to spare the civil population and the prisoners of war in the area of conflict in the Middle East additional sufferings;

(b) Considered that essential and inalienable human rights should be respected even during the vicissitudes of war;

(c) Considered that all the obligations of the Geneva conventions relative to the treatment of prisoners of war of 12 August 1949 should be complied with by the parties involved in the conflict;

(d) Called upon the government of Israel to insure the safety, welfare and security of the inhabitants of the areas where military operations had taken place and to facilitate the return of those inhabitants who had fled the area since the outbreak of hostilities;

(e) Recommended to the governments concerned the scrupulous respect of the humanitarian principles governing the treatment of prisoners of war and the protection of civilian persons in time of war, contained in the Geneva conventions of 12 August 1949;

(f) Requested the Secretary General to follow the effective implementation of the resolution and to report to the Security Council;

2. Notes with gratitude and satisfaction and endorses the appeal made by the president of the General Assembly on 26 June 1967;

3. Notes with gratification the work undertaken by the International Committee of the Red Cross, the League of Red Cross Societies and other voluntary organizations to provide humanitarian assistance to civilians;

4. Notes further with gratification the assistance which the United

Nations Children's Fund is providing to women and children in the area;

5. Commends the commissioner general of the United Nations Relief & Works Agency for Palestine Refugees in the Near East for his efforts to continue the activities of the agency in the present situation with respect to all persons coming within his mandate;

6. Endorses, bearing in mind the objective of the above-mentioned Security Council resolution, the effects of the commissioner general of the United Nations Relief & Works Agency for Palestine Refugees in the Near East to provide humanitarian assistance, as far as practicable, on an emergency basis and as a temporary measure, to other persons in the area who are at present displaced and in serious need of immediate assistance as a result of the recent hostilities;

7. Welcomes the close cooperation of the United Nations Relief & Works Agency for Palestine Refugees in the Near East and the other organizations concerned for the purpose of coordinating assistance;

8. Calls upon all members concerned to facilitate the transport of supplies to all areas in which assistance is being tendered;

9. Appeals to all governments, as well as organizations and individuals, to make special contributions for the above purposes to the United Nations Relief & Works Agency for Palestine Refugees in the Near East as well as to the other intergovernmental and nongovernmental organizations concerned;

10. Requests the Secretary General in consultation with the commissioner general of the United Nations Relief & Works Agency for Palestine Refugees in the Near East, to report urgently to the General Assembly on the needs arising under Paragraphs 5 and 6 above;

11. Further requests the Secretary General to follow the effective implementation of the present resolution and to report thereon to the General Assembly.

The General Assembly July 4 voted on and rejected the Soviet, Albanian, Yugoslav and Latin American resolutions. It approved the Pakistani and Swedish drafts.

The Assembly voted paragraph by paragraph on the preamble to the Soviet draft and on its 4 operative paragraphs. The preamble, accusing Israel of "premeditated . . . aggression" and denouncing as "inadmissible and illegitimate" any Israeli claims to Arab territory, was defeated by a vote of 57 (opposed) to 36 (in favor), with 24 abstentions and 5 absent. The roll-call vote:

In favor—Afghanistan, Algeria, Bulgaria, Burundi, Byelorussia, Cambodia, Cuba, Czechoslovakia, Guinea, Hungary, India, Indonesia, Iraq, Jordan, Kuwait, Lebanon, Libya, Malaysia, Mali, Mauritania, Mongolia, Morocco, Pakistan, Poland, Saudi Arabia, Somalia, Sudan, Syria, Tunisia, Ukraine, Union of Soviet Socialist Republics, United Arab Republic, United Republic of Tanzania, Yemen, Yugoslavia, Zambia.

Opposed — Argentina, Australia, Austria, Barbados, Belgium, Bolivia, Botswana, Brazil, Canada, Chile, Colombia, Costa Rica, Dahomey, Denmark, Dominican Republic, Ecuador, El Salvador, Finland, Gambia, Ghana, Greece, Guatemala, Guyana, Honduras, Iceland, Ireland, Israel, Italy, Ivory Coast, Jamaica, Japan, Lesotho, Liberia, Luxembourg, Madagascar, Malawi, Malta, Mexico, Netherlands, New Zealand, Nicaragua, Norway, Panama, Paraguay, Peru, Philippines, Portugal, Rwanda, Sierra leone, Sweden, Togo, Trinidad and Tobago, United Kingdom, United States, Upper Volta, Uruguay, Venezuela.

Abstaining—Burma, Cameroon, Central African Republic, Ceylon, Chad, China, Congo (Brazzaville), Cyprus, France, Gabon, Iran, Kenya, Laos, Nepal, Niger, Nigeria, Rumania, Senegal, Singapore, South Africa, Spain, Thailand, Turkey, Uganda.

Absent—Albania, Congo (Kinshasa), Ethiopia, Haiti, Maldive Islands.

The first operative paragraph, condemning Israel's alleged aggression and occupation of Arab territory, was defeated by a vote of 57 (opposed) to 36 (in favor), with 23 abstentions and 6 absent. The roll-call vote on the first paragraph was identical to that recorded for the preamble, except that Laos shifted from abstention to a negative vote and Malta, opposed to the preamble, was absent.

The 2d operative paragraph, demanding the withdrawal of Israeli forces to the 1949 armistice lines, was defeated by a vote of 49 (opposed) to 45 (in favor) with 21 abstentions and 7 absent. The roll-call vote:

In favor—Afghanistan, Algeria, Bulgaria, Burma, Burundi, Byelorussia, Cambodia, Ceylon, Congo (Brazzaville), Cuba, Cyprus, Czechoslovakia, Greece, Guinea, Hungary, India, Indonesia, Iraq, Jordan, Kuwait, Lebanon, Libya, Malaysia, Mali, Mauritania, Mongolia, Morocco, Nepal, Pakistan, Poland, Rumania, Saudi Arabia, Senegal (but Senegal announced July 5 that it wished to have its vote changed from "in favor" to "abstaining"), Somalia, Sudan, Syria, Tunisia, Uganda, Ukraine, Union of Soviet Socialist Republics, United Arab Republic, United Republic of Tanzania, Yemen, Yugoslavia, Zambia.

Opposed — Argentina, Australia, Austria, Barbados, Belgium, Bolivia, Botswana, Brazil, Canada, Chile, Colombia, Costa Rica, Denmark, Dominican Republic, Ecuador, El Salvador, Gambia, Ghana, Guatemala, Guyana, Honduras, Iceland, Ireland, Israel, Italy, Jamaica, Lesotho, Liberia, Luxembourg, Malawi, Netherlands, New Zealand, Nicaragua, Norway, Panama, Paraguay, Peru, Philippines, Rwanda, Sierra Leone, Sweden, Thailand, Togo, Trinidad and Tobago, United Kingdom, United States, Upper Volta, Uruguay, Venezuela.

Abstaining—Cameroon, Central African Republic, Chad, China, Finland, France, Gabon, Iran, Ivory Coast, Japan, Kenya, Laos, Madagascar, Mexico, Niger, Nigeria, Portugal, Singapore, South Africa, Spain, Turkey.

Absent—Albania, Congo (Democratic Republic of), Dahomey, Ethiopia, Haiti, Maldive Islands, Malta.

The 3d operative paragraph, demanding that Israel pay war reparations to the Arab states, was defeated by a vote of 54 (opposed) to 34 (in favor), with 28 abstentions and 6 absent. The roll-call vote:

In favor—Afghanistan, Algeria, Bulgaria, Byelorussia, Cambodia, Cuba, Czechoslovakia, Guinea, Hungary, India, Indonesia, Iraq, Jordan, Kuwait, Lebanon, Libya, Malaysia, Mali, Mauritania, Mongolia, Morocco, Pakistan, Poland, Saudi Arabia, Somalia, Sudan, Syria, Tunisia, Ukraine, Union of Soviet Socialist Republics, United Arab Republic, United Republic of Tanzania, Yemen, Yugoslavia.

Opposed — Argentina, Australia, Austria, Barbados, Belgium, Bolivia, Botswana, Brazil, Canada, Chile, Colombia, Costa Rica, Dahomey, Denmark, Dominican Republic, Ecuador, El Salvador, Finland, Gambia, Ghana, Guatemala, Guyana, Honduras, Iceland, Ireland, Israel, Italy, Ivory Coast, Jamaica, Japan, Lesotho, Liberia, Madagascar, Malawi, Mexico, Netherlands, New Zealand, Nicaragua, Norway, Panama, Paraguay, Peru, Philippines, Rwanda, Sierra Leone, Sweden, Togo, Trinidad and Tobago, United Kingdom, United States, Upper Volta, Uruguay, Venezuela.

Abstaining—Burma, Burundi, Cameroon, Central African Republic, Ceylon, Chad, China, Congo (Brazzaville), Cyprus, France, Gabon, Greece, Iran, Kenya, Laos, Nepal, Niger, Nigeria, Portugal, Rumania, Senegal, Singapore, South Africa, Spain, Thailand, Turkey, Uganda, Zambia.

Asbent — Albania, Congo (Democratic Republic of), Ethiopia, Haiti, Maldive Islands, Malta.

The 4th operative paragraph, appealing to the Security Council to undertake "immediate effective measures in order to eliminate all consequences of the aggression committed by Israel," was defeated by a vote of 54 (opposed) to 36 (in favor), with 26 abstentions and 6 absent. The roll-call vote:

In favor—Afghanistan, Algeria, Bulgaria, Burundi, Byelorussia, Cambodia, Cuba, Czechoslovakia, Guinea, Hungary, India, Indonesia, Iraq, Jordan, Kuwait, Lebanon, Libya, Malaysia, Mali, Mauritania, Mongolia, Morocco, Pakistan, Poland, Saudi Arabia, Somalia, Sudan, Syria, Tunisia, Ukraine, Union of Soviet Socialist Republics, United Arab Republic, United Republic of Tanzania, Yemen, Yugoslavia, Zambia.

Opposed—Argentina, Australia, Austria, Barbados, Belgium, Bolivia, Botswana, Brazil, Canada, Chile, Colombia, Costa Rica, Dahomey, Denmark, Dominican Republic, Ecuador, El Salvador, Finland, Gambia, Ghana, Guatemala, Guyana, Honduras, Iceland, Ireland, Israel, Italy, Ivory Coast, Jamaica, Japan, Lesotho, Liberia, Luxembourg, Malawi, Mexico, Netherlands, New Zealand, Nicaragua, Norway, Panama, Paraguay, Peru, Philippines, Portugal, Rwanda, Sierra Leone, Sweden, Togo, Trinidad and Tobago, United Kingdom, United States, Upper Volta, Uruguay, Venezuela.

Abstaining—Burma, Cameroon, Central African Republic, Ceylon, Chad, China, Congo (Brazzaville), Cyprus, France, Gabon, Greece, Iran, Kenya, Laos, Madagascar, Nepal, Niger, Nigeria, Rumania, Senegal, Singapore, South Africa, Spain, Thailand, Turkey, Uganda.

Absent—Albania, Congo (Democratic Republic of), Ethiopia, Haiti, Maldive Islands, Malta.

The Albania draft was defeated by a vote of 71 (opposed) to 22 (in favor) with 27 abstentions and 2 absent. The roll-call vote:

In favor—Albania, Algeria, Bulgaria, Byelorussia, Cambodia, Cuba, Czechoslovakia, Hungary, Iraq, Jordan, Kuwait, Lebanon, Mauritania, Mongolia, Poland, Saudi Arabia, Sudan, Syria, Ukraine, Union of Soviet Socialist Republics, United Arab Republic, Yemen.

Opposed—Argentina, Australia, Austria, Barbados, Belgium, Bolivia, Botswana, Brazil, Canada, Chile, China, Colombia, Congo (Democratic Republic of), Costa Rica, Cyprus, Dahomey, Denmark, Dominican Republic, Ecuador, El Salvador, Ethiopia, Finland, Gambia, Ghana, Greece, Guatemala, Guyana, Honduras, Iceland, India, Indonesia, Iran, Ireland, Israel, Italy, Ivory Coast, Jamaica, Japan, Lesotho, Liberia, Luxembourg, Madagascar, Malawi, Malaysia, Malta, Mexico, Nepal, Netherlands, New Zealand, Nicaragua, Norway, Pakistan, Panama, Paraguay, Peru, Philippines, Portugal, Rwanda, Sierra Leone, Spain, Sweden, Thailand, Togo, Trinidad and Tobago, Turkey, Uganda, United Kingdom, United States, Upper Volta, Uruguay, Venezuela.

Abstaining—Afghanistan, Burma, Burundi, Cameroon, Central African Republic, Ceylon, Chad, Congo (Brazzaville), France, Gabon, Guinea, Kenya, Laos, Libya, Mali, Morocco, Niger, Nigeria, Rumania, Senegal, Singapore, Somalia, South Africa, Tunisia, United Republic of Tanzania, Yugoslavia, Zambia.

Absent—Haiti, Maldive Islands.

The Yugoslav resolution was defeated by a vote of 46 (opposed) to 53 (in favor), with 20 abstentions and 3 absent. The roll-call vote:

In favor—Afghanistan, Algeria, Bulgaria, Burma, Burundi, Byelorussia, Cambodia, Cameroon, Ceylon, Congo (Brazzaville), Congo (Democratic Republic of), Cuba, Cyprus, Czechoslovakia, France, Gabon, Greece, Guinea, Hungary, India, Indonesia, Iran, Iraq, Japan, Jordan, Kuwait, Lebanon, Libya, Malaysia, Mali, Mauritania, Mongolia, Morocco, Nigeria, Pakinstan, Poland, Rumania, Saudi Arabia, Senegal, Somalia, Spain, Sudan, Syria, Tunisia, Turkey, Uganda, Ukraine, Union of Soviet Socialist Republics, United Arab Republic, United Republic of Tanzania, Yemen, Yugoslavia, Zambia.

Opposed—Argentina, Australia, Austria, Barbados, Belgium, Bolivia, Botswana, Brazil, Canada, Chile, Colombia, Costa Rica, Denmark, Dominican Republic, Ecuador, El Salvador, Gambia, Ghana, Guatemala, Guyana, Honduras, Iceland, Ireland, Israel, Italy, Jamaica, Lesotho, Liberia, Luxembourg, Madagascar, Malawi, Mexico, Netherlands, New Zealand, Nicaragua, Norway, Panama, Paraguay, Peru, Philippines, Togo, Trinidad and Tobago, United Kingdom, United States, Uruguay, Venezuela.

Abstaining—Central African Republic, Chad, China, Dahomey, Ethiopia, Finland, Ivory Coast, Kenya, Laos, Malta, Nepal, Niger, Portugal, Rwanda, Sierra Leone, Singapore, South Africa, Sweden, Thailand, Upper Volta.

Absent—Albania, Haiti and Maldive Islands.

Two amendments submitted to the Yugoslav draft June 30—by Albania and Cuba—were defeated in subsequent votes.

The Albanian amendment would have replaced the first operative paragraph with a new one stating that the General Assembly: "Strongly condemns Israel for its aggression against the United Arab Republic, the Syrian Arab Republic and Jordan." The amendment was defeated by a vote of 66 (opposed) to 32 (in favor), with 22 abstentions and 2 absent.

The 2 Cuban amendments to the Yugoslav draft would have (1) added a new operative first paragraph stating that the General Assembly "condemns the aggression committed by . . . Israel against Jordan, Syria and the United Arab Republic, and its principal instigator," the U.S.; and (2) deleted paragraphs 2, 3, 4, 5 and 6 (paragraph 1, calling for the withdrawal of Israeli forces to positions held prior to June 5, would have become paragraph 2). Cuba withdrew the 2d amendment from the voting July 4. The first amendment was defeated by a vote of 78 (opposed) to 20 (in favor), with 22 abstentions and 2 absent.

The Latin American draft failed to be adopted although backed by a vote of 57 (in favor) to 43 (opposed). (Passage required a ⅔ majority of those present and voting, with abstentions counted as votes.) The roll-call vote:

In favor—Argentina, Australia, Austria, Barbados, Belgium, Bolivia, Botswana, Brazil, Cameroon, Canada, Central African Republic, Chad, Chile, China, Colombia, Congo (Democratic Republic of), Costa Rica, Dahomey, Denmark, Dominican Republic, Ecuador, El Salvador, Ethiopia, Gambia, Ghana, Guatemala, Guyana, Honduras, Iceland, Ireland, Italy, Ivory Coast, Jamaica, Japan, Lesotho, Liberia, Luxembourg, Madagascar, Malawi, Mexico, Netherlands, New Zealand, Nicaragua, Norway, Panama, Paraguay, Peru, Philippines, Sierra Leone, Thailand, Togo, Trinidad and Tobago, United Kingdom, United States, Upper Volta, Uruguay and Venezuela.

Opposed—Afghanistan, Albania, Algeria, Bulgaria, Burundi, Byelorussia, Ceylon, Congo (Brazzaville), Cuba, Cyprus, Czechoslovakia, Finland, Guinea, Hungary, India, Indonesia, Iraq, Jordan, Kuwait, Lebanon, Libya, Malaysia, Mali, Mauritania, Mongolia, Morocco, Pakistan, Poland, Rumania, Saudi Arabia, Senegal, Somalia, Sudan, Syria, Tunisia, Uganda, Ukraine, Union of Soviet Socialist Republics, United Arab Republic, United Republic of Tanzania, Yemen, Yugoslavia and Zambia.

Abstaining—Burma, Cambodia, France, Gabon, Greece, Iran, Israel, Kenya, Laos, Malta, Nepal, Niger, Nigeria, Portugal, Rwanda, Singapore, South Africa, Spain, Sweden and Turkey.

Absent—Haiti and Maldive Islands.

The Pakistani resolution declaring Israel's reunification of Jerusalem invalid was adopted by a vote of 99 in favor, with none against, 20 absentions and 3 absent:

Abstaining—Australia, Barbados, Bolivia, Central African Republic, Colombia, Congo (Democratic Republic of), Dahomey, Gabon, Iceland, Italy, Jamaica, Kenya, Liberia, Malawi, Malta, Portugal, Rwanda, South Africa, United States and Uruguay.

Absent—Haiti, Israel and Maldive Islands.

The Swedish draft on humanitarian assistance was adopted by a vote of 116 in favor (among them Israel and most of the Arab states), with none against, 2 abstentions (Cuba, Syria) and 4 absent (Albania, Haiti, Maldive Islands, Saudi Arabia).

After meeting July 5 to hear 17 speakers explain their voting on the resolutions, the Assembly agreed to adjourn until July 12 in an effort to work out a compromise resolution.

After reconvening July 12, the Assembly July 14 adopted a 2d resolution demanding that Israel rescind measures it had taken to reunify the city of Jerusalem under a single administration. The Assembly's new action was in response to a July 10 Israeli government decision upholding the reunification of Jerusalem in defiance of the Assembly's July 4 resolution on Jerusalem. Submitted July 12 by Pakistan and co-sponsored by Afghanistan, Guinea, Iran, Malaysia, Mali, Somalia and Turkey, the new resolution said:

The General Assembly,

Recalling its Resolution 2253 (ES-V) of 4 July 1967,

Having received the report submitted by the Secretary General,

Taking note with the deepest regret and concern of the noncompliance by Israel of Resolution 2253 (ES-V),

1. Deplores the failure of Israel to implement Resolution 2253 (ES-V);

2. Reiterates its call to Israel in that resolution to rescind all measures already taken and to desist forthwith from taking any action which would alter the status of Jerusalem;

3. Requests the Secretary General to report to the Security Council and the General Assembly on the situation and on the implementation of the present resolution.

A 4th operative paragraph, calling on the Security Council to "take the necessary measures" to insure compliance with the resolution, was withdrawn from the voting July 14.

The resolution was adopted by a vote of 99 (in favor) to 0 (opposed), with 18 abstentions and 4 absent. The roll-call vote:

In favor—Afghanistan, Albania, Algeria, Argentina, Austria, Belgium, Brazil, Bulgaria, Burma, Burundi, Byelorussia, Cambodia, Cameroon, Canada, Ceylon, Chad, Chile, China (Nationalist), Congo (Brazzaville), Costa Rica, Cuba, Cyprus, Czechoslovakia, Dahomey, Denmark, Dominican Republic Ecuador, El Salvador, Ethiopia, Finland, France, Gabon, Gambia, Ghana, Greece, Guatemala, Guinea, Guyana, Honduras, Hungary, India, Indonesia, Iran, Iraq, Ireland, Italy, Ivory Coast, Japan, Jordan, Kuwait, Laos, Lebanon, Lesotho, Libya, Luxembourg, Mali, Mauritania, Mexico, Mongolia, Morocco, Nepal, Netherlands, New Zealand, Nicaragua, Niger, Nigeria, Norway, Pakistan, Panama, Paraguay, Peru, Philippines, Poland, Rumania, Saudi Arabia, Senegal, Sierra Leone, Singapore, Somalia, Spain, Sudan, Sweden, Syria, Tanzania, Thailand, Togo, Trinidad & Tobago, Tunisia, Turkey, Uganda, Ukraine, Union of Soviet Socialist Republics, United Arab Republic, United Kingdom, Upper Volta, Venezuela, Yemen, Yugoslavia, Zambia.

Abstaining — Australia, Barbados, Bolivia, Central African Republic, Colombia, Congo (Democratic Republic of), Iceland, Jamaica, Kenya, Liberia, Madagascar, Malawi, Malta, Portugal, Rwanda, South Africa, United States, Uruguay.

Not participating—Israel.

Absent—Botswana, Haiti, Malaysia, Maldive Islands.

In debate after the adoption of the resolution, Israeli Foreign Min. Eban explained that Israel had not participated in the voting because the resolution (1) ignored the "affirmative aspect" of the reunification measures, (2) presented the factual situation inaccurately and (3) was juridically weak. U.S. Amb. Goldberg said the U.S. had abstained in the voting because it believed that peace could be achieved in the Middle East only by attention to all of the area's problems. He emphasized, however, that the U.S. did not "recognize or accept" the measures instituted by Israel. He said the U.S. regretted them and considered them "interim and provisional."

Presenting the draft to the Assembly July 12, Pakistani delegate Agha Shahi had assailed a letter Eban had sent to U Thant July 10. In the letter, Eban had reaffirmed Israel's policy toward Jerusalem. Shahi charged that, whatever the "euphemisms" contained in Eban's letter, "the fact remains that Israel is attempting to absorb and integrate the Holy City within its territory." Soviet Amb. Nikolai T. Fedorenko referred to Eban's letter as "an insolent and provocative defiance of the United Nations and all its members." By its "occupation" of Jerusalem, he charged, Israel was following the "new order" expansion of the "fascist *fuhrers*." Fedorenko reiterated the Soviet position that the "main and vital" question was the withdrawal of Israeli forces from captured Arab territory.

Assembly Returns Issue to Security Council

The Assembly continued debate on the Middle East July 13, met briefly July 17, adjourned and then reconvened July 20, when it voted immediately to postpone discussions for 24 hours. Finnish delegate Max Jakobson had proposed the adjournment because of "information" indicating that behind-the-scenes negotiations might succeed in working out a compromise resolution acceptable to most delegations. Jakobson's proposal was adopted without a dissenting vote. The following day, July 21, the Assembly voted to adjourn "temporarily" and return discussion of the Arab-Israeli crisis to the Security Council for consideration.

The adjournment resolution was presented to the Assembly July 21 by Sweden, Finland and Austria after it had become clear that no compromise on the Middle East impasse was possible. The text:

> The General Assembly,
>
> Having considered the grave situation in the Middle East,
>
> Considering that the Security Council continues to be seized of the problem,
>
> Bearing in mind the resolutions adopted and the proposals considered during the 5th emergency special session of the General Assembly,
>
> 1. Requests the Secretary General to forward the records of the 5th emergency special session of the General Assembly to the Security Council in order to facilitate the resumption by the Council, as a matter of urgency, of its consideration of the tense situation in the Middle East;
>
> 2. Decides to adjourn the 5th emergency special session temporarily and to authorize the president of the General Assembly to reconvene the session as and when necessary.

The resolution was adopted by a vote of 63 (in favor) to 26 (opposed), with 27 abstentions, 5 absent and one not participating. The roll-call vote:

In favor—Argentina, Australia, Austria, Barbados, Belgium, Bolivia, Botswana, Brazil, Bulgaria, Byelorussia, Canada, Central African Republic, Chad, Chile, China, Colombia, Costa Rica, Czechoslovakia, Dahomey, Denmark, Ethopia, Finland, Gabon, Ghana, Hungary, Iceland, India, Ireland, Italy, Ivory Coast, Jamaica, Japan, Laos, Liberia, Luxembourg, Madagascar, Malawi, Mexico, Mongolia, Nepal, Netherlands, New Zealand, Nicaragua, Niger, Norway, Paraguay, Peru, Philippines, Poland, Rumania, Rwanda, Sierra Leone, Singapore, Sweden, Thailand, Togo, Trinidad & Tobago, Ukraine, Union of Soviet Socialist Republics, United Kingdom, United States, Upper Volta, Uruguay.

Opposed—Afghanistan, Albania, Algeria, Burundi, Congo (Democratic Republic of), Cuba, Guinea, Iraq, Jordan, Kuwait, Lebanon, Libya, Malaysia, Mali, Mauritania, Morocco, Pakistan, Saudi Arabia, Somalia, Sudan, Syria, Tanzania, United Arab Republic, Yemen, Zambia.

Abstaining—Cameroon, Ceylon, Congo (Brazzaville), Cyprus, Dominican Republic, Ecuador, El Salvador, France, Greece, Guatemala, Guyana, Honduras, Indonesia, Iran, Israel, Kenya, Malta, Nigeria, Panama, Portugal, Senegal, South Africa, Spain, Turkey, Uganda, Venezuela, Yugoslavia.

Absent—Cambodia, Gambia, Haiti, Lesotho, Maldive Islands.

Not participating—Burma.

The Assembly reconvened Sept. 18 and unanimously voted to place "the grave situation in the Middle East," "as a matter of high priority," on the agenda of the 22d regular session of the UN General Assembly. (The agenda also included the Vietnamese war, disarmament and other major world problems.) The Assembly session opened Sept. 19. Debate was started Sept. 21, and the Assembly adjourned Oct. 25. The major parties to the Arab-Israeli dispute made statements in which they reiterated the arguments they had voiced at the previous emergency Assembly session and Security Council hearings:

U.S. Amb. Goldberg Sept. 21 proposed an 8-point plan to bring peace to the region. It stressed an end to Arab belligerency toward Israel, the withdrawal of Israeli troops from Arab areas, but "within a context of peace," free and innocent passage through international waterways for all nations and the principle that the status of the Old City of Jerusalem "must not be decided unilaterally, but in consultation with all concerned."

Soviet Foreign Min. Gromyko Sept. 22 condemned Israel's "aggression" and occupation of Arab territories. He called for withdrawal of Israeli troops, reimbursement by Israel for material damage inflicted on Syria, Jordan and the UAR in the fighting and compliance by Israel with the UN resolutions to end the annexation of Jerusalem.

Israeli Foreign Min. Eban said Sept. 25 that a permanent settlement and peace between Israel and the Arab states could come about only through direct negotiation between Israel and the Arabs. He warned that the UN must not attempt a substitute for direct negotiations. Eban charged that the Arabs were using the UN as a shelter against "the necessity of peace." By ignoring the UN Charter's emphasis on recognition, negotiation and peace,

Eban said, the Arabs had forfeited their right to invoke the Charter. Eban condemned the Soviet Union for encouraging "extremist Arab policies" and for attempting to "restore the conditions which have led to war."

British Foreign Secy. George Brown Sept. 26 opposed Israel's dismissal of a UN role for Middle East peace. He maintained that "a settlement in the Middle East can only come through our" UN.

UAR Foreign Min. Mahmoud Riad Sept. 29 accused the U.S. of violating its stated policy of supporting "the political independence and territorial integrity of the states in the Middle East." Riad said that the U.S. had stated such a policy many times prior to the outbreak of hostilities June 5 but that afterwards the U.S. had "adopted a position of alignment with Israel and hostility toward the Arab people." Riad said that the Assembly's emergency session had failed to condemn Israeli aggression because of the U.S.' "negative position." He lauded the USSR, which "has stood closely by our side in difficult times," and he reiterated that the UAR would not negotiate with Israel.

Council Meets on Suez Clashes

The UN Security Council convened in emergency session Oct. 24 to consider a new crisis created by Egypt's sinking Oct. 21 of the Israeli destroyer *Elath* in the Mediterranean and Israel's retaliatory shelling Oct. 24 of the UAR's major oil installations at the Suez Canal port city of Suez. The meeting had been requested by Israel and the UAR. The Council Oct. 25 unanimously adopted a resolution calling on Israel and Egypt to halt violations of the cease-fire agreement. The resolution (drawn up by Council Pres. Semjin Tsuruoka of Japan):

The Security Council,

Gravely concerned over recent military activities in the Middle East carried out in spite of the Security Council resolutions ordering a cease-fire.

Having heard and considered the statements made by the parties concerned.

Taking into consideration the information on the said activities provided by the Secretary General . . .

Condemns the violations of the cease-fire;

Regrets the casualties and loss of property resulting from the violations.

Reaffirming the necessity of the strict observance of the cease-fire resolutions;

Demands of the member states concerned to cease immediately all prohibited military activities in the area, and to cooperate fully and promptly with the United Nations Truce Supervision Organization.

In a move to strengthen the truce, UN Secy. Gen. U Thant proposed to the Security Council Nov. 1 the establishment of 9 additional UN observation posts along the waterway and an increase in the number of observers from 43 to 90. Implementation of the expanded inspection system was announced by Thant Dec. 2.

The Security Council Nov. 22 unanimously approved a British resolution calling for the eventual withdrawal of Israeli forces from Arab areas captured in June and for an end to the Arabs' state of belligerency with Israel. It empowered Thant to send a representative to the Middle East "to establish and maintain contacts with the states concerned in order to promote agreement and assist efforts to achieve a peaceful settlement in accordance" with the provisions of the resolution. Thant Nov. 23 announced the appointment of Swedish Amb.-to-USSR Gunnar V. Jarring as his special envoy to the Middle East. The resolution:

The Security Council,

Expressing its continuing concern with the grave situation in the Middle East,

Emphasizing the inadmissibility of the acquisition of territory by war and the need to work for a just and lasting peace in which every state in the area can live in security,

Emphasizing further that all member states in their acceptance of the Charter of the United Nations have undertaken a commitment to act in accordance with Article 2 of the Charter,

1. Affirms that the fulfillment of Charter principles requires the establishment of a just and lasting peace in the Middle East which should include the application of both the following principles: (i) Withdrawal of Israeli armed forces from territories of recent conflict; (ii) Termination of all claims or states of belligerency and respect for and acknowledgment of the sovereignty, territorial integrity and political independence of every state in the area and their right to live in peace within secure and recognized boundaries free from threats of acts of force;

2. Affirms further the necessity (a) for guaranteeing freedom of navigation through international waterways in the area; (b) for achieving a just settlement of the refugee problem; (c) for guaranteeing the territorial inviolability and political independence of every state in the area, through measures including the establishment of demilitarized zones;

3. Requests the Secretary General to designate a special representative to proceed to the Middle East to establish and maintain contacts with the states concerned in order to promote agreement and assist efforts to

achieve a peaceful and accepted settlement in accordance with the provisions and principles in this resolution;

4. Requests the Secretary General to report to the Security Council on the progress of the efforts of the special representative as soon as possible.

The Council's 10 non-permanent members Nov. 3 had turned over the task of drafting a resolution to the body's 5 permanent members—the U.S., Britain, France, the USSR and Nationalist China. The non-permanent members, led by India, Canada and Denmark, had acted after reporting that they had been unable to agree on a proposal to send a special representative to the Middle East to seek a solution within generally agreed principles.

The U.S., Indian and Soviet delegations did not request votes on draft resolutions they had submitted. The resolutions called for Israeli withdrawal from Arab territories, an end to the state of belligerency, the right of all Middle East states to a guarantee of their territorial inviolability and political independence, the right of all states to innocent passage through international waterways and a resolution of the Arab refugee problem. The Soviet resolution differed from India's and the U.S.' in suggesting that Israeli troops be withdrawn "without delay" and in not proposing a UN envoy to the Middle East.

The Israeli government Nov. 23 expressed satisfaction with the Security Council resolution. An Israeli diplomat said: "We can live with it. . . . It's probably the best resolution we could have hoped for under the circumstances."

Describing the Council resolution as "insufficient" and "unclear," UAR Pres. Gamal Abdel Nasser called Nov. 23 for an Arab summit meeting to discuss it. In an address at the opening of the UAR National Assembly's 5th session, Nasser said: "The British resolution is not enough for a settlement of the Middle East crisis. The Soviet resolution was clearer in its interpretation of the situation." Nasser took issue with the British call for "freedom of navigation through international waterways" in the Middle East. He pledged that the UAR would continue to bar Israeli ships from the Suez Canal "no matter what the cost." Nasser said Arab policy remained: no recognition of Israel, no negotiations with Israel, no armistice and no "liquidation of the Palestine question."

Jarring Begins Peace Mission

Dr. Gunnar V. Jarring, U Thant's special envoy to the Middle East, began his peace mission with visits to Lebanon, Israel, Jordan and the UAR Dec. 13-26. Jarring conferred with Lebanese officials in Beirut Dec. 13-14. Then he proceeded to Israel, where he met with Foreign Min. Eban Dec. 14 and with Premier Levi Eshkol Dec. 15. On arriving in Amman Dec. 15, Jarring conferred with Jordanian King Hussein and stayed in Jordan until Dec. 18. Jarring's presence in that country precipitated a demonstration Dec. 17 of 600 students and some faculty members of Jordan University, 7 miles from Amman. The demonstrators carried placards demanding that Israel return the Old City of Jerusalem and the west bank of the Jordan River to Jordan. Jarring flew to Cairo Dec. 18 and conferred with UAR Pres. Nasser and Foreign Min. Mahmoud Riad.

The UN envoy then flew to Cyprus, his base, for a respite. He was reported Dec. 22 to have reported to Thant that in his talks with Arab and Israeli leaders he had received "expressions of willingness to cooperate with his mission." Jarring conferred again with Eban in Israel Dec. 26-27 and with UAR officials in Cairo Dec. 27-28.

Syria, which had denounced the Nov. 22 Security Council resolution paving the way for Jarring's mission, refused to accept the UN envoy.

Mohammed Hassanien Heykal, a close associate of Nasser and editor of the Cairo newspaper *Al Ahram,* had stated in an editorial Dec. 15 that Jarring's mission was "almost foredoomed to failure." But he said the UN envoy's political endeavors would help the UAR by keeping "the crisis alive" and by providing Cairo with needed "breathing space" to reequip and retrain its army for another round of fighting with Israel. "The Middle East crisis should always remain a hot and lively issue and should never be left for a minute to cool down or stagnate," Heykal said.

Thant Defends UNEF Withdrawal

UN Secy. Gen. U Thant submitted a detailed report to the General Assembly June 27 in defense of his May 18 decision to withdraw the UN Emergency Force (UNEF) shortly before the fighting started. Thant explained in his introduction that the report was intended to answer the criticism, "both public and private," aimed at his decision to honor the UAR's request for withdrawal of the force. Thant said that such critical statements were "very damaging to the United Nations and to its peace-keeping role in particular."

Thant acted after a personal *aide-mémoire* of the late UN Secy. Gen. Dag Hammarskjöld had been made public by private sources, who charged that Thant had not acted according to the agreed-upon procedure envisaged for any withdrawal of UNEF. Dated Aug. 5, 1957, the memo gave Hammarskjöld's own account of his Nov. 1956 efforts to persuade the Egyptian government to limit its "sovereign right in the interest of . . . the UNEF operation." The memo was made public June 18 by Stephen M. Schwebel, director of the American Society of International Law and a former U.S. State Department legal adviser on UN affairs. Schwebel had received the document in May from Ernest A. Gross, a former U.S. deputy representative to the UN and consultant to Hammarskjöld.

Thant, in a June 19 statement that was reiterated in his June 27 report, claimed he had known of the Hammarskjöld document and that it had no bearing on his decision to withdraw the UNEF.

Summaries of the contents of the 3 documents:

June 27 Thant report—The events leading to the UNEF withdrawal:

At 8:00 p.m. GMT (Greenwich Mean Time) May 16, Brig. Eiz-el-Din Mokhtar transmitted to the UNEF commander, Maj. Gen. Indar Jit Rikhye, a message from Gen. Mohammed Fawzi, the UAR chief of staff, requesting withdrawal of all UN troops from their positions along the Israeli border. Rikhye refused the request, explaining that he could not take such action without specific instructions from UN headquarters.

UAR troops began moving May 17 into positions between the UNEF posts and the Israeli border. Thant, at 4:00 p.m. NYT (New York time) May 17, conferred at UN headquarters with representatives of the 7 countries having contingents in UNEF and informed them of the UAR demand. Two of the representatives said that if the UAR made a formal request for the withdrawal of UNEF, the question should be brought before the General Assembly and should be coupled with an appeal to the UAR to withdraw its request. Two other representatives (reported to be Yugoslavia and India) said that the UAR was entitled to ask for the withdrawal of UNEF and that the request should be obeyed.

Egyptian forces May 18 began preventing UNEF sentries from occupying their posts and took over the camps of 2 Yugoslav UNEF units. At 12:00 noon NYT Thant received a formal request from UAR Foreign Affairs Min. Mahmoud Riad for the withdrawal of UNEF troops "as soon as possible." Thant told UAR Amb. Mohamad Awad El Kony that he disapproved of the UAR's action and that he intended to appeal directly to Pres. Nasser "to reconsider the decision."

At 5:00 p.m. NYT May 18 Thant met with members of the UNEF Advisory Committee (composed of 4 of the nations providing UNEF troops—Brazil, Canada, India and Norway—and of 3 other nations, Ceylon, Colombia and Pakistan) and with representatives of 3 countries that were not on the committee but that had provided troops for UNEF: Denmark, Sweden and Yugoslavia. After some discussion, Thant decided that he had no alternative but to comply immediately with the UAR request. Although some representatives said that "the ultimate responsibility for the decision to withdraw" rested with the UN, "no proposal was made that the Advisory Committee should exercise the right vested in it . . . to request the convening of the General Assembly" to consider the response to the UAR request.

At about 7:00 p.m. NYT Thant sent a message telling UAR Foreign Min. Riad that he was "proceeding to issue instructions for the necessary arrangements to be put in train without delay for the orderly withdrawal of the force." Thant also said, however, that he had "serious misgivings" about taking such action because he "believe[d] that this force has been an important factor in maintaining relative quiet in the area of its deployment during the past 10 years and that its withdrawal may have grave implications for peace."

Thant sent instructions to Gen. Rikhye later May 18 to order the withdrawal to begin the following day. (The UNEF withdrawal was completed June 17.)

Israeli Amb.-to-UN Gideon Rafael met with Thant May 19 and urged that Thant not condone any changes in UNEF's status before holding international consultations.

The outbreak of hostilities June 5, Thant declared, was not precipitated by the UNEF withdrawal but by the "continuing Arab-Israel conflict." UNEF's effectiveness as a buffer was lost as soon as "the direct confrontation between Israel and the United Arab Republic was revived after a decade by the decision of the United Arab Republic to move its forces up to the [armistice] line. . . ." This occurred before the formal UAR request for withdrawal of the UN force.

The UAR always had assumed that it had the right to terminate UNEF operations at any time, and this right had never been questioned.

Thant had scrupulously observed the agreements requiring consultations before a decision on withdrawal of UNEF. According to the procedure indicated Feb. 26, 1967 by Dag Hammarskjöld, the Secretary General was to first inform the UNEF Advisory Committee, which would then "determine whether the matter should be brought to the attention of the [General] Assembly." Thant said he had consulted not only the Advisory Committee but also all the countries providing troops for UNEF. None suggested that the matter be taken before the Assembly. Thant was aware of the sharp differences of opinion that would be encountered within the Assembly and he "did not believe that any useful purpose would be served by his seeking a meeting" of the Assembly or the Security Council.

Thant gave a chronological account of 1956-57 events dealing with the decision to place UNEF on UAR territory. He cited 2 UN General Assembly Resolutions: 998, of Nov. 4, 1956, calling for a plan within 48 hours, "with the consent of the nations concerned, of an emergency international United Nations Force to secure and supervise the cessation of hostilities"; 1125 (XI), of Feb. 2, 1957, expanding UNEF's powers to "the scrupulous maintenance of the armistice agreement" to be carried out "after full withdrawal of Israel from the Sharm el Sheik and Gaza areas." UNEF's entry into Egypt was announced Nov. 12, 1956, then was postponed for 2 days pending a final agreement with the Egyptian government. Hammarskjöld conferred with Pres. Nasser Nov. 16-18, 1956 and reached an agreement embodied in an " 'aide-mémoire on the basis for the presence and functioning of UNEF in Egypt' (the so-called 'good faith accord')," which was presented to the Assembly Nov. 20, 1956.

Hammarskjöld's recently disclosed private aide-mémoire gave an interprative account of his talks with Nasser. But Thant stressed: "This memorandum is not in any official record of the United Nations. . . . It . . . has no standing beyond being a purely private memorandum of unknown purpose or value. . . . This paper, therefore, cannot affect in any way the basis for the presence of UNEF on the soil of the United Arab Republic as set out in the official documents, much less supersede those documents."

The public good faith accord (presented Nov. 20, 1956) provided that Egypt and the UN would "be guided, in good faith" by the task established in Resolution 998. It was wrong to insist that Egypt should be held to the good faith accord for a "task" that was not stated at the time of the accord and was added to the UNEF mandate only 2½ months later, in the resolution of Feb. 2, 1957; i.e. "the scrupulous maintenance of the [1949] armistice agreement."

Although Israel had tried to get further commitments from Egypt regarding the stationing of UNEF at key points in the Sinai Peninsula pending guarantees of free access to the Gulf of Aqaba, Egypt had never consented to any limitation of its sovereignty. And Israel's consistent refusal to allow the stationing of UNEF troops on its side of the armistice demarcation line, "in the exercise of its sovereign rights," made it "even less possible to consider that Egypt's 'good faith' declaration . . . could constitute a limitation of its rights." The question of Egypt's right to unilaterally order the departure of UNEF, raised by Israel Nov. 23, 1956, could have been solved if Israel had allowed UN troops on its own territory.

The UNEF Advisory Committee had not exercised its option of calling for an Assembly session on the UNEF withdrawal.

Aug. 5, 1957 Hammarskjöld Memorandum—The resolution establishing UNEF Nov. 4, 1956 "did in no way limit the sovereignty" of Egypt. However, in "the interest of political balance and stability in the UNEF operation," Hammarskjöld thought that some limitation of sovereignty was necessary. In talks with then-Egyptian Amb.-to-UN Omar Loutfi Nov. 10-11, 1956, Hammarskjöld contended that, in view of Egypt's vote for the resolution setting up UNEF, he "did not find that a withdrawal of consent could be made before the tasks which had justified the entry had been completed. . . ."

In opposing Hammarskjöld's view, Egypt's then-Foreign Min. Mahmoud

Fawzi contended Nov. 13, 1956 that UNEF should remain out of Egypt "until all misunderstandings were cleared up." Hammarskjöld threatened to bring the matter before the General Assembly if Egypt continued to block UNEF operations and "did not accept my stand on withdrawal as a precondition for further steps. . . ." Egypt then notified Hammarskjöld that it would permit the arrival of troops.

Hammarskjöld decided to follow up by forcing Egypt "into an agreement in which they limited their freedom of action as to withdrawal by making a request for withdrawal dependent on the completion of the task. . . ." Knowing that it would not be possible to get Egypt to accept granting the Assembly the right to decide on the terms for UNEF's withdrawal, Hammarskjöld decided on the "good faith accord" formula. He said the "obvious procedure, if Egypt requested withdrawal, would be as follows: The matter would at once be brought before the General Assembly. If the General Assembly found that the task was completed, everything would be all right. If they found that the task was not completed and Egypt, all the same, maintained its stand and enforced the withdrawal, Egypt would break the agreement with the United Nations." Thus, instead of an agreement *"directly concerning withdrawal,"* the above formula "created an obligation to reach agreement on the fact that the tasks were completed, and, thus, *the conditions for a withdrawal established"* (Hammarskjöld's italics).

Hammarskjöld presented this "good faith accord" to Pres. Nasser at a meeting in Cairo Nov. 17, 1956. The accord was accepted by Nasser, and the Assembly approved it Nov. 20, 1956.

June 19 Thant Statement—The memo contained little that was new and did not "warrant the special significance being attributed to it in some quarters." The document was private, not official. It was said to have been given by Hammarskjöld to friends and "the release of such a paper at this time would seem to raise some questions of ethics and good faith."

The memo was never conveyed to the UAR government, although Thant himself had known of it.

The "task" of UNEF outlined in the accord was "to secure and supervise the cessation of hostilities"; the task of maintaining the armistice agreement was not added to its mandate until after the "good faith accord" had been reached.

Because Israel had refused to allow UNEF troops on its soil, the effectiveness of UNEF as a buffer force was wholly dependent "upon the voluntary action of the UAR in keeping its troops away from the line."

The right of the UAR to move its troops to the armistice line, therefore, could not be questioned. Once such a move did take place, as it did May 17, "UNEF could no longer perform any useful function in maintaining quiet, and its continuing presence on UAR territory lost any real significance."

U.S. & FRENCH VIEWS

Johnson Proposes Peace Program

Pres. Johnson June 19 outlined a 5-point program for peace in the Middle East. He stressed that "the main responsibility for the peace of the region depends upon its own peoples and its own leaders." "Clearly," Mr. Johnson said, "the parties to the conflict must be the parties to the peace. . . . It is hard to see how it is possible for nations to live together in peace if they cannot learn to reason together." The President declared that "troops must be withdrawn," but not without reciprocal actions to establish peace in the region. "There must . . . be [1] recognized rights of national life, [2] progress in solving the refugee problem, [3] freedom of innocent maritime passage, [4] limitation of the arms race and [5] respect for political independence and territorial integrity."

Excerpts of the President's statement, made in a speech at the National Foreign Policy Conference of Educators in Washington:

> The first and the greatest principle is that every nation in the area has a fundamental right to live, and to have this right respected by its neighbors. For the people of the Middle East, the path to hope does not lie in threats to end the life of any nation. Such threats have become a burden to the peace, not only of that region, but a burden to the peace of the entire world.

> In the same way, no nation would be true to the United Nations Charter or to its own true interests if it should permit military success to blind it to the fact that its neighbors have rights and its neighbors have interests of their own. Each nation, therefore, must accept the right of others to life.

> 2d, this last month, I think, shows us another basic requirement for settlement. It is a human requirement; justice for the refugees. A new conflict has brought new homelessness. The nations of the Middle East must at last address themselves to the plight of those who have been displaced by wars.

> In the past, both sides have resisted the best efforts of outside mediators to restore the victims of conflict to their homes or to find them other proper places to live and work. There will be no peace, though, for any party in the Middle East unless this problem is attacked with new energy by all and certainly primarily by those that are immediately concerned.

> 3d, a lesson from this last month is that maritime rights must be respected. Our nation has long been committed to free maritime passage through international waterways, and we along with other nations were taking the necessary steps to implement this principle when hostilities exploded. If a single act of folly was more responsible for this explosion than any other, I think it was the arbitrary and the dangerous announced decision that the Straits of Tiran would be closed. The right of innocent maritime passage must be preserved for all nations.

> . . . 4th, this last conflict has demonstrated the danger of the Middle Eastern arms race of the last 12 years. Here the responsibility must rest not only on those in the area, but upon the larger states outside the area. We believe that scarce resources could be used much better for technical

and economic development. We have always opposed this arms race, and our own military shipments to the area have consequently been severely limited.

Now the waste and futility of the arms race must be apparent to all the peoples of the world. And now there's another moment of choice. The United States, . . . for its part, will use every resource of diplomacy, and every counsel of reason and prudence, to try to find a better course.

As a beginning, I should like to propose that the United Nations immediately call upon all of its members to report all shipments of all military arms into this area and to keep those shipments on file for all the peoples of the world to observe.

5th, the crisis underlines the importance of respect for political independence and territorial integrity of all the states of the area. We reaffirmed that principle at the height of this crisis. We reaffirm it again today, on behalf of all. The principle can be effective in the Middle East only on the basis of peace between the parties. The nations of the region have [had] only fragile and violated truce lines for 20 years. What they now need are recognized boundaries and . . . arrangements that will give them security against terror and destruction and war. Further, there just must be adequate recognition of the special interest of 3 great religions in the holy places of Jerusalem.

During Security Council debate on the Middle East fighting, Pres. Johnson June 8 had praised the growing acceptance of the Council's cease-fire calls by the belligerents. Mr. Johnson said that although "a cease-fire is the urgent first step required to bring about peace in that troubled part of the world, a halt in hostilities will be only a beginning" and "many more fundamental questions must be tackled promptly if the area is to enjoy genuine stability." The Johnson Administration's policies on the Middle East, the President said, were similar to those adopted by 3 previous Administrators. "These policies have always included a consistent effort . . . to maintain good relations with all the peoples in the area in spite of the difficulties caused by some of their leaders. This remains our policy despite the unhappy rupture of relations which has been declared by several Arab states."

De Gaulle Blames Israel for Starting War

French Pres. Charles de Gaulle accused Israel June 21 of starting the war. In a major statement delivered to his cabinet and made public in Paris, de Gaulle said that France "condemns the opening of hostilities by Israel" even though France "disapproved the threat to destroy Israel brandished by her neighbors" and "reserved" its position on Egypt's decision to block the Gulf of

Aqaba to Israeli shipping. De Gaulle recalled his May 24 statement appealing to Britain, the U.S. and the Soviet Union to join France in making effective "their common opposition to the use of arms [in the Middle East]." "At the same time," he declared, "it let each of the 2 parties [Israel and the Arabs] know that it would lay the blame on the one that opened fire first. Today France accepts as final none of the changes effected on the terrain through military action."

De Gaulle held that the Middle East conflict stemmed from "the war [that] was started in Vietnam through American intervention." He said: The violence of the Southeast Asian conflict "cannot but spread disorder not only on the spot but far away." France believed that the Middle East crisis could not be settled peacefully "in the present world situation unless a new international element should come into sight. This element could and should be the end of the war in Vietnam through termination of foreign intervention."

A U.S. response to de Gaulle's remarks was delivered June 21 by White House Press Secy. George Christian. Christian said: "No one close to the situation sees any connection between the Middle East war and the situation in Southeast Asia."

The Egyptian government June 21 expressed satisfaction with de Gaulle's statement.

French Premier Georges Pompidou discussed the Middle East crisis in Moscow July 4 and July 6-9 with Premier Aleksei N. Kosygin and other Soviet leaders. A joint communiqué issued July 9 said France and the Soviet Union had agreed to work for peace in the Middle East and to safeguard the "rights for an independent existence of all peoples of the area." The statement recognized Israel's right to exist, but it said France and the Soviet Union would not recognize Israel's military conquest of Arab territories.

ISRAEL CONSOLIDATES GAINS

Israel Renounces 1949 Borders

In the wake of the Israeli victory, Premier Levi Eshkol and other government leaders made it known that Israel was determined to retain at least part of the territory it had won in the 6-day war. They said Israel would not accept a return to the 1949 armistice agreements setting the frontiers between the Jewish state and the neighboring Arab states. Addressing "all nations of the world" in a speech to the Knesset (parliament) June 12, Eshkol said: "Be under no illusion that . . . Israel is prepared to return to the situation that reigned up to a week ago. Alone we fought for our existence and security. We are entitled to determine what are the true and vital interests of our country and how they shall be secured. The position that existed until now shall never again return. The land of Israel shall no longer be a no-man's-land, wide open to acts of sabotage and murder."

Eshkol denounced the 1949 armistice agreements drawn up after Israel's first war with the Arab states. He charged that those agreements had been used as "time-gaining expedients" by the Arabs to prepare for new war. He called on the world's powers to urge the Arab states to observe the UN Charter, which "obligates them, just as it obligates every other member state, to solve disputes by peaceful means."

Eshkol denounced the Soviet Union for its position in the crisis. He said Moscow had not only failed to criticize Arab policy "but even helped the aggressor" diplomatically.

Addressing himself to "the Arab people," Eshkol concluded: "Just as you have a right to your country, so we have a right to ours. . . . Throughout the generations, Israel in dispersion maintained its spiritual and material links with this country. It was never severed from it even in exile. . . . This historic and spiritual right of ours has been confirmed by international law and forged on the anvil of reality. Today the world realizes that no force can uproot us from this land."

Foreign Min. Abba Eban declared June 11 that peace and stability in the Middle East could be achieved only through direct negotiations between Israel and its Arab neighbors, and not through intermediaries.

The need for direct Israeli-Arab negotiations and Israel's determination to hold on to the land it had conquered had been emphasized June 9 by Defense Min. Moshe Dayan. Speaking in a TV interview (rebroadcast June 11 on the CBS-TV program "Face the Nation"), Dayan said: "I don't think we should in any way give back the Gaza Strip to Egypt or the western part of

Jordan to King Hussein"; Jerusalem, "which is our capital" and was divided, was reunited; Israel must control Sharm el Sheik until its ships were assured passage through the Gulf of Aqaba, and it must have the right to use the Suez Canal. Dayan warned the Arabs that if they refused to enter into direct talks with Israel "then there will be a new map, not of the Middle East, but of Israel. If they don't want to talk to us, . . . then we shall stay where we are."

Information Min. Yisrael Galili said June 10 that Israel "cannot return to the 1949 armistice agreement and boundaries determined by these agreements." These agreements, Galili stated, had been nullified by what he called the latest attack against Israel by the armed forces of the UAR, Jordan, Syria and Iraq.

Israel Reunites Jerusalem

The Israeli government officially merged the Old City of Jerusalem with the Israeli sector of the city June 28. Its action, which ended the *de facto* division of the city in effect since the 1948 Arab-Israeli war, was attacked by the UN, the U.S. and other nations. (The 1947 UN plan for partition of Palestine into separate Arab and Jewish states had provided for the internationalization of Jerusalem. But the city was split into separate Jordanian and Jewish sectors by the 1948 fighting.) Israel reunified Jerusalem in defiance of international demands that the Old City not be annexed and that it be given international status. Israel denied that it had annexed the Old City and said that the merger of Jerusalem had been carried out primarily for administrative purposes.

The re-establishment of a single city of Jerusalem had been approved June 27 by the Israeli Knesset. The only dissenting votes were cast by 3 Communist members. The Knesset also passed a measure providing that the city's religious shrines, holy to Jews, Christians and Moslems, would "be protected from desecration and any other violation and from anything likely to violate the freedom of access of the members of the different religions to the places sacred to them. . . ."

The reunification of Jerusalem came into effect June 28 with a proclamation issued by Interior Min. Moshe Shapiro and with the publication in the government's *Official Gazette* of "The

Declaration of the Extension of the Boundaries of the Jerusalem Municipal Corporation." Under the unifying act, Jerusalem's boundaries also were expanded. The new boundaries extended 9 miles to the north, taking in the Kalandia airport at its northernmost point, and south to a line just one mile north of Bethlehem. Several villages in the south and southeast sectors were absorbed into the newly-merged city. Mt. Scopus, to the northeast, became part of Jerusalem.

Israeli authorities June 29 removed the barriers that had physically separated the Arab and Israeli sectors since 1948. Thousands of Israelis and Arabs then moved freely throughout the city without incident. In another action aimed at solidifying the physical unification of Jerusalem, Israel demolished the Mandelbaum Gate. (The demolition job was completed Aug. 30.) The passage had been the only authorized crossing point between Israel and the Jordanian sectors of Jerusalem from 1948 until June 7, when Israeli forces captured the Old City.

U.S. Pres. Lyndon B. Johnson June 28 expressed opposition to Israel's merger of Jerusalem and said the U.S. would refuse to recognize the action. Mr. Johnson's views were contained in 2 statements—one issued by the White House in response to the Israeli Knesset's approval of the unification bill and the other by the State Department in reaction to Israel's proclamation formally reuniting the city. The first statement recalled the President's statement of June 19 that "there must be adequate recognition of the special interests of 3 great religions in the holy places of Jerusalem." The statement added: "On this principle, he assumes that before any unilateral action is taken on the status of Jerusalem, there will be appropriate consultation with religious leaders and others who are deeply concerned." The 2d statement, said by the State Department to reflect Mr. Johnson's views, asserted that "the hasty administrative action taken today [by Israel] cannot be regarded as determining the future of the holy places or the status of Jerusalem in relation to them."

Israel was reported to have assured the U.S. June 29 that the fusion of the 2 sections of Jerusalem was not an act of political annexation but merely a measure aimed at extending municipal services to areas occupied by Israeli forces.

Israel was reported June 22 to have entered into discussions with representatives of the Vatican, Moslem leaders in Israel and the World Council of Churches on the guaranteeing of access to Jerusalem's Christian, Moslem and Jewish shrines. Pope Paul VI and the Vatican had persistently called for the internationalization of Jerusalem since Israeli forces had captured the Old City June 7. A note circulated at the UN June 23 by Msgr. Alberto Giovannetti, the pope's diplomatic representative at the UN, stated that the religious shrines in Jerusalem "are so numerous throughout the city that it is not possible to separate the 2 questions, namely, that of Jerusalem, and that of the holy places." The Vatican statement said "only an international regime would have the authority and sufficient power . . . to provide for the maintenance of and free access to holy places." Pope Paul said June 26 that "the holy city of Jerusalem must always remain that which it represents—the city of God, a free oasis of peace and prayer, a place of encounter, of elevation of concord for all, with its own international status guaranteed."

The Israeli government July 10 upheld its decision to reunify the city of Jerusalem. It did so despite the UN General Assembly's adoption July 4 of a resolution that declared the city's reunification invalid and demanded that all measures taken toward that end be rescinded. The reaffirmation of Israel's policy toward Jerusalem, transmitted to UN Secy. Gen. U Thant in a letter from Foreign Min. Abba Eban, prompted the reconvening of the General Assembly's emergency special session July 12. The Assembly July 14 adopted a new resolution deploring Israel's failure to implement the earlier resolution and demanding once again that the reunification measures be annulled. Eban's letter was in response to one written by Thant July 5 to draw Israel's attention to the July 4 resolution. In his reply, Eban declared that the resolution's supporters' use of the word "annexation" to describe Israel's action was "out of place." He asserted that the measures adopted by the Israeli Knesset "relate to the integration of Jerusalem in the administrative and municipal spheres and furnish a legal basis for the protection of the holy places in Jerusalem," but did not constitute annexation.

Thant August 15 announced the appointment of Dr. Ernesto Thalmann of Switzerland to undertake a fact-finding mission in

Jerusalem to determine the effects of Israel's reunification of Jerusalem. Thalmann, who was Switzerland's former observer at the UN (1961-66), arrived in Jerusalem August 21. After meeting with Arab and Israeli leaders, Thalmann filed a report that the UN published Sept. 12. Thalmann said in his report: The Israelis reiterated their refusal to relinquish control of former Jordanian Jerusalem as well as other Arab territories captured during the Arab-Israeli war. The Israelis contended that their control of Old Jerusalem was beneficial to the Arabs. The Arabs were willing to cooperate with Israeli authorities, but "they were opposed to civil incorporation into the Israeli state system." Despite the lack of a spirit of revolt, the Arabs feared Israeli racial and religious oppression. They had accused the Israelis of what they called desecration of Moslem shrines. Arabs opposed Israeli rules requiring Israeli censorship of sermons in Moslem mosques.

Israel Resettles Kfar Etzion on West Bank

Premier Eshkol Sept. 24 announced plans for Israeli resettlement of the Etzion section, the site of 4 former Israeli farm communities in the Bethlehem-Hebron area 4 miles inside the west bank of the Jordan River. It had been announced earlier that Israel would establish a similar settlement in Israeli territory bordering the northern section of the captured Golan Heights of Syria, near Baniyas. In response to international protests, Israel explained later that the Etzion move was not a permanent settlement plan but was designed solely for military security. The Etzion area consisted of Kfar Etzion and 3 other nearby communal settlements that had been seized by Jordanian forces in 1948. The site had been used as a Jordanian military camp until its recapture by Israel in June. The vanguard of the Kfar Etzion settlers arrived Sept. 27. They consisted of 15 members of the Israeli army's Nahal Corps, a unit that combined military service with agricultural training. Many of them were children of the 240 original Kfar Etzion settlers who had been killed in the 1948 fighting.

The U.S. State Department Sept. 27 protested the Israeli move into Kfar Etzion. The department said: "If accurately reported, the plans for establishment of permanent Israeli settlements would be inconsistent with the Israeli position as we understand it that they regard occupied territories and all other issues arising out of the fighting to be matters for negotiation." Israeli Amb.-to-U.S. Avraham Harman, meeting Sept. 28 with U.S. Asst. State Secy. (for Near Eastern and South Asian affairs) Lucius D. Battle, explained that Israel was only setting up "military strong points" in the area, and this "does not imply" a change in Israeli policy.

In a protest filed Sept. 28 with the U.S., British, French and Soviet embassies in Amman, Jordanian acting Foreign Min. Shukri al-Muhtadi asserted that the Israeli move into Kfar Etzion was contrary to the UN Charter and a violation of international law.

A 100-member Nahal Corps unit had moved into the Baniyas area Sept. 24 and had started construction work on 17 buildings. The site overlooked the Baniyas River (800 yards to the east), a major tributary of the Jordan River, whose free flow was guaranteed by the Nahal settlement.

Israel Plans to Retain Arab Areas

Premier Eshkol said Oct. 30 that Israel would "consolidate her position" in the Arab territories captured in June and that the situation that had prevailed prior to the conflict "shall never be restored." Speaking to the Knesset, Eshkol said this policy would be followed "in keeping with the vital needs" of Israel's "security and development" because the Arab states were "maintaining their attitude not to recognize Israel, not to negotiate with her, not to conclude with her a peace treaty." Referring to the west bank of the Jordan River and to the Gaza Strip, Eshkol said that prior to the June fighting these areas had been held by Jordan and Egypt "not by right but by force, as the result of military aggression and occupation" during the 1948 war. Eshkol conceded that the 1949 Arab-Israeli truce agreement had recognized Jordanian and Egyptian retention of these territories. "But these agreements have been nullified by military provocation and aggression on their part," he asserted. Eshkol also asserted that signers of the 1949 cease-fire accords had agreed "that the armistice lines had been determined only by military considerations and did not have the character of frontiers."

Eshkol said Israel would "not permit the restoration of the situation" in Syria's Golan Heights "that bore the seeds of havoc and destruction for our villages in the valley. Nor will the situation in Sinai, in the Gulf of Elath [Aqaba] and in the Suez Canal be restored to what it was." Reiterating Israeli opposition to mediation, Eshkol said "there is no sense in entering into discussions on the conditions of settlement" with the Arabs "except in direct negotiations."

In a speech at the opening session of the B'nai B'rith Israel Commission in Jerusalem Oct. 28, Eshkol had stressed the need for more Jewish immigration from abroad to settle in what he called a "greater Israel" that would include the Arab areas occupied by Israel. Eshkol voiced concern that "in greater Israel today" the population was 64% Jewish, 36% non-Jewish. Eshkol said he "did not want to predict right now what the figures and percentages will be 5, 10 and 15 years from now."

ARAB RECOVERY DRIVE

Arab leaders responded to the Israeli victory with pledges to unite to continue their struggle against the Jewish state.

In a message to UAR Pres. Nasser, Jordanian King Hussein lauded Nasser June 10 for his decision to remain in office. Hussein said: "I believe the battle is at its beginning and your presence in the leading role in the UAR is a national necessity for our success in dealing with the results of the setback and facing our great responsibilities in the next stage."

Algerian Pres. Houari Boumedienne prodded the Soviet Union and its allies June 10 to adopt a firmer position in support of what he called the Arab struggle against Zionism and Anglo-American imperialism. To be "neutral means to avoid taking a position," Boumedienne said.

Hussein appealed to Arab leaders June 19 to adopt a realistic policy and accept the defeat by Israel as "a turning point for the better." Speaking at a news conference in Amman, Hussein said: "We would like this to be a turning point in our lives, in our thinking, in our planning, and then we will face up to problems not only here in Jordan but in the whole area."

Nasser appealed to the Egyptian people July 23 for total mobilization to cope with the economic hardships resulting from the UAR's military defeat by Israel. Speaking at a Cairo University gathering of 5,000 persons, Nasser declared that he was re-equipping and revamping Egypt's armed forces to continue the struggle against Israel. He urged all Egyptians to enlist in what he called the "people's resistance organization." Nasser said: "We shall never surrender and shall not accept any peace that means surrender. We shall preserve the rights of the Palestine people."

Arab Meetings

Foreign ministers of 13 Arab states met in Kuwait June 17-18 to map joint political strategy in the wake of the Arabs' military defeat. The conference's final statement, issued by Kuwait Foreign Min. Sheik Sabah al-Ahmed al-Jaber, made no mention of any definitive Arab joint policy. It merely condemned "Israeli aggression" against the Arab states. In a speech opening the conference, Jaber had said that the "deep hurt" inflicted by Israel "requires us to start a new era in Arab relations, an era of solidarity based on absolute confidence in each other." Jaber charged that Israel sought to use its occupation of Arab territories "as a means for bargaining a solution that guarantees [the] aggressors permanent settlement in our homeland." A Kuwaiti official informed the conferees that Kuwait, which had suspended oil shipments June 6, had resumed them June 8 "except to Britain and the U.S." (Saudi Arabia had announced June 15 that it was resuming oil exports but not to "countries which backed Israel.") Algerian Foreign Min. Abdel Aziz Bouteflika told the conferees that at a meeting with Soviet officials in Moscow June 12-13, he and Algerian Pres. Houari Boumedienne had been given a "firm commitment" by the USSR to assist "in wiping out the traces of aggression."

Several other strategy meetings of Arab leaders were held after the Kuwait session. Jordanian King Hussein had conferred with Nasser and Boumedienne in Cairo July 10-11. Boumedienne flew to Damascus later July 11 and conferred with Pres. Nureddin al-Attassi and other Syrian leaders. In a speech broadcast over Damascus radio, Boumedienne urged Syria to press its "fight against Zionism and America." He vowed that Algeria would join "in the forefront of coming battles" against Israel because "this is the best safeguard for the future."

A communiqué issued July 16 at the conclusion of a 2-day strategy conference held in Cairo by the presidents of 5 Arab states announced joint agreement on "the necessary effective steps to eliminate the consequences of imperialist Israeli aggression in the Arab homeland." The statement was signed by Nasser

(UAR), Boumedienne (Algeria), Attassi (Syria), Abdel Rahman
Arif (Iraq) and Ismail el Azhari (Sudan). The communiqué
warned that the Arab states would reconsider their relations with
all countries suspected of aiding Israel. The conferees accepted
Azhari's suggestion that Arab foreign ministers meet in Khartoum,
Sudan to pave the way for a summit meeting of Arab heads
of state.

Arab Summit Conference in Khartoum

Leaders of 13 Arab states held a summit conference in Khartoum August 29-Sept. 1 to formulate a joint policy against Israel.
The parley had been arranged at meetings of the states' foreign
ministers in Khartoum August 1-5 and August 27-28. The summit
conference was highlighted by the adoption of resolutions (a)
pledging a continued non-military struggle against Israel, (b) announcing the creation of an Arab fund to assist the war-ravaged
economies of Jordan and the UAR, (c) lifting the Arab oil boycott
against the West and (d) announcing a UAR-Saudi Arabian
agreement designed to end the Yemeni civil war.

The anti-Israel resolution adopted at the conclusion of the
conference Sept. 1 said the conferees had "agreed to unified efforts
at international and diplomatic levels to eliminate the consequences
of aggression and to assure the withdrawal of the aggressor forces
of Israel from Arab lands, but within the limits to which Arab
states are committed: No peace with Israel, no negotiations with
Israel, no recognition of Israel and maintenance of the rights of
Palestinian people in their nation."

Nasser was quoted as having said at a closed-door meeting that
the UAR was willing to fight Israel but could do so only if financed
by the other Arab states. He was reported to have said that without such Arab aid, a political solution would have to be found.
He was quoted as saying: "Surrender [to Israel] is out of the question, but to carry on the struggle involves certain responsibilities,
military, political and economic. The question is: Are we ready
to shoulder these responsibilities? That is what we must agree on."

The proposed Arab fund, agreed to at the August 31 session,
would provide the UAR and Jordan with £140 million (about
$392 million).

As for the oil embargo, the conferees agreed in principle August 31 to permit each Arab state to decide independently as to how it would act on the recommendations made by Arab finance and petroleum ministers at an August 15-19 meeting they had held in Baghdad. This agreement, in effect, allowed the lifting of the oil embargoes that had been imposed against the U.S. and Britain in retaliation for their alleged military assistance to Israel in the June war. (Saudi Arabia announced Sept. 2 that it had ended its oil embargo and that it would start pumping oil "to all countries without exception." The Algerian Foreign Ministry said Sept. 2 that Algeria would continue to bar the shipment of oil and gas to the U.S. and Britain. Kuwait decided Sept. 3 to resume oil shipments to Britain, the U.S. and other countries boycotted since the start of the Arab-Israeli war.)

Only 8 heads of state of the 13 Arab countries attended the Khartoum conference. Algerian Pres. Houari Boumedienne and Syrian Pres. Nureddin al-Attassi, who were opposed to any compromise on Israel, boycotted the meetings. Boumedienne was represented by Foreign Min. Abdel Aziz Bouteflika. Syrian Foreign Min. Ibrahim Makhos had attended the August 27-28 foreign ministers meeting, but he and the entire Syrian delegation boycotted the formal conference after the ministers rejected Syrian demands for a specific agreement on action to "remove the consequences of Israeli aggression." The Syrian government newspaper *Al Thwara* Sept. 2 assailed the Khartoum conference resolutions on the ground that they would "consolidate rather than eliminate Israeli aggression."

The heads of state who attended the conference were Kings Faisal of Saudi Arabia and Hussein of Jordan, Presidents Nasser of the UAR, Abdullah al-Salal of Yemen, Abdel Rahman Arif of Iraq, Charles Hélou of Lebanon and Ismail el-Azhari of Sudan and Emir Sabah al-Salam as-Sabah of Kuwait. Crown Prince Hassan el Ridha of Libya represented King Idris.

Tunisian Pres. Habib Bourguiba, whose country boycotted the Khartoum conference, had reiterated his plea for an end to the Arab countries' state of belligerency against Israel. Speaking August 23 to leaders of the Tunisian Students Union, Bourguiba described the Arab position as a "dead-end policy." He declared: "Policies adopted hitherto have deprived [the Arabs] of all sympathies. . . . The state of Israel has been recognized by both the United States and the Soviet Union. . . . Its existence is challenged only by the Arab countries. In these circumstances it is useless to continue ignoring the reality and claim to wipe Israel off the map. In so doing, one drives himself into near-isolation." The June war was started, Bourguiba asserted, because, "deliberately and without weighing well the risks, steps had been taken to bar Israel from access to the Gulf of Aqaba." He noted that until then "Israel was satisfied with its frontiers."

Israeli Premier Levi Eshkol declared Sept. 3 that the Khartoum conference decision against recognizing Israel was "against the real interests of the people of the region and is against the principles" of the UN Charter. Eshkol said: "We also have noted the security and political implications of these resolutions" adopted at the Arab parley; "they make the prospects for peace in our region dimmer"; "in contrast to the aggressive intentions of the Arab heads of state, we will stand stanchly in the positions vital to the security and undisturbed development of Israel." Israeli Foreign Min. Abba Eban said Sept. 5 that Israel had detected no signs of moderation in the resolutions adopted in Khartoum. He asserted: "The Arab leaders . . . voted in favor of immobility. Their decision strengthened Israel's need and right to maintain her present position until a new situation is negotiated between herself and her neighbors."

Arabs Get Soviet Political Backing & Arms

The Soviet Union bolstered the Arabs' weakened position with promises of continued support against Israel. These pledges were fulfilled by the replenishment of the depleted Egyptian and Syrian arsenals with generous shipments of Soviet arms. A statement supporting the Arabs' cause was issued June 22 by the Soviet Communist Party's Central Committee at the conclusion of a 2-day Moscow meeting on the Middle East. The statement said: "The most important task is to prevent the aggressor from taking advantage of the results of its perfidious action, to achieve an immediate unconditional withdrawal of the troops of the interventionists from the territories occupied by them behind the truce line, and the payment of indemnity to the United Arab Republic, Syria and Jordan for the damage inflicted by the aggressor."

A Soviet diplomatic mission headed by Pres. Nikolai V. Podgorny visited the UAR June 21-23 and Syria and Iraq July 1-4 to discuss further Soviet aid to the Arab states. Podgorny conferred in Cairo June 21-23 with UAR Pres. Nasser. A joint communiqué issued at the conclusion of the parley said only that the meetings had taken place in a spirit of "traditional friendship" and that both sides had talked about measures to counter what they called the consequences of Israeli aggression. (Before arriving in Cairo, Podgorny had stopped in Belgrade June 20 to confer with Yugoslav Pres. Tito. Podgorny visited Yugoslavia again June 24 on his way back to Moscow and held another meeting with Tito, on the Adriatic island of Brioni.) Podgorny flew June 30 to Damascus, where he conferred July 1-3 with Pres. Nureddin el-Attassi and other Syrian leaders. A communiqué July 3 said Podgorny and the Syrian officials had "reviewed the conditions arising from Israel's aggression against Syria and other Arab countries and practical measures that should be taken to wipe out the results of this aggression." A similar joint Soviet-Iraqi statement was issued after Podgorny conferred with Iraqi leaders in Baghdad July 4.

Soviet Communist Party Gen. Secy. Leonid I. Brezhnev vowed in a Kremlin speech July 5 that the Soviet Union would continue its "political struggle" against Israel in support of the Arab states.

Brezhnev and Soviet Premier Aleksei N. Kosygin conferred in Moscow July 18 with Algerian Pres. Houari Boumedienne and Iraqi Premier Abdel Rahman Arif. A communiqué issued after the talks said the Moscow meeting had dealt with "ways of liquidating the aftermath of Israel's aggression." Boumedienne and Arif returned to Cairo July 19 to brief Nasser on their meeting with the Soviet leaders.

It was reported in Washington in mid-June that the USSR had started to ship planes and other war matériel to Egypt and Syria to replace equipment destroyed or captured by Israel during the war. Diplomatic sources in Washington reported June 14 that Moscow had informed other Communist countries of its intentions to continue to supply the UAR and other Arab countries with military aid.

Israeli sources reported June 14 that 100 Soviet MiGs, tanks, artillery pieces and spare parts had arrived in the UAR since the end of hostilities. A report from Tel Aviv June 15 said: Syria and Egypt had received 200 MiG jets each in recent days; heavy Soviet transport planes capable of carrying jet fighters, tanks or artillery had flown to Egypt in the past week, and the airlift was continuing. Israeli quarters reported the same day that King Hussein had deferred his acceptance of 50 Soviet MiGs offered to Jordan. Hussein was said to have informed Western diplomats in Amman of the offer and to have told them he would prefer not to accept Soviet equipment.

Confirming the existence of a UAR-bound Soviet airlift, Yugoslav and Western diplomatic sources in Belgrade said June 17 that about 200 Soviet transport flights had been made to Egypt in the past 10 days. These sources reported that about 100 Soviet MiG fighters had been disassembled and crated and then flown to Egypt via Budapest.

A *N.Y. Times* report from Beirut June 24 quoted Western diplomats in the Lebanese capital as saying that they had received reports of a Soviet pledge to Cairo of 200 new planes to replace aircraft destroyed in the war with Israel. Fifty Soviet MiGs were said to have arrived in Cairo since the end of the fighting.

A report from Washington July 10 said Egypt had received more than 25,000 tons of Soviet equipment since June 5. The matériel was said to have been delivered by a Soviet fleet of a half dozen ships and several dozen planes. An additional 5,000 tons of Soviet military equipment had been sent in Russian ships to Syria, and an equal amount of war matériel had been delivered to Algeria, which had funneled some of it to Egypt, the report said.

The Soviet news agency Tass reported July 10 that 500 Soviet motor vehicles were on their way to Egypt to replace vehicles destroyed in the Sinai fighting.

The U.S. State Department July 11 expressed "increasing concern" about "reports of continuing shipments of aircraft and other arms from the Soviet Union to the United Arab Republic and other countries of the Middle East." The department said "the great powers should be working toward a limitation of arms and not a resumption of the old race."

Israeli Premier Eshkol said Oct. 11 that the Soviet Union had resupplied the United Arab Republic and Syria with enough arms to "again upset the balance of power in the Middle East." "This influx of Soviet weapons," Eshkol asserted, "has made our position more precarious and made it all the more important that the Western powers permit us to buy the weapons we need to defend ourselves." Eshkol said the Soviet Union had replaced 80% of the planes, tanks and artillery that the Egyptian armed forces had lost in the war. He said Israeli intelligence reports indicated that the new Soviet equipment received by Syria had brought Damascus' weapons strength to nearly its pre-war level.

It was reported in Washington Oct. 11 that U.S. intelligence sources had calculated that Cairo had received more Soviet arms than had previously been estimated but considered that the increase still would not constitute a threat to Middle East peace. Civilian officials in Washington estimated that Moscow had given the UAR 180-200 jets and about 200 tanks. The plane shipments replaced about ⅔ of the UAR planes destroyed in the war, the tanks about ⅓ the losses. U.S. Defense Department officials estimated that the UAR had received 225-240 Soviet jets since the end of the conflict.

U.S. Eases Arms Ban

The U.S. eased its ban on the shipment of arms to the Middle East by announcing Oct. 24 that it would send Israel light jet bombers and provide military equipment to 5 pro-Western Arab countries—Morocco, Libya, Lebanon, Saudi Arabia and Tunisia. A State Department statement explained that "virtually all of the equipment, including jet fighters for Morocco and Libya, was ordered before the Arab-Israeli war in June, when the embargo was imposed." The arms shipment, the statement said, was "not an opening of the floodgates" and did not mean that the U.S. was committing itself to providing more military aid to Middle East countries. Israel was to receive 48 Skyhawk A-45 light attack bombers as had been arranged under a $52 million arms transaction signed in 1966. U.S. officials said first deliveries were to reach Israel in December, as originally scheduled.

Israel had called on the U.S. July 18 to give it "the opportunity" to obtain American arms. Speaking at the National Press Club in Washington, Israeli Amb.-to-U.S. Avraham Harman said the additional arms were necessary "to maintain a minimum level of deterrent strength" and to prevent the shipment of military equipment to the Middle East from turning into "a one-way street." Harman said that instead of responding positively to a U.S.-Soviet limitation of arms shipments to the Middle East proposed by Pres. Johnson June 19, Moscow was "pouring back large quantities" of arms to the UAR and other Arab states.

(The Israeli cabinet Dec. 3 appointed Brig. Gen. Chaim Bar-Lev, deputy chief of staff, to replace Maj. Gen. Itzhak Rabin as chief of staff. Rabin had been named ambassador to the U.S.)

Hussein's Travels & Statements

King Hussein of Jordan went on several diplomatic missions to the West and to the Soviet Union in the aftermath of Jordan's defeat in June. The king's discussions with world leaders on those trips dealt with the new political, economic and military problems that had arisen in the Middle East as a result of Israel's sweeping victory. Hussein apparently sought economic aid and arms to help restore Jordan's war-ravaged economy and its weakened military position. The king's diplomatic tour was marked by public expressions of his views on various aspects of the Middle East situation.

Hussein conferred with Pres. Johnson in Washington June 28. A White House statement said after the 2-hour meeting that Hussein and Mr. Johnson had been unable to arrive at an "identity of views" in their discussions on the Middle East. (Hussein had arrived in the U.S. June 24 to address the UN General Assembly's emergency session on the Middle East.)

Returning to New York June 29, Hussein said: Jordan hoped to rebuild its armed forces with U.S. and British equipment. "We hope there will be no serious obstacle to our attempts to equip our armed forces from the free world. Unless there is some serious obstacle, we will get our arms where we always did." Israel's reunification of the Jewish and Arab sectors of Jerusalem was "a challenge to the United Nations and a completely intolerable and unacceptable development." "My hope is that the world will as a whole do all that is possible to insure the swift withdrawal" of Israeli troops from the Arab lands they had captured during the war. Jordan had "no accurate figures yet on the casualties" its forces had suffered in the war, "but they were very heavy."

On his way back to Jordan, Hussein stopped in London July 1 to confer with British Prime Min. Harold Wilson. Arab acceptance of Israel's right to exist was not the issue in the Middle East, Hussein told newsmen. "What is most important at this stage is the right of Arabs to exist, for us to maintain our identity, our freedom, and for the Middle East to settle down on a proper basis . . . . This could be brought about if there were justice." Hussein met with Wilson July 3 and then flew to Paris, where he conferred July 4 with French Pres. Charles de Gaulle. Before returning to Amman, Hussein went to Rome July 6, met with Pope Paul VI and discussed Middle Eastern problems, including that of the Arab refugees.

Hussein conferred with USSR officials in Moscow Oct. 3-5 on possible Soviet economic and military aid to Jordan. A communiqué issued Oct. 5 on the conclusion of the talks made no specific mention of Soviet assistance. A report from Moscow Oct. 3 had quoted Soviet sources as saying that Russia had offered Hussein large-scale economic aid to help his country recover from the ravages of the war. The Oct. 5 communiqué reaffirmed Soviet intentions to "continue to give to the Arab states" all backing required to "strengthen their defensive capacity." The joint statement condemned Israel. Jordan and the Soviet Union signed an agreement on cultural and scientific cooperation.

Hussein returned to the U.S. Nov. 2 for another round of talks with U.S. officials. (He had completed a series of fresh diplomatic contacts in late October with leaders in the UAR, Algeria, France, West Germany and Britain.) Speaking on the CBS-TV program "Face the Nation" in New York Nov. 5, Hussein asserted that the Arab states had changed their position on Israel and would recognize its right to exist but only as part of an over-all Middle East peace settlement preceded by the withdrawal of Israeli forces from Arab territory they had occupied in the June war. Hussein implied that this did not necessarily mean Arab diplomatic recognition of Israel. Hussein said that Nasser was ready to grant Israeli ships free passage in the Suez Canal and the Gulf of Aqaba "if the right conditions were reached" in a general solution of the Middle East political impasse. Insisting that Israeli forces must withdraw from Arab territory, Hussein said such a pull-back could be "linked" to other problems, such as Israel's shipping rights and the controversy over Arab refugees. "As long as our territories are occupied," Hussein asserted, "we will try to limit our action and concentrate in fact at arriving at a way out through the [UN] Security Council," rather than through direct talks with Israel. The Arabs would not permit Israel "to dictate terms" of a peace settlement "from the position they have acquired" through military conquest, Hussein said.

Hussein said on arriving in Washington Nov. 6 that Nasser shared his views on the Middle East. Hussein conferred later Nov. 6 with State Secy. Dean Rusk and other State Department officials. Hussein was said to have reaffirmed the view that the Arab states would recognize Israel's right "to live in peace and security," would end the state of war that had existed with Israel since 1948 and would permit Israeli ships to use the Gulf of Aqaba and the Suez Canal. A State Department statement on the Rusk-Hussein talks confirmed that the discussions had dealt with "the possibility of early movement toward a peace settlement" in the Middle East.

In an address at Georgetown University in Washington later Nov. 6, Hussein reiterated that the Arabs must accept the proposition "that Israel is a present fact of life. We may not like it, and we may choose not to recognize it, just as we choose not to recognize Red China." Hussein conferred with Pres. Johnson Nov. 8. He left New York Nov. 12 for Europe.

Hussein's statement that the Arabs recognized Israel's right to exist was reaffirmed Nov. 8 by Mohammed H. el-Zayyat, chief spokesman for the UAR government. Zayyat said Cairo's commitment was embodied in Article I of the Egyptian-Israeli armistice agreement of Feb. 24, 1949, which stated: "The right of each party to security and freedom from fear of attack by the armed forces of the other shall be fully respected."

The Syrian government reported Nov. 10 that it had informed the Jordanian ambassador to Damascus Nov. 9 that it disagreed with King Hussein's assertion in the U.S. that he spoke for all Arabs when he said Israel was "a fact of life." The Jordanian ambassador was informed that the Syrian government "had not authorized anyone to speak in its name, particularly about questions which bear on the destiny of the Arab nation."

Jordanian Government & Military Shake-Ups

In the wake of the Israeli victory, Jordan undertook a series of major changes in the government and the armed forces to strengthen its political and military posture.

King Hussein was reported July 13 to have begun a major military reorganization. The plan called for merging several army brigades into at least 2 divisions to provide a more efficient command structure. Jordan's army brigades had been divided between 2 regional commands, one on each bank of the Jordan River. The commander of the west bank area, conquered by Israel, had been placed on leave.

In another move to strengthen Jordan's defenses, Hussein announced July 25 a program to provide military training for an undisclosed number of Jordanian civilians.

Premier Saad Jumaa, 51, and his cabinet resigned July 15 to make way for a new cabinet to cope with the Middle East crisis. Hussein accepted Jumaa's resignation Aug. 1 but called on him to form a new government. Jumaa agreed and announced the formation of a new cabinet Aug. 2. Jumaa retained his additional post as defense minister. The cabinet was similar to the outgoing one except for these 2 major changes: Ahmed Toukan, foreign minister in the previous government, was appointed deputy premier and minister of state; Mohammed Adib al-Aarmiri, head of the accountancy department, replaced Toukan as foreign minister.

Jumaa, who favored close relations with the U.S., resigned Oct. 7 and was replaced the same day as premier by Bahjat al-Talhouni, a supporter of stronger ties with the UAR. In his letter of resignation to Hussein, Jumaa said that circumstances required "re-evaluating the situation in order to confront Israeli threats." Hussein created a new cabinet post—minister for religious affairs and holy places. The position was given to Sheik Abdul-Hammid as-Sayeh, the chief justice of the High Moslem Court in Jerusalem, who had been deported to Jordan Sept. 23 by Israeli authorities. The new cabinet, as had the previous one, included 9 Palestinians. Talhouni, a confidant of Hussein, also held the defense portfolio.

Hussein announced Oct. 8 that he was assuming personal and "direct control" of Jordan's armed forces. His decision was disclosed in a message to Maj. Gen. Amer Khamas, army chief of staff. Hussein had been the nominal supreme commander of the armed forces. Hussein's decision was coupled with an announcement that 4 top Jordanian officers had been pensioned. They included Lt. Gen. Mohammed Ahmed Salim, commander of the western front facing Israel. In another reorganizational move, Hussein Oct. 9 abolished the military posts of commander-in-chief and deputy commander-in-chief. This move resulted in the dismissal of Marshal Habes Majali and his deputy, Lt. Gen. Sherif Nasser Ben Jamil. But Hussein appointed Majali defense minister and named Nasser Ben Jamil as his (the king's) chief aide.

(Amman radio announced Oct. 9 that 4 high-ranking Jordanian officers in the west-bank command, including a major general, had been retired on pension. Forty more army officers were retired Oct. 14.)

UAR Crushes Plot, Amer Commits Suicide

UAR authorities in Cairo August 25 arrested 50 top-ranking military and civilian officials accused of attempting to stage a *coup d'état* against the Nasser government. Among those seized was the alleged leader of the plot, Marshal Abdel Hakim Amer, 47, former deputy supreme commander. Cairo reported Amer's suicide by poisoning Sept. 14.

Amer and the other accused plotters were among the military officers who had been dismissed or pensioned off by Nasser in the wake of the UAR's defeat in June. (400-500 officers were said to have been involved in Nasser's purge of the armed forces.) The principal objectives of the planned uprising were said to be the reinstatement of the dismissed officers and the thwarting of the government's scheduled investigation into the Egyptian armed forces' conduct of the war. Other alleged plotters arrested were ex-War Min. Shamseddin Badran, ex-Maj. Gen. Othaman Nasr, ex-Interior Min. Abbas Radwan and Salah Nasr, who was relieved of his post as head of the General Intelligence Department.

According to Cairo, Amer swallowed poison when police came Sept. 13 to his home, where he had been placed under house arrest Aug. 25, to question him about the plot. He died the following day.

A UAR government source reported Sept. 19 that 181 military officers and civilians, including the 50 seized August 25, had been arrested for security reasons since the outbreak of the June war. The semi-official Cairo newspaper *Al Ahram* Sept. 19 denied a *N.Y. Daily News* report on Sept. 15 that 70,000 Egyptians had been arrested since the end of the war.

Al Ahram reported Oct. 5 that Salah Nasr had been accused of ordering the poison tablets that Amer had used to take his life.

Shukairy Out as PLO Leader

Ahmed Shukairy resigned Dec. 24 as chairman of the Cairo-based Palestine Liberation Organization. A PLO executive member, Yehia Hammouda, was named acting chairman. Six members of the 10-member committee had demanded Shukairy's resignation. In a letter made public Dec. 18, they charged that Shukairy had announced Dec. 7 the formation of a non-existent Jerusalem-based Revolutionary Command Council against Israel. Shukairy was also accused of ineffectual leadership of the PLO.

BORDER FIGHTING

Repeated border clashes followed the cease-fire agreement that ended the Arab-Israeli war in June. The heaviest fighting centered along the Suez Canal truce line, where large concentrations of Israeli and Egyptian forces faced each other on the 2 banks of the waterway. Clashes of lesser severity also flared along the west bank of the Jordan River facing Jordan and on Syria's Golan Heights. Israeli and Jordanian troops also clashed along their borders north of the west-bank area.

The Suez Canal fighting erupted July 1 and continued sporadically throughout 1967. Ground, air and naval forces were involved. UN Security Council intervention led to the stationing of UN observers along the canal in July-August to strengthen the truce, but this had little effect in pacifying the belligerents. The most serious engagement took place Oct. 21 when UAR naval craft sank the Israeli destroyer *Elath* off the northern Sinai coast with the loss of 47 Israeli seamen. The Israelis retaliated 3 days later by shelling major Egyptian oil installations at the canal port of Suez and destroying 80% of its output.

Israel Charges Syria Violates Truce

The first breach of the truce was reported by Israel June 18. An Israeli army communiqué charged that Syrian troops had violated the cease-fire that day by firing on Israeli soldiers north of El Quneitra in Israeli-held Syrian territory. The report said Israeli troops had repulsed the attack, carried out with 3 armored troop carriers. The Israeli communiqué also claimed that "for the last 3 days the Syrians have been trying to create a *fait accompli* by advancing their troops" to alter the truce line established at the conclusion of the recent fighting when the UN-supervised agreement was signed June 11.

The UN Secretariat June 24 made public an Israeli denial of Syrian charges that Israel had executed Syrian prisoners and abused Syrian civilians. Damascus had made the accusations in a note filed June 15 with UN Security Council Pres. Hans Tabor of Denmark. The Israeli reply to Tabor denied "that any prisoners of war were executed or that any other killings took place as alleged in the Syrian letter or that any other maltreatment took place." Israel insisted that "no civilians were expelled from the area and only members of the Syrian army and armed civilians were taken as prisoners and detained. . . ." "Normal life is being restored" in Syrian areas, it held.

An Israeli military communiqué July 3 reported several clashes along the Syrian cease-fire line in the previous 2 weeks. The announcement said the most serious had occurred July 2 when a Syrian patrol had crossed the truce line at Tel Kalya in Israeli-held Syrian territory and machinegunned Israeli positions. The Israelis returned the fire and the Syrians withdrew after a 20-minute exchange of gunfire, the Tel Aviv announcement said. Israel reported a similar exchange of gunfire with Syrian troops along the cease-fire line July 3 about 4 miles north of El Quneitra.

Suez Canal Clashes Erupt

The first serious violation of the June 8 UAR-Israeli cease-fire occurred July 1 when sharp ground and air skirmishes broke out along the Israeli-held eastern bank of the Suez Canal. The fighting continued through July 9. The renewed violence brought the UN Security Council into emergency session July 8. The Council July 10 approved a proposal of UN Secy. Gen. U Thant that UN observers be stationed on the Suez cease-fire line to supervise the truce. Egypt accepted the plan July 10; Israel gave its conditional approval July 11.

In the first clash July 1, Israel reported that an Egyptian force of about 120 men, equipped with armored half-tracks, crossed the canal from the western bank in boats and barges and established a beachhead on the eastern shore near Ras el Ish, 8 miles south of Port Said. According to the Israeli account, Israeli troops counter-attacked and forced the Egyptians to withdraw to the west bank of the canal after a 3-hour battle. The retreating UAR force was said to have left behind most of its equipment. One Egyptian was taken prisoner.

According to Cairo's version, Israeli troops, accompanied by 8 tanks, had tried to advance from their base at El Qantara to Port Fuad, 30 miles to the north. Port Fuad, opposite Port Said at the northern end of the canal, was the only Egyptian-held point on the east bank. The UAR claimed the destruction of 3 Israeli tanks and 3 armored vehicles.

A Cairo report July 2 said that 11 Israeli tanks again had advanced toward Port Fuad but were repulsed by Egyptian defense positions on the east bank. Three Israeli tanks were destroyed, the UAR announcement said. An Israeli report on the resumption of fighting July 2 said that Egyptian forces had precipitated the clash that day with a heavy mortar and machinegun barrage at Israeli positions at Ras el Ish. The announcement said Israeli guns had returned the fire and silenced the Egyptian batteries after a 90-minute duel. Eight Israeli soldiers were reported wounded, one seriously.

A Tel Aviv announcement said Israeli and UAR troops had exchanged fire twice across the Suez Canal at Ras el Ish July 3. No Israeli casualties were reported. The communiqué also reported that later July 3 an Israeli military freight train traveling in Israeli-held Sinai between El Qantara and El Arish, 17 miles east of the canal, had been derailed by mines believed to have been planted by Egyptian saboteurs.

Israel said that its anti-aircraft gunners had shot down one of 2 Egyptian MiG-19 jets that had intruded July 4 over the Israeli-held town of Sudr, on the Sinai Peninsula's Gulf of Suez coast about 35 miles south of the canal. A Cairo announcement July 4 contended that no UAR jets "had been involved in any incident that day."

A Tel Aviv communiqué July 8 said Israeli jet fighters that day had knocked out Egyptian artillery and tanks that had been shelling

Israeli positions at Ras el Ish and El Qantara. UAR forces resumed the shelling of El Qantara 3 hours later. An Israeli military spokesman reported that 5 Israeli soldiers had been killed and 31 wounded in the day's shellings. Tel Aviv's July 8 communiqué also reported that 2 Israeli jets that day had intercepted 4 Egyptian MiG-21s that had penetrated Sinai air space in the direction of El Qantara. The communiqué claimed that one MiG was hit and was seen falling south of Port Said.

The Egyptian high command's account of the July 8 fighting claimed that UAR ground and air forces had thrown back Israeli attacks around El Qantara and Ras el Ish, destroying 3 Israeli tanks and 11 armored vehicles. The command conceded the loss of one MiG over the Port Said-Port Fuad area. Cairo claimed that 6 Israeli planes had bombed the 2 cities, killing one civilian and injuring 7.

An Israeli soldier was killed and 2 others were wounded July 9 when their jeep ran over a mine 6 miles north of El Qantara. An Israeli army spokesman said 7 other mines had been found in the area.

An Israeli military spokesman announced July 11 that Israeli anti-aircraft fire had downed a Soviet-built UAR Sukhoi-7 fighter that day after 2 of the aircraft had intruded over the Sinai desert east of El Qantara. The pilot of the downed plane was believed killed.

Israel announced July 12 that 2 of its motor torpedo boats and a destroyer had sunk 2 of Egypt's Soviet-built P-153 motor torpedo boats late the previous day 22 miles northeast of Port Said. According to the account, the battle took place after the Israeli naval patrol came under fire from the Egyptian boats. The Israelis said they saw no survivors. Eight Israeli crewmen were injured slightly.

Tel Aviv reported July 12 that Egyptian artillery north of Ismailia had fired across the canal for about 5 hours that day. The Israelis returned the fire and reportedly destroyed an Egyptian tank. The announcement said 2 Israeli soldiers had been wounded. The Egyptian high command July 12 claimed that Egyptian forces had destroyed 2 Israeli vehicles and 2 tanks in the exchange of artillery fire. According to the UAR announcement, the Egyptians began shooting only after Israeli guns had started to fire.

Egyptian and Israeli forces engaged in more serious fighting July 14, when Egyptian artillery pounded the east bank of the canal and Israeli aircraft attacked positons on the west bank. An Israeli announcement at UN headquarters in New York July 15 said 7 Israeli soldiers had been killed and 22 wounded in the attack, while 2 others were missing. The UAR representative at the UN said 26 Egyptian soldiers and civilians had been killed by the Israeli fire. The Egyptian high command asserted that Egyptian artillery and anti-aircraft fire had destroyed 5 Israeli planes, 8 tanks, 15 half-tracks, 9 trucks and 2 boats during the battle. It said Egyptian forces had captured 2 crewmen of Israeli boats sent across the canal. Israel accused the Egyptians of precipitating the incident by launching heavy artillery, tank and machinegun fire at Israeli positions at Port Taufiq and El Qantara. An Egyptian military spokesman said the fighting had broken out after the Israelis had attempted to cross the canal at several points between Ismailia and Port Taufiq, 70 miles apart.

In another clash along the canal July 15, Israel said its forces had downed 5 Egyptian MiG fighters and a bomber. Cairo claimed its forces had shot down 3 Israeli fighters. An Israeli military spokesman said that one Israeli plane had been shot down but that the pilot had parachuted safely into Israeli-held territory. Ground fighting was also reported to have broken out in the Port Taufiq area and around Ismailia. An Egyptian military spokesman said UAR planes had attacked Israeli positions on the east bank after the Israelis had opened artillery and mortar fire on the towns of Suez, Ismailia and Kabrit.

UN Sends Truce Observers to Suez

The UN Security Council had convened in emergency session July 8 to consider the Israeli-Egyptian fighting. The meeting, requested by the UAR and Israel, resulted in the stationing of UN observers on the 2 banks of the Suez Canal to prevent further violations of the cease-fire. Addressing the Council, U Thant disclosed that he had proposed this plan July 4 to UAR Deputy Premier Mahmoud Fawzi and Israeli Foreign Min. Abba Eban.

The Council reconvened July 9 and shortly after midnight (July 10) approved Thant's plan for UN observers on both sides of the cease-fire line along the canal. Under the proposal, adopted by consensus and without a vote, Thant was to ask Lt. Gen. Odd Bull, head of the UN Truce Supervision Organization (UNTSO), to seek Israeli and Egyptian agreement to the plan. Thant said that about 25 members of UNTSO's 133-man observer force, supervising the truce on Israel's borders with Syria and Jordan, could be shifted to the Suez cease-fire line pending the arrival of reinforcements.

In Council debate July 9 prior to the adoption of the Thant proposal, Soviet delegate Nikolai T. Fedorenko demanded that the Council condemn Israel as an aggressor and require that Israeli forces be withdrawn immediately from captured Arab territories. Fedorenko said that sanctions should be imposed on Israel if it refused to comply. Fedorenko charged that Israel's military actions were being encouraged by Britain and the U.S.

U.S. Amb. Arthur J. Goldberg and British Amb. Lord Caradon supported the Thant plan.

The Council recessed briefly and reconvened later July 10. UAR delegate Mohamed Awad El Kony informed Thant of Cairo's acceptance of the plan to place UN observers on the Suez cease-fire line. Israeli delegate Gideon Rafael also replied but the contents of his note were not revealed.

Tel Aviv's approval of the Thant proposal was announced by the Israeli government July 11. A Foreign Ministry spokesman said Israel's approval was "conditional on the installation of observation points on both sides of the cease-fire line on a basis of reciprocity."

Final arrangements for stationing the observers was worked out with the UAR July 13 and with Israel July 14. The watch was scheduled to begin officially at noon July 16 but last minute complications in the negotiations with the UAR caused a postponement until 6 p.m. July 17.

The principal stumbling block to an agreement concerned the use of small boats in the canal. In his talks with Gen. Bull July 14, Israeli Defense Min. Moshe Dayan insisted that either both sides should be permitted to operate boats in the canal or both should be barred from doing so. Cairo radio announced July 17, however, that the UAR would consider the presence of any Israeli boats in the canal a violation of the cease-fire, which would be met with force. This matter was to be settled in further negotiations held later in July. Despite a lack of agreement on the navigational issue, the observer plan went into effect.

The UN observer plan was implemented July 17 when an 8-man UNTSO contingent arrived and took up positions, half on one bank of the Suez Canal and half on the other. By July 26 the UNTSO force in the area was increased to 26.

Israel and Egypt later agreed to a proposal to strengthen the mandate of the UNTSO truce observers. The plan was proposed by the UNTSO chief of staff, Gen. Odd Bull at separate meetings with Egyptian and Israeli officials July 19-30. Bull's proposal called for the "stopping of movements of boats" of both nations in the canal for one month and for a halt in all military activity in the waterway. The accord stipulated that boats of the UAR's Suez Canal Authority could operate in the canal but only to assist foreign ships trapped by the blocking of the waterway. Israel agreed to the UNTSO plan shortly after Bull had proposed it July 27. Egypt gave its approval soon after Bull conferred with UAR officials in Cairo July 30. The navigational agreement was renewed Aug. 27 and the ban continued for an indefinite period.

Bull had conferred first with UAR officials in Cairo July 19-24. The Egyptians initially rejected Bull's proposals for an indefinite navigational ban and for the delineation of a specific cease-fire line along the canal. Egypt was said to have insisted on the guarantee of "the principle of non-existence of a cease-fire line" to obviate the possible *de facto* recognition of Israel's presence on the east bank of the canal. Israel demanded that a cease-fire line be drawn down the middle of the canal. Bull reported the failure of his Cairo mission at a meeting in Jerusalem July 26 with Israeli Defense Min. Moshe Dayan. An Israeli government statement issued after the talks said Dayan had agreed to consider Bull's proposed navigational ban. As for the proposed cease-fire line, the statement quoted Dayan as saying that Israel "had already shown United Nations observers the exact boundaries of the areas held by the

Israeli defense forces." Dayan was said to have "requested that a map delineating the cease-fire line on the Egyptian side be sent to Israel as soon as possible." Cairo's failure to do so, Dayan asserted, "could be interpreted only as Egypt's failure to properly respect the cease-fire established by the UN Security Council."

Bull was reported to have later modified his proposal for a ban on navigation by suggesting in a letter to Dayan that Egypt and Israel suspend the operation of small boats in the Suez Canal for one month. Israel accepted the revised plan July 27. Bull returned to Cairo July 30 to discuss this new plan with UAR officials, who agreed to it the same day.

Israeli Defense Min. Dayan charged in a protest filed with UN officials August 7 that Egypt had violated the UNTSO Suez agreement the previous week. Dayan said that armed Egyptian soldiers had been observed aboard canal authority vessels in areas where there were no stranded ships.

(The Egyptian government was reported to have informed maritime powers July 15 that the Suez Canal, blocked since June 10 by sunken ships, would not be opened by Cairo until Israeli forces were withdrawn from the east bank. Washington sources that day said that Egypt had deliberately blocked the canal by sinking some of its ships at both ends of the 108-mile waterway. A report from London July 11 had said that the canal was obstructed at 3 points: 2 Egyptian ships were sunk near the north entrance, south of Port Said; 2 cement-filled floating docks were sunk between Ismailia and the Great Bitter Lake [where 14 merchant ships of 8 nations had been trapped for 5 weeks]; a small Egyptian tanker was submerged at the southern entrance, at the port of Suez.)

Suez Canal Fighting Intensified

Despite the stationing of UNTSO observers along the Suez Canal, Israeli and Egyptian ground and air forces continued their fighting in the vicinity of the waterway. The clashes were particularly intense between August 26 and Sept. 21. Among major actions:

■ An Israeli army spokesman reported that Israeli anti-aircraft guns Aug. 26 had shot down an Egyptian Soviet-built Sukhoi-7 fighter-bomber in the Sinai Peninsula at Bir Gifgafa, about 50 miles east of the canal.

Israeli and Egyptian troops later August 26 engaged in a one-hour exchange of gunfire along the canal after UAR troops opened fire on an Israeli position opposite Ismailia.

■ Israeli and UAR forces fought their most serious clash Sept. 4 across the canal just north of the Gulf of Suez. One Israeli soldier was killed and an Egyptian boat was sunk in 8 hours of sporadic shelling that was halted by the intervention of UNTSO observers.

According to the Israeli report of the incident: UAR guns near the west bank town of Suez had opened up on an Israeli torpedo boat and a landing craft that were cruising south of Israeli-held Port Taufiq, on the Gulf of Suez. Israeli guns returned the fire, which lasted for an hour. The Egyptian shelling resumed an hour later and was stopped by the first of 3 UN-arranged truces. UAR artillery resumed firing 5 minutes later on Port Taufiq and from another gun position 4 miles to the north. UNTSO observers arranged a cease-fire, but UAR guns opened up again ½ hour later. Before the 3d and final cease-fire, Israeli guns sank the Egyptian torpedo boat near the west bank of the Gulf of Suez.

Egyptian authorities contended that the Israelis had provoked the fighting by attempting to enter the canal with "an armed launch, a trawler and carrier" in defiance of a UN agreement that barred military activity in the canal.

But Egypt was accused by the UNTSO of instigating the clashes. In a report filed with the UN in New York Sept. 6, Gen. Bull said that after Egyptian forces had opened fire on an Israeli motorboat about 2 miles south of Port Taufiq, "the incident accelerated rapidly into an exchange of fire where tanks and mortars were used by both sides."

A UAR letter delivered to the UN Security Council Sept. 6 asserted that Egyptian forces had fired in self-defense when 2 Israeli motorboats and a tug had forcibly sought to enter the canal from the Gulf of Suez. Cairo claimed that the Israeli shelling that followed had destroyed Port Taufiq, killed 42 civilians and wounded 161 persons. A subsequent Egyptian report said the casualties totaled 44 dead and 172 wounded.

■ UAR and Israeli forces exchanged fire Sept. 12-13 in the vicinity of El Qantara. Tel Aviv said Israeli troops had opened fire on Egyptian forces on the west bank Sept. 12 after UAR anti-aircraft guns had fired at an Israeli jet. Israeli authorities reported that in the 2-hour exchange an Egyptian artillery battery was set afire and an Egyptian tank destroyed. The report said Egyptian fire damaged UNTSO observers' cars, a church and a mosque in the east-bank part of El Qantara. The Egyptian high command claimed that UAR anti-aircraft fire had shot down an Israeli jet at El Qantara. Israel claimed that the Sept. 13 fighting had started when Egyptian machineguns had opened fire on an Israeli patrol along the east bank of the canal about 5 miles north of El Qantara.

■ An Israeli communiqué Sept. 20 claimed that Israeli tank shelling that day had sunk 3 Egyptian troop-carrying boats in the Suez Canal less than one mile from the southern end of the waterway near Port Taufiq on the eastern bank. Israel charged that the presence of the UAR craft was in violation of the July Egyptian-Israeli agreement, which banned small-craft navigation in the waterway. A UAR Foreign Ministry statement Sept. 20 asserted that no Egyptian ships had been sunk in the canal and that "our armed forces had [made] no embarkations."

■ Israel charged that Egyptian tank shelling and machinegun fire from the west-bank part of El Qantara Sept. 21 had killed 4 Israelis and wounded 6 in the Israeli-occupied part of the town on the east bank. Israeli guns returned the fire. The one-hour exchange was halted after 2 cease-fire agreements were arranged by UNTSO observers. The Egyptian newspaper *Al Ahram* reported Sept. 22 that 23 Israelis had been killed in the El Qantara shellings. An Egyptian spokesman in Cairo reported Sept. 23 that 2 civilians had been killed and 12 wounded in the clash. Three UAR soldiers were reported slain and 7 wounded.

On instruction from UN Secy. Gen. Thant, Gen. Bull arrived in Cairo Sept. 22 from Norway to investigate the Sept. 20 and 21 Suez Canal clashes. Bull conferred Sept. 23 with UAR Foreign Affairs Undersecy. Salah Gohar and UNTSO observers.

■ Israeli and Egyptian forces exchanged machinegun fire in the Ismailia sector Sept. 27. The fighting quickly spread along most of the stretch of the canal from El Qantara to Suez. An Israeli communiqué said 14 persons had been killed on the east bank during the ensuing 9-hour tank and artillery duel. Ten of those slain were said to be civilians. UNTSO observers had made 6 attempts to halt the fighting. Ismailia Gov. Mobarik Rifai charged Sept. 27 that the Israelis had shelled Ismailia for 7 hours that day and had killed 36 civilians and seriously injured 85.

The fresh outbreak along the canal was reported Oct. 2 to have spurred the further evacuation of civilians from the city of Suez. 60,000 of the city's 250,000 inhabitants had left previously. Civilians were being evacuated also from Ismailia. The UAR government said Oct. 2 that more than 150 civilians had been killed and at least 500 wounded in mortar and artillery shelling along the Suez Canal since July 14.

Israeli Premier Levi Eshkol had visited Israeli positions on the east bank of the Suez Canal Sept. 6. Later Eshkol toured an Israeli base in the Sinai desert and told troops: "When I stood on the bank of the Suez, I said to myself, here I stand, not far from the ruler of Egypt. If I could talk to him as premier of Israel to the president of Egypt, I would propose that we seek the way to an understanding. But the [Arab] summit conference at Khartoum [held August 29-Sept. 1] determined irresponsibly that there is to be no peace with Israel. If Khartoum is their proclaimed position, our reply is, 'We are here.' "

UAR Sinks Elath, Israelis Shell Suez Oil Center

In one of the most violent post-war clashes, missiles fired from UAR naval craft Oct. 21 sank the 2,300-ton Israeli destroyer *Elath (Eilat)* off the northern coast of the Sinai Peninsula. Forty-seven Israeli sailors lost their lives, and 91 were wounded.

The sinking of the *Elath* was followed by heavy Israeli shelling of the UAR's major oil installations at the port city of Suez Oct. 24 during a 3-hour artillery exchange across the southern end of the Suez Canal.

The 2 incidents led to the convening of an emergency meeting of the UN Security Council in New York Oct. 24 to prevent a possible renewal of large-scale warfare between Israel and the UAR.

The Israeli version of the Oct. 21 naval incident was provided Oct. 22 by Commodore Shlomo Erel, naval commander. Erel said: The *Elath* was on routine patrol in international waters and was 13½ miles off UAR-held Port Said when it was hit amidships by a missile. A few minutes later a 2d missile struck the engine room, and 1½ hours later a 3d rocket smashed into the burning destroyer and sank it. A 4th missile exploded in the water a few minutes later and caused more casualties. Nineteen Israeli sailors were killed in the attack, and 28 were reported missing and presumed dead. 155 crew members were rescued.

Erel said the rockets had been fired from Soviet-made missile patrol boats of the *Komar* class believed to have been positioned inside Port Said. Erel said the rockets were Russian, "the most advanced type," but he doubted that they had been fired by Russians. Israeli military leaders said it might have been the first time sea-to-sea missiles were used in combat.

The Egyptian newspaper *Al Ahram* reported Oct. 22 that the *Elath* had been "hit and sunk by 2 Egyptian rocket-launching vessels that surprised the Israeli destroyer while trying to enter Egyptian territorial waters northwest of Port Said."

(U.S. officials in Washington Oct. 23 identified the missile used as the Soviet-made ship-to-ship type called the Styx by the Western allies. The Styx, about 20 feet long and shaped like an airplane, traveled at subsonic speed, was equipped with a 1,000-pound high-explosive warhead and had a range of 20-25 miles. The Egyptians had acquired the missiles in 1962 when the Soviet Union gave Cairo 3 *Komar*-class guided-missile vessels. The 75-ton attack craft traveled at a top speed of 40 knots and carried 2 launchers for Styx missiles.)

Israeli Premier Levi Eshkol charged in a nationwide address Oct. 22 that the UAR attack on the *Elath* was unprovoked and was a violation of international navigation laws and of the truce agreement. Israeli Defense Min. Moshe Dayan asserted Oct. 23 that UAR Pres. Nasser had "renewed hostilities" with Israel by sinking the *Elath*. Dayan held that "there was only one reason" for the attack: "the desire to renew hostilities exactly as they existed 5 months ago," when the UAR closed the Strait of Tiran to Israeli shipping.

An Israeli communiqué Oct. 24 said that Israeli artillery that day had pounded the UAR canal port city of Suez and destroyed about 80% of Egypt's oil-refining capacity there. The announcement reported that during a 3-hour artillery duel across the southern end of the canal, Israeli guns had set ablaze fuel tanks and 2 refineries. The tanks had a capacity of 590,000 tons and the refineries had a combined annual production of 5 million tons, although it was believed the plant had not been operating at capacity. The plant at Alexandria became Egypt's only intact oil installation. The Israeli communiqué said the fighting had started when UAR artillery north of Port Taufiq, just south of Suez, opened fire on Israeli units on the eastern bank of the waterway. The communiqué added: Israeli forces "returned the fire." One Israeli soldier was slightly wounded. The firing stopped 3 hours after a cease-fire call issued by UN observers.

A UAR communiqué accused the Israelis of starting the Suez shooting. It said "the enemy lost heavily in arms and men": one Israeli jet was downed, and 10 Israeli tanks, 4 armored cars and 5 rocket launchers were destroyed. (A Cairo report Oct. 25 said 8 UAR civilians and 3 soldiers had been killed and 60 civilians and 32 soldiers wounded in the shelling.)

Israeli-Jordanian Fighting Erupts

Fighting erupted on the Israeli-Jordanian frontier August 1 for the first time since the June cease-fire. Sporadic clashes continued through August 4.

A Jordanian account of the August 1 incident said that Israeli troops had opened fire first on Jordanian soldiers at the wrecked Damiya Bridge over the Jordan River (20 miles southeast of Nablus) and that the Jordanians had fired in return. The Amman report said that following a 10-minute exchange, 3 Israeli tanks had deployed near the bridge and opened fire with machineguns. The Jordanians said they again fired back. No casualties were reported on either side. Israel acknowledged the 2 separate clashes but claimed that the Jordanians had provoked the fighting.

Israel reported August 2 that 3 Israeli soldiers had been injured in 2 separate clashes with Jordanian troops that day. One man was wounded when the Jordanians attacked an Israeli army patrol between Jericho and Beisan, Israeli army headquarters reported. Two more Israelis were wounded in a 2d exchange about 3 hours later. According to Amman's account of the August 2 clash, Israeli troops had opened fire on Jordanian forces as Israeli troop carriers and jeeps approached the Damiya Bridge.

Israeli and Jordanian soldiers again exchanged fire August 3-4 about 4 miles north of the Damiya Bridge, but no casualties were reported.

A series of Jordanian-Israeli border clashes Nov. 18-21 was marked Nov. 21 by an Israeli air strike against Jordan, the first since the June war. The Israeli raid was in retaliation for the Jordanian tank shelling of Israeli observation posts on the west bank, 12 miles southeast of Nablus. Two Israeli soldiers were reported killed and a 3d wounded in the ground action. Another Israeli was thought to have been killed when his plane was downed by ground fire.

A Jordanian communiqué said 2 Israeli planes had been downed on the east bank Nov. 21 and that the pilot of one had been killed. Accusing the Israelis of having opened fire first on Jordanian military posts in the Shuna area, west of Amman, Jordan said Jordanian retaliatory fire had destroyed Israeli tanks and armored cars and 2 Israeli military posts and the troops manning them.

Jordan reported Nov. 20 that Israeli tanks and artillery on the west bank, firing that day at an Arab refugee camp at Karameh on the east bank, had killed 14 persons and wounded 28. In apparent reference to the same incident, Israeli authorities reported Nov. 20 that Israeli artillery that day had fired "to silence Jordanian positions." The Israelis conceded that shells might have landed in inhabited areas in Karameh, where Jordan, according to the Israelis, had set up artillery. The Karameh area, it was believed, was being used as a staging area for Arab terrorist attacks on Israeli villages in the Beisan Valley.

ARAB RESISTANCE TO ISRAELI RULE

By July Israeli authorities in control of territory taken from Jordan began to encounter Arab resistance. Arab defiance first took the form of non-cooperation with occupation rule: teachers in East Jerusalem (formerly the Old City of Jerusalem) went on strike, merchants closed their shops, and former Jordanian officials and resistance-minded Arab activists issued manifestos and declarations attacking the Israeli presence. These verbal and passive manifestations of opposition to Israeli occupation quickly escalated in August to sporadic armed attacks against Israeli troops and positions. Many of the raids were carried out by El Fatah, the Syrian-based saboteur group, which had mounted similar raids against Israel before the war. The terrorist operations on the west bank quickly spread to Israel proper and, in some instances, led to direct confrontations between Israeli and Jordanian troops.

Despite the renewal of violence, Israeli rule in the west bank of the Jordan River was never seriously challenged. Israel retained a tight grip on the conquered areas by ferreting out and smashing El Fatah and other organized Arab groups suspected of sabotage and by arresting Arab leaders accused of fomenting unrest. The Israeli armed forces also blew up Arab buildings suspected of being used as bases for terrorist assaults.

Arab Campaign of Defiance

Arab leaders in East Jerusalem and elsewhere on the west bank were reported July 25 to have begun a campaign to rally the Arab populace to defy Israeli rule. Leaflets distributed in East Jerusalem by 2 Arab nationalist groups (the Palestine Popular Struggle Organization and the Liberal Youth of Jerusalem) warned Arabs against collaborating with Israeli authorities. Five persons were temporarily detained by Israeli authorities for distributing the leaflets.

Among other acts of non-cooperation in July and August: 8 former west-bank Jordanian judges declined to serve under the Israelis; Arab newspaper owners in East Jerusalem refused an

Israeli invitation to resume publication; a letter published July 25 by members of the disbanded Municipal Council of former Jordanian Jerusalem announced their refusal to serve on East Jerusalem's governing City Council on the ground that they were "not yet ready for full cooperation." The former Jordanian officials agreed, however, to assist in the operation of municipal services.

The most serious act of Arab defiance occurred July 24 when 25 Moslem religious leaders, notables and former political officials, meeting in East Jerusalem's Aksa mosque, issued a manifesto challenging the authority of the Israeli Ministry of Religious Affairs to deal with Moslem religious activities. The statement also said that the Arabs "did not recognize the annexation" of the Old City of Jerusalem by Israel.

Four signers of the Arab manifesto were seized by Israeli authorities in East Jerusalem July 31 and banished to the northern Israeli towns of Safed, Tiberias and Hadera. All 4 were charged with "incitement to subversion" against Israel. They were Jordanian Jerusalem's ex-Gov. Anwar Khatib, son-in-law of Hebron Mayor Sheik Muhammed Ali Jabari, who favored cooperation with Israel; Dr. Daoud el-Husseini, former Jordanian parliament member and leader of the Palestine Liberation Organization on the west bank; Abdul Mehsen Abdul Mehzar, member of the disbanded Jordanian Jerusalem Municipal Council; Ibrahim Baka, a lawyer and former Jordanian parliament member. (Israeli authorities announced Sept. 28 that Khatib would be allowed to return to East Jerusalem.)

East Jerusalem Arabs staged a one-day strike August 7 in protest against Israeli control of the Old City. The city's 2,000 Arab-owned shops and restaurants were closed, all business activity came to a halt, and Arab bus companies suspended service to and within Arab areas of East Jerusalem. The strike was called by the Committee for the Defense of Arab Jerusalem. Leaflets distributed by the committee in the previous 48 hours called on the city's Arabs not to "tolerate for a day their imperialist Zionist occupiers."

Israeli authorities cracked down August 8-25 on Arab civilians who continued to defy Israeli rule in occupied territories.

Israeli forces August 8 padlocked 4 stores in East Jerusalem and issued warrants for the arrest of 5 alleged leaders of the August 7 general strike. The Israelis accused the 4 shopkeepers of having persuaded other merchants to join the strike. An Arab-owned bus company that had participated in the stoppage had its franchise suspended, and its routes were taken over by an Israeli bus firm. (The 4 closed stores and the Arab bus company were permitted to resume business August 20.) The East Jerusalem shopkeepers were reportedly angered by the Israeli business taxes and duties they were required to pay.

Israeli authorities Aug. 9 arrested 2 of the alleged Arab strike instigators named in the August 8 warrant. They were Hafez Tahboub, 40, a former Jordanian district judge, and Mussa el-Bitar, 50. Both were accused of being among the organizers of the Committee for the Defense of Arab Jerusalem, which had distributed leaflets calling for the strike. Tahboub was also one of the 25 Arab leaders who had signed the July 24 manifesto defying the authority of the Israel Religious Affairs Ministry and rejecting Israel's incorporation of Old Jerusalem.

Merchants in El Arish in the northern Sinai Penisula closed their shops August 19 in protest against Israeli occupation. Arab civilians blocked traffic by placing stones on the main street and raised an Egyptian flag. The civil disobedience campaign was staged in response to leaflets, issued August 18, that called for a general strike. Israeli authorities imposed a total curfew and detained 20 Egyptians as alleged instigators. The curfew was lifted August 21. An Israeli spokesman attributed the strike to "hostile Egyptian elements," the 5,000 former UAR officials, professionals and merchants who were awaiting repatriation to Egypt.

Israeli troops August 9 had dynamited 3 houses in the west-bank city of Nablus. 2 of the buildings were said to have contained illegal arms; the 3d reportedly had been used as a refuge by a sniper August 8.

Israeli military authorities August 9 arrested in Bethlehem 40 Arabs identified as members of the El Fatah terrorist organization. Israeli authorities said the group's members confessed that they had planned to blow up installations on the west bank and in Israel and to foment subversion among the Arab inhabitants.

Israeli troops August 25 dynamited 5 buildings in the west-bank town of Abu Dis, near Jerusalem, and arrested 6 Arabs after Arabs had fired that day on an Israeli security force. Three Israeli soldiers were wounded.

Despite Israeli countermeasures, Arab inhabitants of the west bank increased their campaign of defiance in September. Resistance was manifested by intensified armed attacks and a teachers' strike. The Arabs' armed raids spread to Israel itself, for the first time since the end of the June war. Among events of September:

■ Mines planted by Arab saboteurs derailed the first 3 cars of an Israeli Haifa-bound freight train Sept. 15 near the west-bank city of Tulkarm, but nobody was injured. Israeli authorities arrested 9 Arab suspects, imposed a curfew on several villages in the Tulkarm area and blew up 4 houses in Irtah Sept. 16. Israeli army authorities said 3 saboteurs had been traced to Irtah.

■ Arab teachers in public schools in the northern part of the west bank stayed away from classes when school opened Sept. 4. Most of the students also boycotted classes in response to a school strike appeal that had been circulated in leaflets the previous day in Ramallah, Nablus and Jenin. Most of the schools in the Hebron and Bethlehem areas, in the southern part of the west bank, opened on schedule.

Israeli police Sept. 4 arrested Husni Ashab, former Jordanian inspector of education for the Jerusalem District, and one of his assistants. The 2 were accused of attempting to prevent the opening of East Jerusalem schools (scheduled for Sept. 15) and for urging noncooperation with Israeli authorities.

The East Jerusalem school strike went into effect Sept. 15. Israeli authorities Sept. 18 managed to get 6 of the city's elementary schools opened by bringing in 30 teachers, mostly Arabs from the west bank. (By Oct. 6, it was reported, Israeli authorities had reopened 22 public schools for Arab children in East Jerusalem.)

■ Merchants in Nablus staged a general strike Sept. 19 to coincide with the opening of the UN General Assembly in New York. The walkout had been called for the entire west bank and East Jerusalem, but Nablus, traditionally a center of Arab nationalism, was the only area where the strike was fully effective. Police arrested 10 persons in Nablus. The strike had been called by the Supreme Committee for National Arab Guidance.

■ A rising wave of Arab terrorism on the west bank, believed to have emanated from Nablus, brought stern Israeli action in the city Sept. 23. Martial law was imposed, the 7-hour curfew was lengthened to 14 hours, soldiers stepped up their search for hidden arms, and the shops that had participated in the Sept. 19 general strike were padlocked. Nablus merchants defied the Israeli authorities, staged another general strike Sept. 24 and shut 70% of the city's stores.

An Israeli policeman had been attacked with hand grenades and a submachine gun by 2 Arabs in Nablus Sept. 23. One of the Arabs was killed in an exchange of gunfire with other Israeli policemen; the 2d was captured. Israeli police Sept. 24 arrested 13 Arabs in a cave 9 miles southeast of Nablus and captured a cache of weapons. The Arabs resisted arrest, and 4 were wounded in an exchange of gunfire. Several Arabs had been arrested in Nablus for alleged membership in El Fatah.

■ Arab sabotage also spread to Israeli territory. Several apartments and a printing shop in Israeli Jerusalem were blown up Sept. 19. A factory near Hadera, 25 miles northeast of Tel Aviv, was dynamited Sept. 20. Police arrested 9 Arab suspects Sept. 20 in connection with the Jerusalem incident.

Arab terrorists Sept. 25 dynamited a home at Omez, a farm settlement about 20 miles northeast of Tel Aviv, and a factory at nearby Givat Habiba. A 3-year-old child in the home was killed. Israeli authorities discovered near Givat Habiba, leaflets indicating that the attack had been carried out by El Fatah.

■ Israeli police in East Jerusalem Sept. 23 arrested and deported to Jordan Sheik Abdul Hammid as-Sayeh, 55, president and acting chief justice of the High Moslem Court. Sayeh, the spiritual leader of Arabs on the west bank, was accused of fomenting resistance to Israeli rule and of engaging in "hostile activities in Jerusalem and the west bank." Sayeh also was accused of leading the Supreme Committee for National Arab Guidance.

Israelis Smash Arab Sabotage Ring

Israeli police officials in Jerusalem announced Oct. 12 the arrest of 24 members of El Fatah and the capture of large quantities of arms. The police commissioner of Jerusalem, Shaul Rosolio, said that "by these arrests we have thwarted a wave of planned sabotage that would have been carried out in the next few weeks." The weapons taken in and around East Jerusalem included machine-guns, light mortars, explosives and anti-tank guns.

The 24 Arabs were accused of participating in the sabotage campaign in the Jerusalem area since Sept. 17. Prior to their arrests, more than 100 other suspects had been seized throughout the west bank.

Israeli army sources were reported Sept. 28 to have linked the Syrian government, and to some extent Algeria, with the guerrilla operations. Captured Arab terrorists were reported to have told Israeli authorities that they had been trained by Syrian and Algerian officers at 3 camps in Syria. One camp, at Duma, near Damascus, was said to be a base of the Palestine Liberation Front, whose members had carried out widespread raids against Israel before the war. Trucks of the Palestine Battalion of the Iraqi army, stationed in Jordan, were said to have moved the saboteurs from Syria to Jordanian territory near the Jordan River. This action had been carried out despite repeated assertions by Jordanian King Hussein that he opposed terrorist attacks but favored passive resistance to Israeli rule by west-bank Arabs. (In a statement made Sept. 5, Hussein had said: He considered that the "renewal of guerrilla activities on Jordanian territory occupied by Israel would be a crime against our Palestinian brothers," but he was "proud of the resistance by our brothers on the west bank . . . to all attempts by the enemy to make them collaborate.")

Among other developments involving Arab terrorism:

■ An Israeli military court in Hebron Oct. 1 sentenced Moustafa Youssef Ahmed Hemayes to life in prison for carrying arms, forging documents and belonging to a terrorist group. Hemayes was a leader of the Palestine Liberation Front.

■ Israeli army authorities reported Oct. 2 that 4 Arab raiders had crossed the Jordan River from Jordan the night of Oct. 1 and attacked the northern Israeli village of Hamadia in the Beisan Valley, 3 miles from the river. An Israeli soldier on leave was shot to death. This was the first time since the end of the war that Arab terrorists had come directly from a neighboring state for a raid against Israel.

■ An Israeli policeman was slightly wounded Oct. 2 when terrorists in Nablus fired on a police jeep. A curfew was imposed in the area as police searched for arms and men.

■ Arab saboteurs Oct. 6 broke into the compound of the headquarters of the UN Truce Supervision Organization in Jerusalem and dynamited the antenna. Damage was reported to be slight.

■ Arab terrorists from Jordan Oct. 15 again struck in Israel's Beisan Valley, blowing up a dining hall, a transformer house and a trailer truck in the Maoz Haim communal settlement. Six marauders were believed involved in the attack. The raiders left El Fatah leaflets as they retreated back to the Jordan frontier, 2 miles away.

■ Israeli authorities Oct. 20 announced the capture of 11 Syrian-trained infiltrators of the Palestine Liberation Front Oct. 16 in a cave in the west bank's Jenin area.

■ A top El Fatah commander was reported by Israeli authorities Nov. 3 to have been captured in Jerusalem earlier that week. He was identified as Maj. Faisal el-Husseini, 25. Israeli authorities said he had entered Jerusalem 3 weeks earlier to set up a sabotage network in the west bank.

Jordanian Troops Aid Terrorists

An Israeli communiqué Nov. 5 charged Jordanian forces that day had for the first time intervened on behalf of irregular Arab saboteurs attacking Israeli territory. The communiqué claimed that Jordanian artillery had shelled Israeli positions near the Beisan Valley settlement of Sde Eliyahu (17 miles south of the Sea of Galilee) to screen the escape of Arab terrorists who were spotted and came under Israeli retaliatory fire. The saboteurs were said to have set off dynamite charges in a grain silo and warehouse in the settlement.

Israeli troops Nov. 7 killed 7 Arab infiltrators in a clash 3 miles northeast of Hebron on the west bank. The fighting erupted when Israeli troops challenged the infiltrators, who had been spotted by helicopter observers.

Israel warned Amman Nov. 7 of possible Israeli retaliation against Jordan for Jordan-organized raids. An Israeli state radio broadcast said: "After the past 5 months it must surely by now be understood that Israel's warnings are to be taken seriously. Israelis will not be misled by the vague and often confused public utterances of [Jordanian] King Hussein. They will judge their intentions by the actions of the king and his army in the near future."

Ahmed Shukairy, head of the Palestine Liberation Organization, had declared in Beirut Oct. 13 that Arab terrorist raids on the west bank were only "the first phase of a popular Palestinian war." He added: "The passive resistance of Palestinians are merely preliminary signs, not only for escalation of defiant guerrilla action but also to develop that action into the nature of a popular war." The elimination of "traces of Israeli aggression must take place at home, not in the United Nations, and by Arab, not international means."

Continued Arab armed attacks in November prompted the Israelis to return to their retaliatory practice of blowing up Arab buildings after removing their occupants. Several buildings in the Gaza Strip town of Dir el-Ballah were destroyed Nov. 27 in retaliation for the slaying of a youth in the neighboring Israeli settlement of Gan Shlomo, Israeli officials reported Nov. 28. Eighteen Arabs had been arrested in connection with the murder. It was reported Nov. 29 that the Israeli army during the previous 2 weeks had levelled all the 800 buildings in the west-bank village of Jiftliq, 12 miles south of Nablus. Israeli authorities described Jiftliq as a base for Arab terrorists.

Israeli forces Dec. 7 wiped out an Arab terrorist base in a cave near Nablus. Army, border police and security personnel killed 6 Arabs, captured an undisclosed number of prisoners and seized a cache of arms that included Soviet and Chinese Communists weapons.

The Jordanian government charged Dec. 8 that the Israelis Dec. 7 had expelled 200 Jordanians of the Nuseirat tribe from the west bank near Jericho to the east bank of Jordan. Saleh Nazhan, *muktar* of the tribe, told Jordanian authorities that prior to their eviction, the Israelis had destroyed almost all of the victims' homes, the local school and a mosque and had killed several men. The Israelis claimed the raid was in retaliation for the inhabitants' hiding of Arab saboteurs, Nazhan said.

Israeli officials announced Dec. 21 the smashing of an Arab attempt to revive a widespread sabotage campaign against Israeli control of the west bank. Israeli military authorities said that 54 Arab suspects had been seized and that 2 had been shot in a roundup that had started in Ramallah Dec. 15. Subsequent arrests were carried out in Jenin, Nablus and East Jerusalem. Two of the suspects were deported Dec. 20 to Jordan. They were Kemal Nasser, a poet, and Ibrahim Baqer. Both had been active in fomenting opposition to Israeli rule in the west bank since the end of the June war.

ARAB REFUGEE PROBLEM

Thousands of Arab civilians fled from the west bank of the Jordan River to Jordan's remaining territory on the east bank in the wake of Israel's seizure of the west bank during the fighting on the Jerusalem-Jordanian front. The evacuees came from such west-bank cities as Jerusalem, Ramallah, Jenin and Jericho and included many Palestinian refugees who had left the area that became Israel during the Arab-Israeli war of 1948. In the Syrian border areas occupied by Israel, several thousand Arabs also fled their homes.

Answering charges that Jordan's west-bank Arabs were being ousted or pressured to leave their homes, Israel insisted that the refugees were leaving voluntarily. The Israeli government provided free bus transportation for many of the refugees to the Allenby Bridge and other points at which the Jordan River could be crossed. (The Allenby Bridge, on the main road from Jerusalem to Amman via Salt, had been wrecked in the fighting but still could be crossed on foot.)

The UN Relief & Works Agency (UNRWA) sought to ease the plight of the refugees by providing them with food, medicine and shelter.

Estimates of the numbers of Jordanian refugees varied according to the source of the information. Preliminary figures released by the Jordanian government June 16 indicated that about 200,000 had gone to the east bank of the Jordan River. An Israeli Foreign Office spokesman June 21 estimated the number to be 50,000-60,000. Laurence V. Michelmore, commissioner general of UNRWA, reported to UN officials in New York June 20 that at least 100,000 Arabs had left for the east bank. Of this number, he said, about 80,000 were from Palestinian refugee camps. Michelmore said that some of the 100,000 refugees had been persuaded to return to the west bank. Preliminiary reports from southern Syria, Michelmore said, indicated that 50,000 persons, including 10,000 refugees of the 1948 war, had moved to the Damascus-Dera region to the north.

Prior to the outbreak of hostilities June 5, more than 940,000 Arabs had lived on the west bank, more than 500,000 of them classified as residents of the area and Jordanian citizens and 440,000 of them as refugees of the 1948 war. (About 275,000 refugees from that conflict lived on the east bank.) Palestinian refugees in the Gaza Strip totaled 400,000.

While some refugees sought to return to their homes on the west bank, a larger number of Arabs in the areas occupied by Israel crossed to the east bank into Jordan.

Israel Allows Refugees to Return

The first of several directives permitting west-bank Arab refugees to return from the east bank to their homes was announced by the Israeli government July 2. The regulation applied to those who had fled between June 5 and July 4, and the potential returnees were required to prove they were west-bank residents and were not security risks. August 10 was set as the deadline for the filing of applications of return, but at first no time limit was set for the return itself. The Israeli directive specifically barred the return to the west bank of the Palestine refugees who had been displaced by the 1948 war and since then had lived in camps on the east bank directly opposite the Israeli-occupied city of Jericho.

Israeli Defense Min. Dayan had expressed opposition the previous week to a wholesale return of Arab refugees to the west bank. Dayan said he had no objections to the reuniting of Arab families, "but if the 100,000 who left would feel like coming back, I would not be for letting them come back. Why should we? We are 2½ million Jews here, and the last contact that we had with these people was that they wanted to destroy us. That was just 20 days ago, if you recall." Dayan visited the Allenby Bridge July 3 to determine why west-bank Arabs continued to cross the wrecked span to the east bank. Dayan speculated that many Arabs were leaving to rejoin their relatives in Amman and other parts of Jordan. "In some cases," he said, "the family wage earner is in Kuwait or Saudi Arabia and they cannot receive his assistance unless they go to Amman." Others, Dayan pointed out, "simply would rather live under Arab rule than under Israeli. We are not Arabs, let's face it."

King Hussein of Jordan, in London to meet with British Prime Min. Harold Wilson, said July 3 that the Israeli decision to permit the return of Arabs to the west bank was "a welcome development. Only time will tell whether this offer was sincere." Hussein estimated that 120,000-150,000 Arabs had fled the west bank.

Jordanian Premier Saad Jumaa urged former west-bank Arabs July 5 to return to their homes, but he vowed at the same time that "we shall not hesitate to shed every drop of our blood" to regain the Jordanian area captured by Israel. Jumaa asserted that 200,000 Arabs had fled the west bank because of "Israeli pressure, insults and humiliation." But the Arabs should return to the west bank "even if they will suffer under Israeli domination" because it would "upset the enemy's plans" and facilitate the return of the west bank to Jordan, Jumaa said.

The first authorized repatriation of Arab refugees from the east to the west bank started July 18. About 160 Jordanian civilians, described as hardship cases, crossed into Israeli-held territory over the Allenby Bridge.

The resettlement movement, however, was suddenly suspended July 19 following a dispute over the refugee application form. Jordan demanded that the words "State of Israel" be deleted from the form and replaced by the emblem of the International Red

Cross (IRC), which was assisting in the repatriation. At meetings with IRC mediators in Amman, Jordanian authorities had twice rejected an Israeli proposal that the applications carry the Red Cross symbol in addition to the Israeli government identification. Jordan feared that acceptance of the phrase "State of Israel" would imply recognition of Israel. The Jordanians also had rejected IRC suggestions that the 2 governments hold direct talks on the dispute. The suggestions had been accepted by Israeli Defense Min. Dayan at a meeting in Tel Aviv July 14 with IRC Pres. Samuel A. Gonnard. Dayan also had agreed to the immediate return to the west bank of hardship cases among the Arabs seeking repatriation.

Negotiations on the application dispute produced August 6 an agreement permitting resumption of the return of Arab refugees to the west bank. With the IRC acting as mediator, Jordanian and Israeli representatives agreed that the Israeli application forms would carry the names of the State of Israel, the Kingdom of Jordan and the IRC.

As a result of the suspension of the repatriation movement during the negotiations, Israel extended the deadline for filing repatriation forms from August 10 to August 31.

Jordanian Finance Min. Abdel Wahab Majali, also chairman of Jordan's Higher Committee for Refugees, urged August 7 that refugees from the west bank return to their former homes to help their "brothers to continue their political action and remain a thorn in the flesh of the aggressor [Israel] until the crisis has been solved."

In response to international pressures, Israel agreed August 29 to permit Arab refugees to return to the Israeli-occupied west bank after the Aug. 31 deadline that had been set by the Israeli cabinet. But the Israelis informed UN Secy. Gen. U Thant Sept. 13 that they would not permit a wholesale return of Arab refugees. Under the Israeli rules announced August 29, all potential returnees whose applications had been approved would be allowed to go back to the west bank. Israel had approved 21,000 of 130,000 Arab refugee application forms. But only 14,000 approved refugees had elected to return since the full-scale authorized reentry operation had started August 18. Israel had agreed to accept the remaining

7,000 if special arrangements could be made for them. Israeli officials also had indicated that the additional 109,000 Arabs on the east bank could be brought back to the west bank if Jordan agreed to negotiate their return directly with Israel. The IRC had estimated that 170,000 Arabs had applied to return to the west bank.

At its August 13 meeting, the Israeli cabinet had voted to subject Arabs returning to Israeli-occupied territory to rigid security checks. An Israeli government source said after the cabinet meeting that "several cabinet ministers felt that we should cancel the [Arab refugee] deal altogether" in view of recent Jordanian government statements allegedly aimed at inciting the returning refugees to resist Israeli authority on the west bank. In a note to UN Secy. Gen. Thant August 16, Israeli delegate-to-UN Gideon Rafael had charged that the Amman government's campaign of "vituperation and direct incitement" was "not only designed to aggravate the situation, but is placing serious obstacles in the way of implementation of the policy of permitting the return of refugees to their homes."

Among developments preceding the Israeli decision to extend the August 31 deadline for the return of the Arab refugees to the west bank:

■ A joint protest note filed with the UN Security Council August 19 by 12 Arab nations charged Israel with a "systematic policy" of discouraging the return of Arab refugees to their homes in Israeli-occupied Jordan and Syria in order to "accommodate more Jewish immigrants." The note, signed by Saudi Arabian delegate Jamil M. Baroody, accused Israel of "oppression and psychological intimidation" of Arabs in Israeli-occupied areas.

■ Israel August 22 rejected a Jordanian request to permit Arab refugees to return to the west bank after August 31. Israel spurned the request at a meeting with Jordanian officials near the Allenby Bridge. Later August 22 Jordanian Foreign Min. Mohamed Adib al-Ameri said in a statement of protest: "The United Nations resolutions concerning repatriation of refugees to their homeland has not limited the period of repatriation. No one from either side, Israel or Jordan, can define or limit this period as long as there is a suitable reason for giving refugees an opportunity to return home."

■ The U.S. was reported August 24 to have appealed to Israel to extend the refugee deadline so "that all those wishing to return to the west bank would be allowed to do so."

■ U Thant, in a note delivered August 25 to Gideon Rafael, urged an extension of the August 31 deadline. Thant said that an extension was the only way to insure compliance by Israel with the UN General Assembly resolution calling for the repatriation of all Arab refugees.

In a note made public Sept. 13, Israel informed Thant it was not extending the August 31 deadline for the general return of refugees. But the note, delivered by Rafael, announced these 2 concessions: (1) Israel would accept applications from west-bank residents for the admission of relatives currently living on the east bank; (2) applications based on hardship cases would be considered.

Thant August 19 had issued a report on the plight of the Arab refugees. He stated that the 323,000 Arabs who had fled into Jordan, Syria and the UAR had aggravated the Palestine refugee problem, endangered Jordan's economic future and placed a heavier burden on the already debt-ridden UN relief operations. Thant said the UNRWA would require an additional $10 million in 1967. The U.S. mission at the UN informed Thant August 30 that the U.S. had contributed $9.9 million for Arab refugee relief since the end of the Arab-Israeli war; $2 million of the sum had been donated to UNRWA.

The British Foreign Office had announced August 31 that British Amb.-to-Israel Michael Hadow had urged Israel to extend the August 31 refugee deadline.

(Israeli authorities announced that as of August 29 Gaza Strip Arabs could freely cross into the west bank. When the area had been under UAR control, the UAR had required Gaza Strip Arabs to obtain permits to leave the area. During the previous 2 weeks an estimated 500 Arabs a day had left the Gaza Strip for the west bank. Before then the strip's population had comprised 315,000 Arab refugees and about 120,000 indigenous Arabs.)

Refugee Return Suspended

A planned return of an additional 6,200 Arab refugees from the east bank to west bank, scheduled to resume Sept. 17, failed to take place. Israel attributed the failure to Jordan's refusal to cooperate in arrangements for their return. The potential returnees were former west bank residents who had been granted Israeli permits to come back but were unable to do so by the August 31 deadline. Israel had announced the extended grace period for their return Sept. 11.

Israeli and Jordanian officials had discussed the matter at the Allenby Bridge Sept. 15. Amman then informed Israel Sept. 16, through the International Red Cross, that there would be a delay in the planned limited resumption of the refugees' return. According to Israel, the Jordanians gave no reason for the delay. Jordanian representatives were to resume talks with the Israelis Sept. 20 but they failed to appear. The Israeli refugee representative said Israel would make no effort to bring back the 6,200 refugees until Jordan filed a request for their return.

UNRWA Commissioner Laurence V. Michelmore, in an annual report filed with the UN General Assembly Oct. 19, said that only a "small fraction" of the Arab refugees on the east bank who had applied to return to their homes in the west bank had been able to do so. Michelmore said he and his UNRWA staff at Amman had found that "Jordanian authorities did all that was humanly possible to insure those whose applications to return were approved were promptly informed and were given every assistance in recrossing the river." According to Michelmore's report: Since August 12, when Israel had first issued applications for the return to the west bank, the Jordanian government had reported that 40,000 forms had been completed for 150,000 of the 200,000 Arabs who had fled to the east bank. Israel said that during this period it had received 32,000 completed application forms for 100,000 people. Jordan reported that Israel had approved and issued 5,122 permits for 18,236 refugees. According to Israel, the figure was 5,797 permits for 20,658 persons. Jordan said that 14,150 refugees had returned to the west bank by August 31; Israel said 14,056 had done so. The number of refugees who had registered with UNRWA who had been permitted to return to the west bank "is reported to be only about 3,000 of the 93,000 who crossed to the east bank before July 4 and who were therefore *prima facie* eligible to return in accordance with the conditions stipulated" by Israel.

A spokesman for Israel's UN mission Oct. 19 denied Michelmore's statement that only a "small fraction" of the west-bank refugees had returned to their homes. Michelmore's remarks that Jordan was cooperative in facilitating the return of the refugees also was challenged. The Israeli spokesman recalled that the Israeli representative to the UN had informed UN Secy. Gen.

Thant in a letter Sept. 11 that "from the outset . . . Jordan created artificial obstacles" in preventing the return of refugees "by insisting on specious formalities."

In October Israel announced a program for the reunion of divided families on both banks of the Jordan River. The plan envisaged the readmission of 40,000 Arabs to the west bank. 300 applications had been received. The return of refugees in this category resumed Nov. 27 with the arrival on the west bank of 7 persons.

Israel Counts Refugees

An Israeli census report, issued Oct. 3, listed 288,000 fewer refugees under Israeli control than had been listed by the UNRWA.

The Israeli count, made in September, found an estimated 1,000,000 Arabs in the Arab areas captured by Israel in June. They included 340,000 refugees of the 1948 war. 600,000 Arabs were found living on the west bank, exclusive of former Jordanian Jerusalem. 120,000 of these were listed as refugees. (The UNRWA reported 311,182 refugees in the west bank as of the end of August; it had listed 430,000 refugees on the west bank before the June fighting. Jordan's 1961 census of the west bank had recorded 830,000 persons.) The Gaza strip population, according to the Israeli census, totalled 365,000, including 220,000 refugees. (317,000 Gaza Strip refugees had been listed on UNRWA's rolls as of May 31.) 67,000 Arabs lived in East Jerusalem (formerly Jordanian Jerusalem) and were considered Israeli citizens since Israel had absorbed the sector after the war, the report said. 33,000 persons were reported in the northern Sinai; 30,000 of them lived in El Arish. The Israeli census listed 6,400 residents in the Golan Heights; 80,000 had lived there before Israeli forces captured it from Syria.

(The Egyptian Middle East News Agency reported Oct. 9 that 700 Arabs had left El Arish that day for Egypt. The refugees were reported to have crossed the Suez Canal at El Qantara. Nearly 900 more Egyptians in the Sinai Peninsula, mostly women and children, crossed the Suez Canal into UAR territory Oct. 16.)

Israel Proposes 5-Year Plan

Israel Dec. 14 submitted to the UN Special Political Committee a 5-year plan to solve the Arab refugee problem. The plan was conditioned on a general peace settlement between Israel and the Arab states. The proposals, presented by Israeli delegate Michael S. Comay, were outlined in general terms; the details were to be made public after they were discussed privately with other UN delegates, who, in turn, were to transmit them to Arab leaders. Comay suggested direct Israeli discussion of the plan with the Arab countries in which the refugees resided and the countries contributing funds to aid the refugees. Israel offered to extend technical aid and advice toward the rehabilitation of the Middle East's 1½-million displaced Arabs (UN estimate) and toward their "integration into the economic life of the region."

Comay said his government would oppose an "open-door" policy for the return of Arab refugees to areas held by Israel "unless and until" there was a general understanding on other problems.

Arab delegates at the UN Special Committee Dec. 15 rejected the Israeli proposal on the ground that it was linked with a general Middle East peace settlement.

INDEX

A

AARMIRI, Mohammed Adib al- — 169

ABDULLAH, Capt. Adnan — 37

ABRAHAM (Hebrew patriarch) — 1

ABU Agweigila (or Abu Uwaygilah) (Sinai Peninsula) — 77

ABU Dhabi — 86

ABU Dis (west bank of Jordan River) — 186

ACRE (Israel) — 10

AFFULEH (Israel) — 17

AFGHANISTAN — 52, 129, 131-138, 140

AFLAK, Michel — 20

AIR Warfare — See JUNE 1967 War

AL — Arabic names bearing this prefix are indexed by surname (e.g., thus: BITAR, Salah al- — under 'B')

AL Ahram (Egyptian newspaper) — 50, 91, 144, 171, 180, 181

AL Arish — See EL Arish

AL Asifa (or El Asifa) (military arm of Al Fatah, Arab nationalist guerrilla organization) — 12, 16, 23, 24, 40

AL Awja—See EL Auja

Al-Ba'ath (Syrian newspaper) — 23

ALBANIA — 124, 127, 132-138, 140

AL-Diffa (Jordanian newspaper) — 21

ALEXANDRIA (United Arab Republic) — 182

AL Fatah (or El Fatah) (Arab terrorist group) — 12, 16-18, 22-26, 41, 184, 186, 188, 189

ALGERIA: Arab unification — See ARAB Unification. Armament arrangements — See ARMAMENT Arrangements. Armed forces — 42, 52, 67, 70. Foreign relations (misc.) — 83, 163. Guerrillas — See ARAB Guerrilla Forces. Petroleum boycott — 85-86, 161. UN policy — 132-136, 138, 140. Warfare — See under 'W'

AL Gomhouria (Cairo newspaper) — 80

AL Kuntillah — See KUNTILLA

ALMAGOR (Israel) — 16, 23

AL Moharrer (Beirut newspaper) — 16, 38

AL Qunaytirah — See EL Quneitra

AL Thwara (Syrian government newspaper) — 161

AMER, Lt. Gen. (later Field Marshal) Abdel Hakim — 12, 13, 15, 21, 116, 170-171

AMERI, Mohamed Adib al- — 195

AMERICAN Society of International Law — 145

AMMIAD (Israel) — 40

ANTI-Semitism — See JEWS & Judaism

AQABA (Jordan) — 47, 51

AQABA, Gulf of (or Gulf of Elath): Closed to Israeli shipping — 42, 46-51, 53, 54, 57-64, 70, 98, 99, 118, 127, 151, 153, 157, 162, 167, 168. Elath — See under 'E.' Fighting — 38, 74, 76, 78. Geography — 47. Israel regains use — 11, 78. Map — 76. Sharm el Sheik — See under 'S.' Sinai Campaign of 1956 — 9. UNEF withdrawal — 147

ARAB Guerrilla (or commando) Forces — 6, 7, 11. See also subheads under JUNE 1967 War. Al Asifa (or El Asifa) — 12, 16, 23, 24, 40. Al Fatah (or El Fatah) — 12, 16-18, 22-26, 41, 184, 186, 188, 189. Fedayeen — 8. Heroes of Repatriation — 38. Palestine Liberation Organization — 15, 32

200

S

DATE DUE

GAYLORD   PRINTED IN U.S.A.